DRAGON LADIES

Asian American Feminists Breathe Fire

Edited by Sonia Shah
Preface by Yuri Kochiyama
Foreword by Karin Aguilar-San Juan

South End Press
Boston, MA

Cover design by Beth Fortune
Printed in the U.S.A.

Library of Congress Cataloging-in-Publication Data
Dragon ladies : Asian American feminists breathe fire / edited by Sonia Shah.
p. cm.
Includes bibliographical references and index.
ISBN 0-89608-576-7 (cloth).—ISBN 0-89608-575-9 (pbk.)
1. Feminism—United States. 2. Feminists—United States. 3. Asian American women. I. Shah, Sonia.
HQ1426.D845 1997
305.48'895073—DC21 97-22918
CIP

03 02 01 4 5 6 7

Contents

III. Global Perspectives

IV. Awakening to Power

Preface: Trailblazing in a White World

A Brief History of Asian/Pacific American Women

By Yuri Kochiyama

Struggle is a way of life for all who inhabit this world, but particularly for women of color in a white-dominated world. Asian/Pacific Island women, like their colored counterparts, have had to fight to participate as equals with whites in U.S. society. Sometimes they have had to almost literally "move mountains" that once seemed immovable to get to where they are today.

Let's begin with Queen Liliuokalani of Hawaii. In 1893, she was dethroned and deposed by U.S. military action. The United States acquired more than 2 million acres of land, and the Hawaiian kingdom was decimated.

Queen Liliuokalani was a titled native Hawaiian, with rank, prestige, influence, and some wealth. After her dethronement, she called on her people to join together: "There is still time to save our heritage. Never cease to act because you fear you may fail. The voice of the people is the voice of God." Today, her people, the kanakas, are fighting for sovereignty. And among the passionate, brilliant leaders are women warriors like the sisters Mililani and Haunani-Kay Trask, Dr. Lilikala Kameleleihiwa, and Kawehi Kanui Gill.[1]

At the turn of the century, Hawaii's women pioneers were poor immigrants from Japan, the Philippines, China, and Korea who worked in the pineapple and sugar cane plantations. They, too, are part of our legacy. Their back-breaking work and years of privation and hardship never vanquished them.

The same was true for Asians who migrated to the U.S. mainland. California desert lands flowered into farmlands through years of toil, with women working side by side with men, returning home at the end of the day to cook, wash, and care for the children.

After World War II, and when immigration laws finally changed in the mid-1960s, more and more Asian women were allowed into the United States. Asian women took jobs in the garment and textile industries, where they faced gender discrimination and institutionalized racism. Asian women in the labor movement were instrumental in improving work conditions. Chinese labor activist and social worker Au Quon McElrath was one of the early union advocates for workers in Hawaii who organized for better pay, better work conditions, health benefits, and maternity leaves.

As women's committees in unions were organized, workers began negotiating for daycare centers and educational seminars. Filipina nurses in the 1970s organized against unfair labor practices in U.S. hospitals. Today, the Asian Pacific American Labor Alliance (APALA), with representatives such as May Chin and Mae Ngai of New York and Katie Qwon and Jai Lee of California, leads the way on many critical issues, such as fighting against Proposition 187, an anti-immigrant bill adopted in California.

Asian/Pacific American women trailblazers in the cultural arts would be too numerous to name, but some stand out in particular. One such cultural artist is Janice Mirikitani, whose powerful poetry has become renowned in Asian/Pacific circles. One of Mirikitani's early poems focuses on her mother, who broke her silence by speaking at the 1981-82 Congressional hearings on Japanese internment during World War II. Mirikitani also plays a significant role as director of myriad community and church-related services at Glide Memorial Church in San Francisco, a unique grassroots-oriented congregation whose soup kitchen project feeds thousands of people daily.

More and more Asian/Pacific American women are winning elected offices and are being appointed to important positions in their communities and the government. Women such as Wilma Chan, Mabel Teng, and Jean Quon, once grassroots political activists, are now elected supervisors in education.

Merle Woo is an educator who is also a lesbian socialist and a radical, not exactly her colleagues' "cup of tea" at prestigious University of California at Berkeley. Her controversial actions ran the gamut from supporting student participation in teach-ins and boycotts to establishing an autonomous Third World College. Woo was fired from the Asian American Studies program in 1982. In 1983, she filed complaints in federal and state courts charging the university with violating her First Amendment rights. She also charged the university with discriminating against her for being a trade unionist, a lesbian, and a socialist feminist affiliated with Radical Women and the Freedom Socialist Party. Woo sparked national and international support, and in 1984, she won a cash settlement and a two-year contract with the Department of Education. Still, she was not allowed to pursue her career in Asian American Studies, which was her original choice. She left Berkeley to teach at San Francisco State University. Her fight was an inspiration to socialists, radicals, and feminists. Woo's openness and pride in her lesbianism helped other women come out of the closet.

One of the most awesome Asian women of contemporary times was Caridad Guidote, a dynamic Filipina Catholic nun, who worked at the InterChurch Center in New York City. A Filipina nationalist, liberation theologist, and international human rights advocate, Guidote traveled to Nicaragua in 1984 to write a comprehensive book comparing the revolution in Nicaragua with the struggle in the Philippines. She spent her last years in the heart of strife-torn Nicaragua, working in the cotton fields with revolutionaries and sleeping in barns. Very few young Asian Americans went to Nicaragua in the 1980s, when thousands of White, Black, and Latino movement activists ventured into the struggles of Latin America. Yet Guidote saw in the Sandinista leadership "compassion without paternalism, practical gut-level love for country and people."

Guidote passed away in 1988; her book, as yet unpublished, exposes U.S. involvement in sabotaging the Nicaraguan revolution. Through her remarkable life and efforts to tell the story of a people other than her own, Guidote has blazed a trail into the international arena.

Since the first Venceremos Brigades in the early 1960s, dozens of Asian Americans of varied ethnic backgrounds have volunteered to do construction work or to pick fruit in the orange groves of Cuba in support of the revolution. More than half have been women. Asian American women from the Bay Area of California to the urban centers of New York City, Chicago, Philadelphia, and even Honolulu have packed their bags and flown to the small Caribbean country that freed itself from U.S. domination, to learn the meaning of revolution and hard work.

In the realm of recent domestic conflicts, perhaps the one that has brought home most forcefully the polarization of ethnic communities is the unforgettable turbulence of the 1992 Los Angeles riots. Most news coverage of the riots and statements by reporters, elected officials, and movement activists of every background showed little empathy for or understanding of the Korean community, which lost many people and more than 2,000 stores. One person who gave voice and visibility to those who suffered was Elaine Kim, Professor of Asian American Studies at Berkeley. Kim's candid remarks about the riot, its aftermath, Black grassroots leadership, Korea Town leadership, the Los Angeles police department, the mayor's office, Korean churches, Korean shop owners, and the still-pervasive stereotypes of Asian Americans, gave vital insight into all aspects of the tragedy.

In New York City, one of the most active pan-Asian organizations is the Committee Against Anti-Asian Violence (CAAAV). CAAAV has monitored day-to-day abuses against Asian Americans by police officers, such as racial slurs, illegal car searches, and trumped-up charges. CAAAV organizes immigrant Asian cab drivers and also works with Blacks, Latinos, and concerned Whites to form coalitions and organize rallies, demonstrations, picket lines, and marches.

Women are almost always at the helm of CAAAV, which elects its leadership. The string of women spokespersons and organizers includes Dr. Mini Liu, Milyoung Cho, Monona Yin, Eunja Lee, Anannya Bhattacharjee and Jane Bai, who have held the reins because of their diligent, dedicated commitment and their ability to get along with people of varied backgrounds, ages, genders, and sexual preferences.

As past and present struggles reveal, Asian/Pacific American women in white-dominated U.S. society will continue to take up the challenge of blazing a trail toward equality and social justice.

Notes

1. Mary Choy, a quietly unpretentious Korean American activist from Honolulu, was recently eulogized by sovereignty leaders as one of the staunchest supporters of Hawaii's struggles.

Foreword: Breathing Fire, Confronting Power, and Other Necessary Acts of Resistance

By Karin Aguilar-San Juan

The Asian American women's movement was the focus of a March 28, 1997, feature article in *Asianweek.* One positive aspect of the article was its mention of ongoing efforts to mobilize Asian American women, including a new organization called the National Asian Pacific American Women's Forum (NAPAWF). An unfortunate aspect of the article was its title, "Two movements in one," which reanimates the familiar notion that race comes first, then comes gender.

In celebrating the return of Asian American women to the Asian American social movement of the 1990s, the *Asianweek* article unintentionally rendered invisible the efforts and accomplishments of Asian American women from 1968 to 1997. In those three decades, needless to say, Asian American women have been involved in many kinds of struggles, from confronting domestic violence to implementing affirmative action, from teaching Asian American Studies to organizing for the rights of immigrant workers. The recent visibility of Asian American women activists in groups like NAPAWF should not invalidate the efforts of women before them to create social justice, since gender inequality is implicated in each of those struggles.

By highlighting this example from *Asianweek*, I do not mean to overlook the well-meaning intentions of the author or the publication, nor do I intend to suggest that the article did greater harm than good to the feminist movement. But by casting the Asian American women's movement as a two-for-one deal, the article brings to mind the entrenched gender bias that prevails in Asian American politics: the idea that gender is implicated in power relationships only when gender inequality is explicitly prioritized as a problem. The whole point of launching a feminist critique of society is to draw attention to the way gender hierarchies inform every aspect of social life. This critique disenables patriarchal power and shifts the experience of women from the margins to the center.

The fact of the matter is that from its very conception as an organizing principle, Asian America has masked a series of internal tensions. In order to produce a sense of racial solidarity, Asian American activists framed social injustices in terms of race, veiling other competing social categories such as gender, sexuality, ethnicity, and nationality. The relative absence of gender as a lens for Asian American activism and resistance throughout the 1970s until the present should therefore be read as neither an indication of the absence of gender inequality nor of the disengagement of Asian American women from issues of social justice. Many Asian American activists (including some of the authors in this book) refute the label "feminist" although their work pays special attention to the experience of women. Sometimes this feeling reflects a fear of alienating men—a consequence that seems inevitable if men are unable to own up to their gender privilege. At other times, the antipathy toward feminism reflects the cultural insensitivity and racism of white, European feminists.

By creating this anthology, Sonia Shah suggests an Asian American feminist paradigm with its own cultural and political reference points. This paradigm should not be referred to as an "addendum" to Asian American politics or as a "variant" of white feminism, because those terms force Asian American feminism into the margins of other political frameworks. A point that bears repeating is that Asian American feminism, like other movements initiated by women of color, does not depend on a mechanical process of adding up oppressions.

I have heard too many community activists explain the intersection of gender and race by referring to disembodied identities, fractions of human experience: "First I am a person of color, then I am a woman. That makes me doubly oppressed." According to this way of adding, a white man has the most whole identity; his experience is treated as the norm. The notion that the Asian American women's movement consists of "two movements in one" relies on this convenient but unreasonable arithmetic. Instead, Asian American feminism is an articulation of the necessary overlap of many social and historical processes of hierarchy and injustice.

This overlap is necessary in the sense that Asian American feminists must think, write, and act from their particular gendered and racialized contexts. Although in theory we can isolate one dimension of social life (the experience of being female) from another (the experience of being Asian American), in fact such a one-dimensional moment never exists.

The chapters in this book illustrate a variety of activist approaches to the principles of feminism and to the complex realities of Asian American life. Whether the topic is domestic violence, sexual exploitation, the environment, or punk rock, each approach wrestles in some way with the intersection of gender and race, gender and imperialism, or gender and tradition. Asian American feminists redefine the usual sites of feminist struggle: the home, the family, and the body. As America's "perpetual foreigners," Asian Americans have a complicated relationship to the idea of "home," particularly to the extent that home indicates nationhood or nationality. Asian American families often span multiple generations and multiple continents, involving intricate social bonds. For Asian Americans, the inscription of gender on the body is prefigured by the colonial relationship of the Orient to the West. Protecting women's bodies in this scenario cannot be fully accomplished by an appeal to personal control over one's health or desires.

Because Asian American feminism emerges in a context that is not already encapsulated by the prevailing sites of feminist struggle, the ideas and accomplishments of Asian American feminists need to be considered on their own terms. As they struggle for empowerment, they find there is no perfect solution, no political formula. Anyway, Asian American political resistance is not predicated on such cleanliness. Instead, as these women show, activism involves an opening up of possibilities, an acknowledgment of fragile bonds, and most important, an articulation of a commitment to justice.

Introduction: Slaying the Dragon Lady

Toward an Asian American Feminism

By Sonia Shah

Why publish a book on Asian American feminism? Many fine works on Asian American women have been published in recent years, from anthologies such as the recently released *Making More Waves, Our Feet Walk the Sky,* and *The Very Inside* to literary collections, such as *The Forbidden Stitch, The Politics of Life*, and *Unbroken Thread*,[1] to name just a few.

But this book is fundamentally different. It focuses explicitly on the political perspectives of Asian American women, describing a growing social movement and an emerging way of looking at the world: Asian American feminism. As I argue below, an Asian American feminist perspective—more than being Asian American or a woman—can animate and unite Asian American women into a lasting and fruitful social movement.

Works on Asian American women often take as their focal point their experiences, tacitly assuming *something* is similar or unifying in Asian American women's experiences, despite the obligatory disclaimers to the contrary.[2] As critics and scholars have long pointed out, the experiences of Asian American women are fantastically diverse. We are a group of people with different nationalities, languages, religions, ethnicities, classes, and immigration status. I agree that there *is* something unifying in women's varying experiences. But in works on Asian American women, that something is left undefined—it is vaguely referred to, if at all, as something about being from Asia, or about stereotypes, foods, and career choices.

All of the above similarities do exist, to varying degrees. But, I think, in the end, that those similarities are only skin-deep, not enough to make relations between different Asian American women any more likely than relations between Asian women and any other group of people. Indeed, the differences are at times much bigger, more real, more visceral and emotionally laden than the similarities, which are so often abstract.

To critics who would then say, well then, how does it make sense to talk about Asian American women at all? I would respond: it makes as much sense as it does to talk about white people or black people or Latinos. These racial groups admit just as much, if not more, diversity within their ranks than they have similarities. In the end, they are historical constructs, kept in place by social and political institutions, in service of a hierarchical, racially biased society. White people include poor Irish Catholic illegal immigrants, rich WASPS, and Jewish intellectuals. They are at least as different as they are similar. But it makes sense to talk about them as a group because they all share the same rung on the racial hierarchy, which, in many areas of life, is the most significant determinant of their social status in the United States. More than their shared language, ethnic heritage, or class, their *whiteness* determines who they live with, who they go to school with, what kind of jobs they get, how much money they make, and with whom they start families.

Similarly, the reason to talk about Asian American women as a single group is because we all share the same rung on the racial hierarchy *and* on the gender hierarchy. It is not that our lives are so similar in substance, but that our lives are all monumentally shaped by three major driving forces in U.S. society: racism and patriarchy most immediately, and ultimately, imperial aggression against Asia as well. As long as those systems of distributing and exercising power continue to exist, it will continue to make sense to talk about Asian American women as a group (as well as other racial and gender groups.)

Explicitly defining this book as one *not* about Asian American women, but rather exploring the topic of Asian American feminism, is the embodiment of the above point. There is no *political* point in just talking about Asian American women's experiences, even as the very question rests upon the years of vital scholarship and creative work done on detailing that experience. What it makes *political* sense to talk about is how the forces of racism, patriarchy, and imperialism specifically affect Asian American women. And, most importantly, how Asian American women counter resistance to those forces. In other words, about a racially conscious, international feminism: Asian American feminism.

Dragon Ladies: A Brief Political History

Empress Tsu-hsi ruled China from 1898 to 1908 from the Dragon Throne. The *New York Times* described her as "the wicked witch of the East, a reptilian dragon lady who had arranged the poisoning, strangling, beheading, or forced suicide of anyone who had ever challenged her autocratic rule."[3] Decades later, scholars such as Sterling Seagrave attempted to balance this self-servingly racist caricature of Empress Tsu-hsi. But the shadow of the Dragon Lady—with her cruel, perverse, and inhuman ways—continued to darken encounters between Asian women and the West they flocked to for refuge: the 1996 Meriam Webster dictionary describes a dragon lady as "an overbearing or tyrannical woman."

Far from being predatory, many of the first Asian women to come to the United States in the mid-1800s were disadvantaged Chinese women, who were tricked, kidnaped, or smuggled into the country to serve the predominantly male Chinese community as prostitutes.[4] The impression that *all* Asian women were prostitutes, born at that time, "colored the public perception of, attitude toward, and action against all Chinese women for almost a century," writes historian Sucheng Chan. Police and legislators singled out Chinese women for special restrictions and opprobriums, "not so much because they were prostitutes as such (since there were also many white prostitutes around plying their trade) but because—as Chinese—they allegedly brought in especially virulent strains of venereal diseases, introduced opium addiction, and enticed white boys to a life of sin."[5]

While Chinese men bought Chinese women's sex and displayed their bound feet to curious Americans (at the St. Louis World's Fair, for example),[6] white women took to "saving" their disadvantaged sisters. Protestant missionary women brought policemen with hatchets to brothels to round up Chinese women into Mission Homes, where everything from personal mail to suitors was overseen by the missionary women.[7] Chinese women who were not prostitutes ended up bearing the brunt of the Chinese exclusion laws that passed in the late-1800s, engendered by the missionaries' and other anti-Chinese campaigns.

During these years, Japanese immigration stepped up, and with it, a reactionary anti-Japanese movement joined established anti-Chinese sentiment. During the early 1900s, Japanese numbered less than 3 percent of the total population in California, but nevertheless encountered virulent and sometimes violent racism. The "picture brides" from Japan who emigrated to join their husbands in the United States were, to racist Californians, "another example of Oriental treachery," according to historian Roger Daniels.[8]

U.S. immigration policy towards Asians has in large part been shaped by its perceived labor needs. Early Chinese and Japanese immigrants were actively recruited from the poorer classes to work as manual laborers on the railroads and elsewhere. As has been widely noted, before the immigration laws were radically changed in 1965, few Asian women emigrated to the United States. But it bears noting that despite the fact that they weren't in the country, Asian women shouldered much of the cost of subsidizing Asian men's labor. U.S. employers didn't have to pay Asian men as much as other laborers who had families to support, since Asian women in Asia bore the costs of rearing children and taking care of the older generation.[9]

Asian women who did emigrate here in the pre-1960s years were also usually employed as cheap laborers. In the pre-World War II years, close to half of all Japanese American women were employed as servants or laundresses in the San Francisco area.[10] The World War II internment of Japanese Americans made them especially easy to exploit: they had lost their homes, possessions, and savings when forcibly interned at the camps. Yet, in order to leave, they had to prove they had jobs and homes.[11] U.S. government officials thoughtfully arranged for their employment by fielding requests, most of which were for servants.

The 1965 immigration act brought in a huge influx of immigrants from Asia to fill primarily professional positions in the United States. Asian engineers, physicians, students and other professionals flocked to the country, drastically altering the face of Asian America and Asian American politics.

Making Waves, Big and Small

The first wave of Asian women's organizing formed out of the Asian American movement of the 1960s, which in turn was inspired by the civil rights movement and the anti-Vietnam War movement. While many Asian American women are quick to note that women's issues are the same as men's issues—i.e. social justice, equity, human rights—history shows that Asian American men have not necessarily felt the same way. Leftist Asian women in Yellow Power and other Asian American groups often found themselves left out of the decision-making process and their ideas and concerns relegated to "women's auxiliary" groups that were marginal to the larger projects at hand. Some Asian male activists rationalized this by

> pointing to their own oppression, arguing that they had a "right" to the sexual services of "their" women, after years when Asian women were excluded from the country. Moreover, they saw services from women as "just compensation" for the sacrifices they were making on behalf of the "people."[12]

As Asian American scholar Gary Okihiro notes, "Europe's feminization of Asia, its taking possession, working over, and penetration of Asia, was preceded and paralleled by Asian men's subjugation of Asian women."[13] Asian women naturally gravitated together in response to men's patronizing attitudes and some formed ambitious, radical political projects. Eager to advance "the correct line," most of these early groups petered out over sectarian conflicts. They were unable to inspire large numbers of Asian or other women or to hammer out unity amongst themselves.

While earnest, hardworking, and vital, these early Asian women radicals couldn't compete with the growing reality that for many Asian American women, there was money to be made. The highly educated and affluent Asian immigrants who came to the United States after 1965 were eager to be incorporated into the U.S. economy, and could be treated as a sort of second-tier professional class by U.S. employers. Not surprisingly, large organizations of primarily middle-class East Asian women, such as Asian Women United and the Organization of Asian Women, flourished during these years. These groups devoted themselves to educational and service projects, rather than to directly resisting social injustices.[14] Their popularity was at least partly affected by the fact that they helped professional Asian American women, in various ways, get and keep better jobs. The National Network of Asian and Pacific Women, founded in 1982 under the auspices of a federal grant, provides a case in point. As William Wei writes:

> It has been castigated for catering to middle-class women who are mainly interested in enhancing their employment opportunities....[The Network believes that] it will be the professionals, rather than the workers, who will be in the vanguard of social change in the United States. Besides, its leaders claim, when it organizes activities that focus mainly on middle-class women, it is merely responding to the wishes of the majority of its members.[15]

Whatever oppositional sparks organizers of these groups may have had were easily squelched by the triple pressure created by the growing model minority myth and multiculturalism's identity politics. Conservative and mainstream institutions who wanted to advance racialized theories supported model minority myth-making because it implied there was a "good" minority in tacit opposition to the "bad" minorities—African Americans and Latinos. At the same time, the model minority myth helped countless struggling Asian Americans start businesses and send their kids to Ivy League schools, and was thus consciously upheld by Asian American community leaders. The ongoing condemnation of white supremacy by African Americans and others was answered by liberals with the benign image of multiculturalism: a scenario in which white people don't exploit black people, but white, brown, yellow, black, and red live together harmoniously. White feminists and other liberals advanced this feel-good fantasy with celebrations of Asian American culture and people. The result was a triple pressure on Asian women to conform to the docile, warm, upwardly mobile stereotype liberals, conservatives, and their own community members all wanted to promote.

The political context of the 1990s is significantly different, and likewise colors Asian women's organizing in this decade. Today, Asian immigrant professionals are less vital to the labor market and are thus, in a familiar cycle, being forced down the status ladder.[16] Affirmative action policies that benefited them are being dismantled. Laws that restrict their access to public assistance and legal rights have been enacted.[17] China and Japan are once again being invoked as evil empires—due now to their financial strength—as a new Yellow Peril is sweeping the country.[18]

At the same time, Asian immigration laws have changed such that the new Asian immigrant is not educated and professional but working-class or poor. Trade agreements such as NAFTA and GATT have broken down protections for workers and the environment in order to secure a free-wheeling capitalist global economy, and Asian workers in Asia and in the United States, especially women, are suffering the worst of it—laboring under worse working conditions and being forced to compete for the most degraded, worst-paying jobs.[19] As Miriam Ching Louie points out, the U.S. workforce is "increasingly female, minority, and immigrant." For example, in San Francisco's garment industry—its largest manufacturing sector—90 percent of the workers are women: 80 percent of those are Chinese-speaking, and less than 8 percent are unionized.[20]

Activists have responded to these new changes with a renewed labor movement and new worker campaigns that cross borders and industries. Asian women organizers have been at the forefront of these campaigns. Most significant among these is the groundbreaking campaign by Asian Immigrant Women Advocates (AIWA) to organize Asian seamstresses against a powerful fashion designer, Jessica McClintock. AIWA's Garment Workers Justice Campaign was launched in May 1992 to secure $15,000 in back wages for Asian immigrant seamstresses who had been stiffed by their employer, Lucky Sewing Company. Instead of going after the sewing shop, which had declared bankruptcy, AIWA aimed its campaign directly at the designer who used the shop's labor. (This was a vital strategic move, as manufacturers often seek to immunize themselves against workers' grievances by subcontracting with shops for whose working conditions they don't take responsibility.) Not only did this campaign, which in the end secured a generous settlement for the seamstresses, establish a vital precedent for labor organizing, it politicized hundreds of young Asian American women across the country. AIWA staff inspired the seamstresses to outrage by showing them McClintock's fancy boutiques and organized Asian American women college students to stage protests at McClintock stores nationwide.[21]

With worker campaigns such as AIWA's, new issue-oriented organizations such as the National Women's Health Organization, and rejuvenated Asian battered women's organizations, a new generation of activists is springing up. They are uncovering the hidden history of previous generations of Asian women activists. With fewer and fewer class interests to divide them, they are shaping a new movement, one that goes beyond just agitating for our little piece of the ever-shrinking pie. They are putting poor immigrant and refugee Asian women at the forefront of their organizing, they are thinking globally, and they are making the connections among the politics of labor, health, environment, culture, nationalism, racism, and patriarchy: connections that have in the past eluded left activists.

An Asian American feminist movement is *the only movement* that will consistently represent Asian American women's interests. As the chapters in this book illustrate, neither the feminist movement nor the Asian American movement have taken Asian American women's interests into consideration on their agendas. But it's much more than that. An Asian American feminist movement is vital for the larger project of uncovering the social structure, with its built-in injustices and inequities, that affect us all. In today's global economy, in which nothing is certain for anyone save the most elite of the elite, this is a project that vitally concerns the majority.

My goal in publishing this book is to describe, expand, and nurture the growing resistance of Asian American women. I hope this book will provide a common ground for Asian women and girls and their allies. In so doing, it provides a set of issues, terms, ideas, and stories for folks to talk about—whether it is to debunk and decry them or to transform them into an agenda for action. As the pieces in this book show, Asian American women are already making their movement happen. A different sort of Dragon Lady is emerging—not a cold-blooded reptile, but a creature who breathes fire.

Notes

1. Kim, Elaine H., Lilia V. Villanueva, and Asian Women United, ed. *Making More Waves: New Writing by Asian American Women*. Boston: Beacon Press, 1997; Women of South Asian Descent Collective, ed. *Our Feet Walk the Sky: Women of the South Asian Diaspora*. San Francisco: Aunt Lute Books, 1994; Lim-Hing, Sharon, ed. *The Very Inside: An Anthology of Writing by Asian and Pacific Islander Lesbian and Bisexual Women*. Toronto: Sister Vision, 1994; Lim, Shirley Geok-Lin, ed. *The Forbidden Stitch: An Asian American Women's Anthology*. Corvallis, OR: Calyx Books, 1989; Houston, Velina Hasu, ed. *The Politics of Life: Four Plays by Asian American Women*. Philadelphia, Temple University Press, 1993; Uno, Roberta, ed. *Unbroken Thread: An Anthology of Plays by Asian American Women*. Amherst: University of Massachusetts Press, 1993.

2. Lim, in her introduction to *The Forbidden Stitch*, describes Asian American women's cultural and other diversity, but then points to Asian American women's "plural singularity," as their unifying principle. *The Forbidden Stitch* was the first anthology of Asian American women's writings to appear in the United States. In the 1997 anthology *Making More Waves*, the editors' preface states that they "wanted…to go beyond simply representing the various Asian ethnic groups." Still, their book is a celebration of diversity—"an attempt to weave history and memory with desire and possibility in such a way that multiple identities emerge as irregularities and discontinuities, beautiful and unpredictable, in the pattern."

3. Seagrave, Sterling. *Dragon Lady: the Life and Legend of the Last Empress of China*. New York: Knopf Books, 1992.

4. In 1860, over 80 percent of the Chinese women in San Francisco were prostitutes. Yung, Judy. "The Social Awakening of Chinese American Women." Ed. Ruiz, Vicki L., and Ellen Carol DuBois. *Unequal Sisters: A Multicultural Reader in U.S. Women's History*. New York: Routledge, 1990. 247-48.

5. Sucheng, Chan. "The Exclusion of Chinese Women, 1870-1943." *Entry Denied: Exclusion and the Chinese Community in America, 1882-1943.* Ed. Sucheng Chan. *Philadelphia: Temple University Press, 1991. 97-99, 138.*

6. Yung 248-49.

7. Pascoe, Peggy. "Gender Systems in Conflict: The Marriages of Mission-Educated Chinese American Women, 1874-1939." Ed. Ruiz, Vicki L., and Ellen Carol DuBois. *Unequal Sisters: A Multicultural Reader in U.S. Women's History*. New York: Routledge, 1990. 142-145.

8. Daniels, Roger. *The Politics of Prejudice: The Anti-Japanese Movement in California and the Struggle for Japanese Exclusion*. New York: Atheneum and the University of California Press, 1973. 1, 44.

9. Bonacich, Edna, and Lucie Cheng, eds. *Labor Immigration Under Capitalism: Asian Workers in the United States before World War II*. University of California Press, 1984. 5-34.

10. Glenn, Evelyn Nakano. "From Servitude to Service Work." Eds. Ruiz, Vicki L., and Ellen Carol DuBois. *Unequal Sisters: A Multicultural Reader in U.S. Women's History*. New York: Routledge, 1990. 408-410.

11. Glenn 413.

12. Wei, William. *The Asian American Movement.* Philadelphia: Temple University Press, 1993. 76.

13. Okihiro, Gary. *Margins and Mainstreams: Asians in American History and Culture.* Seattle: University of Washington Press, 1994. 68.

14. Wei 72-100.

15. Wei 98.

16. Zamichow, Nora. "Education Fails Some Immigrants: Professionals in Other Countries Often Forced into Menial Positions." *The Boston Globe*. 28 May 1996.

17. "Actions by States Hold Keys to Welfare Law's Future." *The New York Times*. 1 October 1996: A22.

18. Conservative writer William Safire summed it up when he responded to campaign fundraising scandals allegedly involving illegal contributions from Asian nationals. Safire decried "the penetration of the White House by Asian interests" and "the Asian connection," calling Asians and Asian Americans "aliens" and "favor-hungry foreigners" who "shell out." Safire, William. "Absence of Outrage." Op-ed. *The New York Times*. 10 October 1996: A33.

19. Brecher, Jeremy, and Tim Costello, *Global Village or Global Pillage: Economic Reconstruction from the Bottom Up*. Boston: South End Press, 1994.

20. Louie, Miriam Ching. "Immigrant Asian Women in Bay Area Garment Sweatshops: 'After Sewing, Laundry, Cleaning, and Cooking, I Have No Breath Left to Sing.'" *Amerasia Journal* 18.1 (1992): 1-26.

21. Delgado, Gary. "How the Empress Gets Her Clothes: Asian Immigrant Women Fight Fashion Designer Jessica McClintock." Ed. Anner, John. *Beyond Identity Politics: Emerging Social Justice Movements in Communities of Color*. Boston: South End Press, 1996. 81-94.

Acknowledgments

Thanks first and foremost to all the contributors, who worked with such care and thoughtfulness on their essays for this book, and were patient and supportive throughout. Thanks to my friends at South End Press—Anthony Arnove, Dionne Brooks, Loie Hayes, Anoosh Jorjorian, and especially my editor, Lynn Lu—and also to the many interns who volunteered to help develop this project. Thanks finally to my family and especially my sister, Seema, and always, M. and Z.

I. Strategies and Visions

Juliana Pegues
Photograph by Chris Durazo

Strategies from the Field

Organizing the Asian American Feminist Movement

By Juliana Pegues

Talking on the phone to a friend of mine, another Asian American woman who has worked in both broad leftist political spaces and identity-based circles, I tell her about this essay. That I am attempting to articulate my frustrations with the tried and tired models for organizing. I ask her what she thinks, for any comments she has.

"Aiyah!"

I wait for her to finish, then realize she is done. "Is that it? Aiyah?"

"That's it," she responds. "What more is there to say?"

To be honest, I know how she feels. As a feminist and lesbian who has participated in identity-based organizations and the white-dominated leftist movement, I am frustrated with the difficulty in organizing with both.

Many of us on the margins have experienced the racism, class elitism, sexism, and homophobia of white-male-dominated leftist organizations. On the other hand, we've also encountered a lack of political analysis among those with whom we share ethnic, gender, and sexual identities. How, then, should Asian American feminists build organizations? With whom should we work? Where is our place in social change movements, and how do we uniquely affect how movements are shaped?

Aiyah, indeed.

Limitations of the Left

I am sitting on the floor of the local anarchist center, my back resting on an old plaid couch someone has donated, every other piece of mismatched furniture and most of the available floor space occupied by other activists. The door to the storefront remains open, and the occa-

sional flapping of the screen door provides the only breeze on an otherwise hot and humid summer day. I'm sure most of us would rather be outside basking in the sun, but our political commitment compels us to sit—wilt, really—surrounded by the mild smell of mildew in this old office space. We are here for a "community meeting on racism," called in response to vandalism of our storefront by local Black teenagers, who most likely perceive our center to be a white establishment in their community of color.

"Maybe we should call the police?" volunteers Marcus, a young, red-haired punk. He must be new to the scene.

"No way!" "No cops!" A chorus of voices shoots him down.

"They are expressing their righteous anger in a racist society," Tom, seasoned anarchist and de facto leader in this supposedly leaderless organization, says.

"Right on!" "Right on!" A few clenched fists fly.

"Yes," says Dave, "it is understandable that they feel threatened after four hundred years of oppression."

The group listens as one white male after another expounds on the evils of racism, interrupted only by the occasional few words from a white woman.

I look over at Juanita, the only other person of color in this motley crew of rag-tag revolutionaries, and roll my eyes. My Chicana sister returns the sentiment with a half-hearted smile and a wink, but her expression soon returns to a serious frown as the discussion continues.

"But we're not the enemy," says Tammy, Tom's lover. "Maybe we can talk to them."

"Talk to them?" questions Dave. "We can't, really. What could we say? As white people, it's really our job to understand them. We really can't say anything to them."

"Precisely," adds Tom.

"Yeah, what can we do? We're all white," says Rick.

"Ahem," Juanita pointedly clears her throat, and few activists miss her glare.

"Well, mostly white," says Tom.

"Exactly," Dave nods towards Juanita.

"Yes," Joyce joins in. "What can we do? We're mostly white."

My eyes glaze over. Snippets of the continuing discussion drift past me.

"I feel so bad...I try so hard not to be racist..." "I think we have to overcome our whiteness, be traitors to our race..." "Isn't there a Black man in the socialist youth group at the university? We should ask him..." "I really have worked on my racism..." "I think these African American youth will change once they see we are really down with them..." "I feel sooo bad..."

As their voices drone on, my gut churns, and I feel a rising red heat, a slow burning sensation that spreads throughout my body; I notice that my fingers are shaking. Still, I say nothing.

"Well, what do you think, Juliana? What do you think, Juanita?" Rapid-fire questions that give no space for answers.

"I don't know," Juanita spits out, her black eyes shooting fire. "Maybe you should figure it out yourselves."

Juanita quickly dismissed, all eyes turn to me. I swallow, pause. Swallow again. "Well, it seems to me that you aren't treating this like a real issue, you aren't treating these Black teenagers like real..."

"I know exactly what you are saying," Tom jumps in. "We need to walk our talk, get to know what their issues are."

"What is that Malcolm X quote?" asks Dave.

"Oh, I know which one you are talking about," Rick responds. "I can't remember exactly what he says, but I know which one you are talking about."

And so it continues.

A few months later, I bump into Marcus, red hair now bleached blonde, sporting a new "Question Authority" button on his black-hooded sweatshirt.

"Hey, Juliana," he says. At least he didn't call me Juanita. "How come you don't come to meetings anymore? I'm on the core collective now, and we could really use your energy."

"Yeah, sure," I mutter, turning to walk away.

"Hey," he adds, "if you see Juanita, bring her with you. We sure could use her righteous anger."

As I quickly depart, he calls out, "On with the revolution!"

As a young, mixed-heritage Chinese American woman, Taipei-born and Alaska-raised, I organized my first protest on a small liberal arts campus in southern California against U.S. troops in Honduras. I came to academia from my quickly rising working-to-middle-class family. Somewhat a punk and somewhat a hippie, I participated in peace, women's, and environmental causes. These activities invigorated my spirit, and I found I was not paying as much attention to my schoolwork. I dropped out and moved to Seattle, where I lived in my first women's collective household and worked in a vegetarian restaurant. The Emerald City is where I became hooked on politics and started identifying as a radical. The large protests were thrilling, and I met students, workers, squatters, and artists. Everyone was political and came with some leftist bent. An eager sponge, I listened and learned.

My political environment exposed and analyzed societal institutions, helping me make sense of my life and experiences. I became enraged with injustice and inspired by struggle. I encountered people who spoke critically about the U.S. government and its policies—people intent on eradicating oppression and creating a new world. I believed in this new world and wanted to be part of it. In the company of self-identified revolutionary anarchists and radical socialists, I found friends and allies, a community.

Unfortunately, it didn't last forever. While becoming confident as a politically aware person, I became increasingly confused about my own place in the struggle, particularly around my racial identity. During those years I was politically active in cities on both coasts and in the Midwest, but I met only a handful of other Asian American activists. Although there are and were many Asian American activists in the United States, there were few in the circles I was involved with.

The groups I worked with adamantly espoused anti-racist and anti-sexist rhetoric, but time and time again refused to accept internal criticism from women and people of color, and leadership from anyone but a white male was unheard of. My growing awareness of these dynamics led me into direct conflict with the white male leadership in leftist circles. When I angrily challenged a comrade who claimed that all Asian Americans were well-off and therefore not concerned with political matters, he scolded me for being "disruptive." My anger was either ignored or deemed overreactionary.

After being hired by a peace and justice nonprofit organization, I was first introduced to the board by the hiring committee, with my assets as an Asian American glowingly highlighted. The three-hour board meeting proceeded with a lengthy discussion of a recent anti-racism workshop the all-white board had attended. Several members of the board complained resentfully that the workshop was an unnecessary waste of time, while others chided them for thinking this, carefully mentioning all the Black friends they had. Just as one member was guiltily recalling ignorant perceptions she used to have, I cut in to say that I thought the conversation was not really appropriate at a board meeting without specific direction and facilitation, and especially in front of a person of color. The discussion ended, but not before several people responded, incredibly, that they weren't aware I was a person of color. After the board meeting, I was approached by many board members who wanted to continue their individual thoughts on race relations, explaining how they weren't really racist. Two board members wanted to give me a hug. With no other person of color available at the time for a reality check, I actually wondered if I had done something wrong.

Another time, I was invited to speak to a group of students about anti-Asian immigrant bashing. Afterwards, I was complimented by their professor, a European American socialist feminist, on how lucky they were to find an Asian American woman like me, since it is so hard to find smart Asian American speakers with a political analysis.

Coming out as a lesbian further separated me from the white male world. I could no longer hear the passionate words of white activists without irony and cynicism creeping in. I left the left bitter and disillusioned, hurt and angry.

My story is not unusual; many of us have experienced this type of marginalization working within the U.S. left. The current political landscape includes trade unions who scapegoat workers from other countries and immigrants within our borders, communist groups with political manifestos calling homosexuality an aberration in a decadent bourgeois society, and a socialist organization that claims a white member who raped a working-class Black teenage girl was "framed" and is actually a political prisoner.

The organizations I participated in and interacted with were unable to comprehend being majority white in an honest way. Many nearly white groups are unwilling to be exclusively white, but in reality they cannot accommodate the agendas of people of color. People of color are invited in or recruited to escape accusations an all-white group would be subject to from other communities of color. But the reality is that these groups in many cases act as all-white groups internally, and white perspectives and standards are the norm.

In addition to the individual inability of majority white leftist groups to deal with race internally, stereotypes of Asian Americans are embedded in left ideology as well. "We should not underestimate our invisibility either in U.S. politics in general, or on the left," cautions writer and activist Karin Aguilar-San Juan. "Myths about Asian Americans belittle the damage done by the discrimination we face, obscure the complexity of experience, and make our contributions to the struggle against racism invisible." This invisibility keeps us isolated, feeding into the belief that Asian American activists are few and far between, reinforcing the notion among white leftists that we are apolitical or conservative. Time and time again white activists have expressed to me how surprising it is to meet an Asian American activist.

Noel Ignatiev, cofounder and editor of *Race Traitor*—a self-proclaimed "journal of the new abolitionism" that publishes articles and promotes dialogue about white people defying whiteness—was interviewed in the revolutionary anarchist newspaper *The Blast.* (The interview was also reprinted in the *Utne Reader*.) When asked why he referred to race relations in terms of Black and white people, Ignatiev replied that the term "people of color" wasn't useful, using Chinese Americans to prove his point. "Chinese are people of color, and in the past they suffered fierce oppression in this country, and still suffer the effects of prejudice, but would anyone argue that Chinese in America today constitute an oppressed race? They have been defined as an ethnic group, indeed the 'model minority.'" That this longtime radical activist and anti-racist scholar can make such a claim is frightening. His comment illustrates the obliviousness of white anti-racists to the persistent and virulent oppression Chinese Americans, and all Asian Americans, face today.

Ignatiev's comments also emphasize a prevalent notion on the left that race is a Black/white issue. When race is seen in Black-and-white terms, Asian American activists remain invisible, and our issues are ignored. "The Black cause was the most important," Mai, a young Vietnamese American activist, complained of the anti-racist group she was involved in. The group consistently balked at taking action against racism directed at non-Black people of color, including police harassment of Native Americans. "They didn't want to pursue it; they wanted to pursue Black issues."

Asian American women also have to contend with stereotypical images of Asian women as exotic. Before coming out, I was subjected to continuous male fascination with my heritage and more compliments about my appearance than my viewpoints. One leftist friend referred to me as his "little Mao." Asian American women are considered a safe bet for leftist groups; we boost their proportions of people of color, yet are expected to be cute, well-behaved, hard-working, and obedient. As Nisei poet Mitsuye Yamada writes,

> I am weary of starting from scratch each time I speak or write, as if there were no history behind us, of hearing that among women of color, Asian women are the least political, or the least oppressed, or the most polite. It is too bad not many people remember that one of the two persons in Seattle who stood up to contest the constitutionality of the Evacuation Order in 1942 was a young Japanese American woman.

These and other barriers seem designed to ensure the participation of only a few people of color in majority white leftist organizations, leaving many radical Asian American women isolated from political communities and organizing.

Ineffectiveness of Identity Politics

I am sitting in Shau Wen's living room, surrounded by plates with bits of Singapore rice noodles, Gai-lan with oyster sauce, rice, and kimchi starting to harden, chopsticks fallen into the half-eaten remains. Papers are strewn about, a few even crumpled and tossed into a convenient corner. Images of women smiling, playing, and kissing adorn the walls, along with a promotional poster for the movie "The Joy Luck Club." From her perch atop a bookshelf, Shau Wen's cat Sappho, a fat grey tabby with green eyes, surveys the dozen or so Asian and Pacific Islander lesbian and bisexual women sitting in a semblance of a circle.

We have been meeting together, this local group, for over a year, organizing educational and visibility actions. Frequently we meet socially for official and unofficial potlucks and mahjong games. But no one is playing now. We are organizing a regional retreat for Asian and Pacific Islander lesbian and bisexual women. Hour Three of our retreat planning meeting finds us discussing the financial aid policy.

"No, I will not change my mind," Shau Wen states. "Any woman who wants financial aid should have it." Many nodding heads support this statement.

"I think it is a good idea," Nancy softly joins in, "but we have to have some sort of guidelines. I get really mad that college students always get financial aid. What about working-class women? Women in college have a lot of privilege."

"That's really too harsh," says Meena. "My father was college-educated, but coming here as an immigrant, he never had it easy, and he worked menial jobs for the rest of his life."

"Can we get back to making a decision?" Me-Kyung asks. "I really need to leave soon."

"Okay," says Alice, "the way I see it, we need to come to a consensus on general guidelines, then set up a committee to do it."

"That's what I said half an hour ago," blurts May Lee. "No one ever listens to what I say." She gets up and moves next to her girlfriend Lisa.

Trinh clears her throat and shifts in her chair. "I'm sorry we didn't listen to you earlier, May Lee. But let's go ahead and set up guidelines, okay?"

"So it should be need-based, right?" I join in. "And could we just let the APLB's registering ask for the amount they need?"

"And then a committee could make final decisions if we have limited funds," adds Alice.

"I think that's a really good idea," Pramilla backs it up. "Are we ready to ask for a consensus?"

"I want to be on the committee," Nancy joins in.

"Me too, then," Shau Wen states. "Any woman who wants financial aid should have it."

"Shau Wen," Nancy sighs, "that's too idealistic."

I look around the room to see that half of the women are sitting at the edges of their seats, ready to jump, while the other half looks ready to fall asleep. Me-Kyung barely covers a yawn, and May Lee is busy picking fuzz out of the carpet.

"I am wondering," says Trinh, "what women who haven't spoken think. Me-Kyung? May Lee? June? Lisa?" May Lee shrugs; June just nods.

Me-Kyung looks at her watch and adds, "I just would like to make a decision soon. I am really tired and we have been going at this for hours."

Lisa starts fidgeting. "I have something to say. It's really been bothering me, but this conversation has been taking us too long. I think we are just babying other APLB's. We're giving women enough notice. If they can't earn the registration—and it is just not that expensive—maybe they shouldn't come. We are wasting way too much time on this."

June is now nodding more vigorously. "I wasn't going to say anything because there is always this PC air in this group, but I agree with Lisa."

"We are not a welfare service," Lisa emphatically adds.

"I cannot believe you said that." Shau Wen is pursing her lips. "That is so classist."

June rolls her eyes, and Lisa throws her pen across the room. As it slides down the beige wallpaper, Trinh looks at Shau Wen and says under her breath, "Classist? You're the college professor."

"What about women who can't save?" Nancy raises her voice. "Single mothers? Poor rural women? Disabled women?"

"Hey, unless they come rolling up in a wheelchair," says June, "I don't think they are that disabled. I think they can save the money."

I sit among those stunned to silence. Breathing hard, breathing angry. The well-worn fabric of community quickly unraveling.

"Can we table this?" asks Me-Kyung.

After my departure from leftist communities to find more supportive spaces, I scooted to the opposite end of the movement spectrum. I joined a women of color discussion group and went to Asian cultural association meetings. I became very active in Asian and Pacific Islander Lesbian and Bisexual (APLB) organizing. I immediately found what was missing in leftist circles: recognition as an Asian American queer woman and validation of and sensitivity to my experiences. This new community was extremely affirming, and I was accepted unconditionally. At local, national, and global levels, from Minneapolis radio interviews and readings to the thrill of marching with other Asian queers from around the world at Stonewall 25, I met other queer Asian women with energy and passion who cared about this world we live in.

I thought that because we were all Asian American, women, and queer, we would have the same political views on ending oppression. Coming from my experience with the left, I assumed that there were avenues for political organizing, both within my new APLB family and the larger queer community. This was not the case.

When I verbally confronted an out Nazi marching in Gay Pride, I was stopped by Pride "marshals" who informed me that anyone who is gay has a right to march, even with a swastika. At a lesbian of color meeting, an Asian American woman repeatedly used the term "poor white trash." When challenged on the offensiveness of such a term, she launched into stereotypical descriptions of poor whites to "show" why they are more racist/sexist/homophobic than rich white people. Lambda Legal Defense and Education Fund, a national law organization that champions gay and lesbian rights, used the racist Broadway play "Miss Saigon" as a benefit fundraiser, even after meeting with a coalition group mobilized by Asian and Pacific Islander queers who opposed the play's imperialist content.

These disturbing examples point to the underlying paradoxes of organizing based on identity. In a society in which O.J. Simpson is seen as an African American hero by certain communities while African American political prisoner Mumia Abu-Jamal rots behind prison bars, we need to look at the dangers of identity-reductionist thinking. Addressing Asian American activists, Aguilar-San Juan warns, "In the 1990s we must take care not to subsume ourselves solely in efforts to build Asian American pride. Reducing race to a matter of identity, rather than expanding our experience of racism into a critique of U.S. society, is detrimental to our movement."

By their very nature, identity-based organizations must remain apolitical, in order to be inclusive to all those with the shared identity, including right-wing Asian Republicans, lesbians who seek only their own visibility, and pro-life activists in women's organizations.

The insular camaraderie based on common identity experience also makes it difficult to challenge privilege within groups, and many identity-based groups that attempt to address issues of unequal power are destroyed through internal conflict. When political differences develop and tensions erupt, members often just leave, and the group fades away. Alternatively, endless amounts of time are spent discussing and re-discussing certain issues, and consensus between those with fundamentally different beliefs and convictions is never reached.

I was an active member of a lesbian of color organization in which incidents of racial hostility occurred. Left unchallenged, gossip and ignorance grew. When inter-ethnic issues were finally discussed and various resources presented (a facilitator experienced in cross-racial relations, additional group discussions and literature), it was very easy for those unwilling to change to resist or ignore them. Though there were several other factors that led to the group's eventual demise (control issues, different friendship circles, and burnout), cross-racial hostility was one of the most salient ones. Similarly, I witnessed the destruction of a consensus-based APLB group that could not agree on issues related to feminism and class, and folded after several all-day attempts at reconciliation. Amie, an activist involved in APLB and Korean adoptee support groups, concludes, "It doesn't work if people aren't committed to each other. And how can I be committed to people who aren't serious about social change?"

Organizing Strategies for Radical Asian American Women

To build movements in a consistent and long-reaching way we must look at new models. We must think more strategically. As Asian American feminists and activists, we have valuable skills and experiences. Many of us have been marginalized in broad political circles and frustrated in identity-based groups. Our analysis is critical in building new strategies and envisioning new movements.

Many believe that political and identity-based spaces are mutually exclusive, to the extent that each group usually defines the other as its antithesis. More useful, however, is viewing each model as exclusive but with positive aspects worth incorporating. Identity-based community organizing and an explicit political agenda can successfully complement each other, as evidenced by recent labor organizing.

In the United States during the 1980s, a number of community-based labor organizations formed to address the needs of Asian American workers. Significantly, the majority of this organizing occurred outside of the white-male-led AFL-CIO. Groups such as Asian Immigrant Women Advocates (AIWA) and the Chinese Progressive Association (CPA) organized not around the traditional trade-unionist model of shop organizing, but rather on the basis of ethnic identity.

In Boston in 1985, Chinese women workers, in conjunction with CPA and a coalition of students and community members, waged an 18-month struggle for job retraining and replacement after the closure of a large garment factory left 350 workers out of a job. Their eventual victory solidified a leadership base of Chinese immigrant women who went on to form the CPA's Workers' Center, an emerging activist organization in which Asian immigrant workers are decisionmakers.

AIWA was founded in 1983. Its membership consists of women in the San Francisco-Oakland Bay Area and Santa Clara's "Silicon Valley." As part of its ongoing activities, AIWA offers workplace literacy classes for immigrant women to learn English while simultaneously learning about their rights as workers, immigrants, and women. In 1992, AIWA launched the Garment Workers Justice Campaign, which effectively organized national support among workers, students, and community activists to secure corporate responsibility toward Asian immigrant women sweatshop workers. Their success in organizing a four-year-long national boycott against designer Jessica McClintock not only secured gains for the exploited sweatshop workers, but also developed leadership among Asian immigrant women and inspired a growing number of young Asian American activists.

These groups are usually viewed as marginal to both the organized U.S. labor movement and Asian American identity movements. But they have established a track record of organizing success precisely because, as marginal groups, they have organized for themselves, setting a progressive social agenda that is at the same time community-based. Asian American feminist and radical activists can look to Asian American community-based labor organizing for genuine leadership in a movement for social change. We can also look to older groups, including the Combahee River Collective, a Black feminist group that met in Boston in the 1970s and 1980s, and Out of Control, a lesbian committee that supports women political prisoners, which formed in the early 1980s and is still active today.

Not all such efforts have been successful. Unbound Feet, a collective of six Chinese and Korean American women writers, formed in 1979 to perform their work, connecting writing and feminism. According to their original Statement of Purpose:

> As writers and cultural workers, we believe in the power of words as a tool for radical social change.... We do not believe in isolating political struggles...but believe that real equality can only come about by all oppressed groups working together.

A year and a half later the group had dissolved over disagreement as to whether the group should focus on artistic expression of identity or on more direct political activism. Some members of the group felt bullied into political action, deeming it "time-consuming." "We already spend too little time on our art." Others stated,

> Today we have a split, not over petty issues or personal differences....We will take political stands, particularly when issues affect us as women, as Asian Americans, as lesbians, as radicals, and as multi-issue feminists.

Unbound Feet is an important example of an attempt to build a group on identity and political vision, and should be studied both for its contributions to Asian American feminism and also for its eventual failure to successfully integrate identity, artistic creation, and political organizing.

To successfully form issue-based identity groups, we must clearly define whom we are willing to work with, both in terms of identity and political beliefs, pro-actively designating our own space. At a very basic level, this means taking a personal responsibility to determine priorities—performing outreach, coming to group consensus over shared identity and political beliefs, and making a commitment to express this to other communities. Creating loose affinity groups would allow for both a sense of community belonging and a sense of purpose.

With affinity groups established, identity-based organizations can then be useful for networking and finding like-minded individuals. While recognizing the limitations of identity-based spaces, they provide necessary support and a logical place for affinity groups to reach out to political allies.

Established affinity groups can also work with leftist groups, regardless of the leadership of such groups. Affinity groups working with other political groups can control their level of involvement in leftist coalitions. Coalitions are vital to larger movement organizing, and affinity groups with expressed political agendas allow for solidarity with others in bottom-up, grassroots mobilizations.

This is, of course, just a blueprint for a possible organizing strategy, and there are still many issues to address. Should affinity groups have open membership or be exclusive collectives? Which issues should they choose to take on and how?

Still, this vision of a radical Asian women's movement has already begun to take shape. It begins when a young Asian American learns of Yuri Kochiyama's activism and tells me, "just to hear about her is a total inspiration," and counts the days until she not only meets Yuri Kochiyama but is involved in political actions at her side. It begins with an APLB member marching at Gay Pride with a sign that reads, "Gay white soldiers in Asia? Not my Liberation!" and ends with the absence of all soldiers, gay and straight, from any imperialist army. It begins with protesting with my Asian American sisters at a local boutique that exploits immigrant seamstresses and becomes a rallying cry for the rights of all workers around the world. It begins here, with all our joy and pain in politics and identity, and carries us to the day when Asian American women are active and vital in a grassroots political movement for sweeping social change.

Sources

I would like to acknowledge the Asian American women activists I interviewed and note that they requested that their full names not be used. I would also like to thank Joanna Kadi for her editorial suggestions and support in writing this essay.

Aguilar-San Juan, Karin. "Linking the Issues: From Identity to Activism." *The State of Asian America: Activism and Resistance in the 1990s*. Ed. Karin Aguilar-San Juan. Boston: South End Press, 1994. 1-15.

Anner, John, Introduction. *Beyond Identity Politics: Emerging Social Justice Movements in Communities of Color*. Ed. John Anner. Boston: South End Press, 1996. 5-13.

Chow, Esther Ngan-Ling. "The Feminist Movement: Where Are All the Asian American Women?" *Making Waves: An Anthology of Writing By and About Asian American Women.* Eds. Asian Women United. Boston: Beacon Press, 1989. 362-377.

Omatsu, Glenn. "The 'Four Prisons' and the Movements of Liberation: Asian American Activism from the 1960s to the 1990s." *The State of Asian America: Activism and Resistance in the 1990s.* Ed. Karin Aguilar-San Juan. Boston: South End Press, 1994. 19-69.

Ignatiev, Noel. "Treason to Whiteness Is Loyalty to Humanity." *Utne Reader*. Nov./Dec. 1994. 82-86. Reprinted from *The Blast*, June/July 1994.

Yamada, Mitsuye. "Asian Pacific American Women and Feminism." *This Bridge Called My Back.* Eds. Cherríe Moraga and Gloria Anzaldúa. New York: Kitchen Table—Women of Color Press, 1983. 71-75.

Critical Visions

The Representation and Resistance of Asian Women

By Lynn Lu

The Australian film *The Adventures of Priscilla, Queen of the Desert*[1] made a huge splash worldwide with its refreshing celebration of carnivalesque camp and its sympathetic portrayal of three male drag performers (including a male-to-female transsexual) who journey across a physically and emotionally arid landscape. In one scene, the trio (whose outlandish costumes and makeup more often make them look like clowns than queens) is aghast to encounter a scantily clad Asian woman gleefully outperforming them by shooting ping-pong balls out of a certain body cavity. Confronted by their own ultimate shortcomings as female impersonators, they can only gape in wonder. The woman, a Filipina ex-prostitute who has conned a drunken client into marrying her, eventually walks out on her white benefactor, declaring, "I no like you anyway. You got little dinga-*ling*." Needless to say, I eventually walked out on the film, feeling similarly dissatisfied. Cinematic attempts at comic relief at the expense of Asian characters are hardly unusual, but never before, to my knowledge, has the myth of Asian women's hypersexual appetite and skill—in the form of propulsion power and a tight grip—been so graphically depicted on screen.

It's no secret that the exotic mysteries of our sex have long held a tight grip on the Western (male) popular imagination. A parade of familiar stereotypes populates our cultural landscape: concubine, geisha girl, mail-order bride; dragon lady, lotus blossom, precious pearl. In this environment, Asian women thirst for realistic and three-dimensional images of ourselves that will not dissolve like mirages as we draw near.

In media-driven U.S. culture, representations of Asian women play a significant role in both reflecting and shaping our status, our self-image, and our potential. As we struggle for visibility and recognition of our diversity, we not only face blatantly offensive depictions of ourselves, but also continually come up against the power of racist, heterosexist, classist, and imperialist ideologies to adapt and pervert our demands by creating new versions of old stereotypes. The closing distance between American and Asian cultures—through popular media, private business, and international trade—has introduced new opportunities for appropriation, exploitation, and commodification of our images under the guise of multiculturalism. Our increasingly global, worldly wise, politically correct culture has raised awareness of ethnic difference—and raised the stakes in the representation game.

Vogue magazine, for example, reports that the fashion world is eagerly embracing Asian culture (as well as the millions of dollars it brings in): "We are…entering a century when we will see truly integrated and universal fashion."[2] Designer Calvin Tsao attests, "I see the beginnings of it already in the fashion magazines—coolie pants worn with Reeboks!" (It hardly seems polite to burst his bubble by asking whether those pants belong to the same coolies who made the Reeboks.) But, *Vogue* cautions, "We aren't talking about Suzie Wong in red brocade." That would be too literal: "The last thing [one] would want is to look as if [one] had just got off the boat." The Asian look may be in, but impoverished immigrants are not.

Designer Josie Natori advises, "Forget ethnic, think international." But as ethnicity and race are subsumed under the rubric of a new "international" cosmopolitanism, cultural traits become mere commodities, and the context and specificity of our experiences vanish. As this "Asian invasion" of a cultural kind belatedly focuses attention on Asian women's unique difference, then, it also puts our bodies and images even more squarely in the public domain, makes us readily available to anyone, renders us accessible for any use, while diverting attention from the deeper, often harsh realities of our lives. Only the stylish surface of Asianness, and not the realities of Asian experience or existence, are in vogue.

Romeo Gigli, whose fashions have had "an oriental slant" (!) for years, seeks what the West "found" in the East in the 1960s. He declares, "We take from the East what we need in the West. The last time the East had a big vogue here was in the sixties....Now we need that serenity and sensuality again, as an escape from our driven society." The point, it seems, is to *look* Asian without actually *being* Asian, to take the essence of Asian culture and mutate it into something the West would not be embarrassed to be seen in—to take what is aesthetically pleasing without all the political baggage. "Eastern women," *Vogue* tells us, "know how to be sexy without exposure—in the sari and the sarong or the discreet side slits of the ankle-length Vietnamese *ao dai* or the Chinese cheongsam." Our clothes promise that we too, will be serene and sensual (read: compliant and servile)—for Asian women know how to please without making strident, overt demands and offer up our exotic talents without unloading the burden of our marginal status. What was that about Suzie Wong in red brocade again?

Okay, okay, it's too easy to go after the fashion world, where the whole point is to be superficial. Yet, taking Natori's advice to "think international" for a moment reveals urgent and deeply rooted problems in the fashion industry that no amount of frills can disguise, such as, say, the exploitation of Asian women's labor abroad and at home. Los Angeles designer Richard Tyler "attributes his success to his exceptionally hardworking and enthusiastic workforce, which is mainly Chinese," *Vogue* tells us. "There is an atmosphere of happiness throughout the company—joy to be here and to be able to give their children a better life and education," Tyler gushes, seemingly oblivious to the economic, social, and political forces that funnel Chinese immigrants into low-wage, low-security jobs in the sweatshops of the fashion industry.[3]

Such complexities do not make pretty pictures and cannot be contained by one-dimensional media images. Yet, as Asian women, our response has often been to counter negative representations of ourselves with equally simplistic images that buy into and reproduce the messages of the dominant culture we inhabit, whose codes, significations, and assumptions we can't help but internalize, even as we struggle to escape their influence. We now have our own Woman Warrior, our own Joy Luck Club, our own successful role models in Hollywood, on Capitol Hill, in the Fortune 500, and on the evening news. But proving that some Asian women can succeed on the terms of the dominant culture fails to question the injustices that remain in place.

Attempts to show that we can be "All-American Girls," as in the TV show starring Korean American comedian Margaret Cho, gets us nowhere. When that sit-com made its debut on national television in 1994, it depicted the same-old story of an American family trying to attain the same-old American dream, though with the added novelty—and comic relief—of Asian faces and an occasional accent. Cho, the star and creator of the show, broke TV's glass ceiling, but only to validate a vision of assimilated, integrated Asians happy to have their unequal share of the pie. As always, we are welcome as long as we claim to be just like everyone else. Cho asserts that Asian women in the United States are better equipped than ever before to resolve the distinct demands of "two very different cultures." She says, "we can create our own identity. One that satisfies our parents that we take pride in our roots, cherish our rich ethnic heritage and have the possibility of becoming doctors and lawyers. But also an identity that says its OK to love America, lose face for a living, and even wear [the stage makeup color] Asian Yellow #5."[4] As we work to smooth out the wrinkles in our hybrid existence, however, we are forced to wear our race as a mask to put on or remove only when the mainstream deems it acceptable or necessary.

A close examination of other new, hip incarnations of Asian women that have recently surfaced reveals the conventional messages they continue to communicate, even as they entertain and thrill in their novelty, even as we welcome their challenge to outdated options. In the ongoing repackaging and commodification of Asian femaleness, difference is superficial, only skin-deep, and influence is measured in dollar signs, purely by market value. As we appear in worldly wise and aggressively assertive versions of old stereotypes, we continue to be presented, received, and read in essentially the same old ways. The pleasure we derive from seeing ourselves in the spotlight comes at the price of more visible marginalization.

Model Jenny Shimizu's astronomical rise to stardom represents a bona fide breakthrough for Asian American visibility. As a Japanese American butch lesbian and tattooed woman, Shimizu has emerged on the scene as a trailblazer (helped along by her discovery by Calvin Klein and rumors of a liaison with Madonna). "Currently the only Asian-American in supermodel contention," her presence has graced numerous catwalks and magazine covers worldwide. While Shimizu has opened up the possibility of Asian American entrée into the fashion world, it is both because of and in spite of her race. "America isn't the blond, blue-eyed world of models anymore," Shimizu says. Indeed, it is now the world of integrated fashion. A recent profile in *The Advocate* doesn't even see any need to discuss her race, and the fashion world seems to have absorbed the former auto mechanic effortlessly into its elite crowd. Like the white women before her, Shimizu marvels, "now I'm traveling places I've never been and drinking Evian." Yet even Shimizu acknowledges the fleeting nature of fashion trends, and is prepared to return to her former lifestyle when her star fades. Rather than transforming the industry, Shimizu seems to be just another pretty face.[5]

In that other realm of potentially transgressive and transformative cultural production, the music scene, a certain kind of Asian female influence has been equally enthusiastically embraced. The rock group Cibo Matto combines savvy sampling and surreal lyrics to create a hip, catchy sound that is a hybrid of American street smarts and Asian sweetness. Heavily hyped by *The New York Times, The Village Voice,* and *Rolling Stone,* the "sample-oholic Japanese megababes" Yuka Honda and Miho Hatori are praised for their "global genius," namely, their creative use of English and a diverse collage of musical styles.[6] Their broken-English, little-girl whispers have a distinctive Asian accent, and their lyrics are an apparently arbitrary mix of nonsequiturs and neologisms about food: "My weight is 300 pounds—My favorite is beef jerky—I'm a vagabond, I'm a vagabond." Cibo Matto is being celebrated largely for constructing a vibrant musical space, but out of empty imitation and insubstantial signs.

By serving up the global residue of American cultural influence worldwide in decidedly unironic, "palatable" form, Cibo Matto is the perfect poster group for the apolitical multicultural atmosphere mainstream critics adore. Their music is thankfully "free of any overt social agenda" and "without an ounce of dogma or pretense." In fact, the critics seem to imply, it is utterly, "charmingly" vacuous, "goofy," "dorky," and "cute." Such diminishing praise is, as critic Christopher Norris acknowledges, "doubly unsavory when [it] smack[s] of racialized condescension." Yet Norris goes on to display his own backhanded and belittling compliments, gushing that Cibo Matto's debut album, *Viva! La Woman,* "would be one of the most sensual and transporting records I've ever heard even if I couldn't understand a single word." He goes on to praise the group's broken-English sensibility, which other critics join in calling "crazed" and "trendy" (in the best possible senses of the words, of course).

Norris practically brands Cibo Matto a pair of idiot savants: "I've never heard a learned tongue work so impressionistically in rock. I find myself wondering whether Honda and Hatori are putting us on. Are they actually native English speakers, or are they pop's Joseph Conrad?" Even I'm not so cynical as to think the group could have sold out *that* much; and yet, if Cibo Matto were all a linguistic hoax, it would serve the critics right as they attempt to outdo each other's nonsense-worship. The critical response to Cibo Matto's global, postmodern brand of music reveals the vulnerability of Asian women's cultural production to a pro-global, pomo brand of condescending criticism. In the hands of the starmakers, *Viva! La Woman* merely prolongs the lifespan of degrading images of Asian women.

As our cultural marketplace has made room for more diverse cultures and images, ultimately the pressures of the profit-minded, corporate-controlled marketplace squeeze out any transgressive meaning or potential we seize for ourselves and reduce us to mere novelties that merely spice up the status quo, keeping it ever fresh and tasty—and palatable. Our difference is merely another fashion or food taste. Indeed, Asian women's exotic cultural and sexual differences are routinely compared with our strange foods, which become a stand-in for a different cultural taste or sensibility. One anthology of contemporary Japanese writing, *Monkey Brain Sushi: New Tastes in Japanese Fiction* is introduced this way: "At once *haute* and irreverent, Japanese writers today are serving up slices of verbal *sushi* that bite back."[7] Likewise, Cibo Matto (whose name means "food madness" in Italian) inspired one reviewer to write, "Like fugu, the Japanese delicacy that can kill if it's not prepared correctly, *Viva! La Woman* is as scary as it is delicious."[8] The slightly threatening image of food that bites back is a subtle reminder that the foreign remains dangerous; one must eat or be eaten.

As bell hooks writes in her insightful essay on the appropriation and ingestion of black culture, "Eating the Other,"

> The commodification of Otherness has been so successful because it is offered as a new delight, more intense, more satisfying than

> normal ways of doing and feeling. Within commodity culture, ethnicity becomes spice, seasoning that can liven up the dull dish that is mainstream white culture.

Moreover, the desire to incorporate the essence of the other without being transformed, without losing one's dominance over it, leads to a fascination with the consumption of cultural characteristics that prevents them from taking hold with any real importance or influence. The ease with which cultural characteristics are erased of meaning and context in popular forms such as fashion, movies, and music, makes constant close attention to the circulation and reception of images vitally important. "The overriding fear," warns hooks, "is that cultural, ethnic, and racial differences will be continually commodified and offered up as new dishes to enhance the white palate—that the Other will be eaten, consumed, and forgotten." She concludes, "We cannot...accept these new images uncritically."[9]

Yet that is precisely how Asian women are expected to respond to our representation in mainstream U.S. culture. We are told, in Cibo Matto's words, to "Shut up and eat!" Meanwhile, any attempt to participate in the ethnic foodfest can easily backfire. While Western critics may never acknowledge their continuing biases and condescending views, many Asian American cultural workers openly embrace the same views—and cater to them—in a short-sighted bid for visibility. Take, for example, the recent anthology, *On a Bed of Rice: An Asian American Erotic Feast.* This groundbreaking collection, "dedicated to the voice of Asian American desire," aims to validate and empower Asian Americans who write openly, honestly, and explicitly about sexuality, by challenging stereotypes and presenting a wide range of perspectives. At the same time, however, it also presents us literally as objects to be consumed. The book's cover, which features a delectably nude Asian woman coyly hiding her crotch behind an ornate fan, resonates with unself-conscious similarities to racist soft porn.[10]

Such attempts at subverting the status quo may fall flat, but they do open up the possibility that we, too, may appropriate the intended messages of conventional images and impose our own meanings on them. Even the most egregious of racist images can simultaneously offer radical alternative readings and possibilities to those able to recreate, refigure, and reinterpret them on multiple levels. The degrading face-value images of Asians increasingly on offer in mainstream film and media just as often contain surprisingly subversive messages within their dominant political context.

For example, Filipina American writer Jessica Hagedorn draws unexpected inspiration from the astonishingly racist and oft-protested film, *Year of the Dragon.*[11] The film's main female character is an Asian American journalist, Tracy Tzu (played by Eurasian actress Ariane), who becomes involved with a Vietnam-vet-turned-cop, Stanley White (Mickey Rourke), in spite of the fact that he slaps her, denigrates her race, and routinely insults her: "I hated you before I even met you. I hated you on TV. I hated you in Vietnam." These unmistakably racialized characters (even their names are explicitly marked) pursue a corrupt Chinatown gang in New York City. Tzu's initially reluctant support of White is portrayed as a direct betrayal of her community, but her eventual acquiescence to his mission and his brutality are later justified when she is gang-raped by men of her own race. White can thus rescue Tzu from what critic Gina Marchetti describes as "the supposedly menacing excesses of Asian culture."[12]

Against the backdrop of this standard narrative, Hagedorn sees a glimmer of hope in the Jade Cobra Gang girls, characters whose unabashed aggressiveness and clear contempt for the macho white cop (who eventually kills them in a shootout) pose a dangerous challenge to society's expectations. Hagedorn writes, "My pleasure in the hard-edged power of the Chinatown gang girls in *Year of the Dragon* is my small revenge....The Jade Cobra girls remain defiant, fabulous images in my memory."[13] By taking an active role as critical spectator, Hagedorn can get beneath the surface to impose an openly oppositional subtext that interrupts the film's inevitably conventional progress and allows her to celebrate and appreciate the visual spectacle while reading her own politics into the scene. This process acknowledges the spectator as a conscious participant in a dialogue rather than a passive observer. An actively oppositional critical faculty can thus shift the terms of cultural representations and give them transgressive meaning.

Ultimately, such subversive readings may do little more than temporarily disrupt the mainstream, but when this occurs on seemingly infinite levels with seemingly infinite responses and transformations, the effect can be dizzying enough to disrupt and change the terms of old debates forever. Witness the example of "Miss Saigon," the Broadway hit musical based on the opera "Madama Butterfly." During the casting of the show, Asian American actors fought for the right to play the Asian and Eurasian characters, roles which were instead given to Anglo actors. Other activists saw beyond the obvious issues of job discrimination and racial authenticity to the need to challenge the broader patriarchal and imperialist message of the show's story, which takes place during the Vietnam War and focuses on a Vietnamese prostitute, Kim, who, abandoned by an American soldier, kills herself to secure her Amerasian son's future in the West.[14] Meanwhile, many gay Filipinos identify ironically with this image of Asian femininity by impersonating Miss Saigon in drag, mimicking the show's melodrama in their mannerisms, and aspiring to Kim's notoriety and the fame of the Filipina singer, Lea Salonga, who originated the role.[15] Each of these active spectators critically calls into question the meaning of white actors in yellow-face, martyred women, and persistent sexual stereotypes through their self-conscious, self-referential, queer and raced inversions of those images.

If transgressive meaning can be found even in these places, then, must we accept that all representations are equally valid and equally harmless? Perhaps the real message every image broadcasts is that what you see is never all you get. What looks like a positive role could limit us even further; what looks like blatant discrimination could present new, radical ways of thinking. But by engaging critically with popular media images, by producing both critical representations and critical readings, we force the dialogue to another level, continually exceeding and redrawing the boundaries.

The realm of cultural production holds the potential to provide mass education, political analysis, and of course, popular entertainment, as alternatives to the same old stereotypes. The triumphant celebration of Asian women's increasing visibility in many areas of U.S. society has inspired the important and innovative work of many visionary writers and artists.[16] Backed by a vibrant, sustained activist movement, their work helps us to reclaim our history, shape our future, and envision the unimaginable. Meanwhile, the development of critical perspectives places us in the crucial role of the beholder—not just the consumer—of cultural products and messages. As we produce both new images and new ways of reading critically, we expand our options and keep representations of Asian women from solidifying into rigid, limiting roles. As our images proliferate and mutate, we may not like what we see, and we may not be seen as we like. But our critical presence in the production and reading of unruly representations ensures our continuing participation in the battle to control our own destinies and to make our voices heard.

Today, U.S. audiences seeking the next exotic movie sensation are turning eastward to Hong Kong martial arts flicks. This genre has gained cult status in the West by providing low-budget, camp aesthetics as an alternative to Western production values and narrative conventions—an alternative that can be both appreciated and ridiculed. Even here, the critical challenge of viewing Asian women as active subjects within the finite constraints of on-screen fantasy can offer valuable clues for resistance to the rigid constraints of real life.

The film *The Heroic Trio*[17] portrays three righteous heroines whose amazing fighting skills are a welcome antidote to those of the ping-pong ball variety. The women in this trio are gratifyingly sexy and strong, and they easily cross gender roles and explode expectations of docile Asian women. With slapstick humor, exaggerated melodrama, and self-conscious irony, they defy male authority figures to fight injustice and evil, all the while struggling to maintain personal relationships built on trust and loyalty. Their strength does not derive from diminishing others, and all are equally worthy of their attention, as they save everyone from policemen to pet kittens. Their powers remain hidden behind conventional alter egos, yet when unleashed, they astound and amaze. When, at the end of the film, one of the heroic trio is shown knitting contentedly while she and her husband watch a news clip of her fantastic feats, things appear to have returned to normal. But we know what she is capable of now, and things will never be the same.

Of course, in the fantasy world of *The Heroic Trio,* liberation requires supernatural powers, and the good gals always win. It remains to be seen whether we will take the cue to uncover our own hidden strengths with which to astound and amaze, and whether we will win our fight against injustice. If Western culture has long imagined our untold sexual prowess, we have only just begun to realize our untold political powers—and they ain't seen nothin' yet.

Notes

1. *The Adventures of Priscilla, Queen of the Desert* (dir. Stephan Elliott, Australia, 1994).

2. All quotes in the following four paragraphs are from Howell, Georgina. "Eyeing the East." *Vogue.* May 1994: 220-222.

3. Helen Zia. "Made in the U.S.A." *Ms.* January/February 1996: 66-73; Gary Delgado, "How the Empress Gets Her Clothes: Asian Immigrant Women Fight Fashion Designer Jessica McClintock." *Beyond Identity Politics: Emerging Social Justice Movements in Communities of Color.* Ed. John Anner. Boston: South End Press, 1996. 81-94.

4. Cho, Margaret. "Losing Face for a Living." *Glamour.* November 1994: 79.

5. Min, Janice, and Allison Lynn. "Popular Mechanic." *People Weekly.* 2 May 1994: 126-28; Interview with Jenny Shimizu. *The Advocate.* 7 March 1995: 53-54.

6. Quotes in the following three paragraphs are from Cibo Matto. *Viva! La Woman.* Warner Brothers, 1996; Farley, Christopher John. "Not Your Father's Hip-Hop." *Time.* 12 February 1996: 79; Norris, Christopher. "Global Genius." *New York.* 5 February 1996: 58-59; Rev. of *Viva! La Woman* by Cibo Matto. *Details.* March 1996: 191; Verna, Paul, ed. Rev. of *Viva! La Woman* by Cibo Matto. *Billboard.* 3 February 1996: 69; Weisel, Al. Review of *Viva! La Woman* by Cibo Matto. *Rolling Stone.* 8 February 1996: 50-51.

7. Birnbaum, Alfred, ed. *Monkey Brain Sushi.* New York: Kodansha, 1991.

8. Weisel 51.

9. hooks, bell. "Eating the Other: Desire and Resistance." *Black Looks: Race and Representation.* Boston: South End Press, 1992. 21-39.

10. Kudaka, Geraldine, ed. *On A Bed of Rice: An Asian American Erotic Feast.* New York: Anchor/Doubleday, 1995.

11. *Year of the Dragon* (dir. Michael Cimino, USA, 1985).

12. Marchetti, Gina. "Conclusion: The Postmodern Spectacle of Race and Romance in *Year of the Dragon.*" *Romance and the "Yellow Peril": Race, Sex, and Discursive Strategies in Hollywood Fiction.* Berkeley: University of California Press, 1993. 202-21.

13. Hagedorn, Jessica. "Asian Women in Film: No Joy, No Luck." *Ms.* January/February 1994: 74-79.

14. Yoshikawa, Yoko. "The Heat is On Miss Saigon Coalition: Organizing Across Race and Sexuality." *The State of Asian America: Activism and Resistance in the 1990s.* Ed. Karin Aguilar-San Juan. Boston: South End Press, 1993. 275-94.

15. Manalansan, Martin F., IV. "Searching for Community: Filipino Gay Men in New York City." *Asian American Sexualities: Dimensions of the Gay and Lesbian Experience.* Ed. Russell Leong. New York: Routledge, 1996. 51-64.

16. See the work of Hanh Thi Pham, Theresa Hak Kyung Cha, Kimiko Hahn, and Shu Lea Chang, among others.

17. *The Heroic Trio* (dir. Jacky To, Hong Kong, 1992).

A Slippery Path

Organizing Resistance to Violence Against Women

By Anannya Bhattacharjee

It was 1989 in New York City when we, the group of women who started Sakhi, first began to imagine concrete ways to build a community of South Asian women in the United States.[1] Although we originally came from different class backgrounds in South Asia, we occupied more or less the same economic status in the United States. We had professional college degrees and carried with us ideas of success and habits of professionalism arising out of our training and education in fields such as law, science, finance, and film. Some of us had been politically active in other communities in the United States and hungered to work with our own. We identified ourselves as South Asian, as we recognized historical commonalities shared by peoples from this region and were drawn to the notion of transcending nationalistic divisions.[2] We also identified ourselves as women of color, with roots elsewhere because of our immigration status and our heritages in the "Third World." We imagined building a community based on this gendered and ethnic identity. (Although I use the pronoun "we," much of what I say tells my story. Needless to say, I do not mean to speak for others. However, my assessment is that, although as individuals each one of us no doubt differed in various ways, we did have a collective understanding of our realities which made our collaboration possible.)

We decided to focus on domestic violence because we recognized that domestic violence is a serious problem in our communities and that resistance to domestic violence had an established tradition in this country. As middle-class, professional, educated women, when we looked for role models in the women's movement, we located women such as ourselves: professional, educated, and aspiring. Domestic violence organizations were the most established, high profile organizational form that we saw in the women's movement. We were excited by what was a clearly recognizable structure and a goal to work towards. We did not wish to emulate totally the hierarchical, service-providing structure of some of the existing domestic violence organizations, as some of us were firm believers in the importance of building a feminist collective. We spoke to existing organizations, such as Manavi, New York Asian Women's Center, and Sanctuary for Families. We were impressed by their operations and dreamed of our own.

Our collective sentiments were not unlike that of many women before us and after us. The battered women's movement has a prominent standing in the women's movement and in mainstream political and cultural processes in this country. Asian American women have started many domestic violence organizations at various levels of operations, funding, and size in their communities across the country.[3] In the South Asian community, for example, the growth of domestic violence organizations has been one of the most visible progressive activities. In the last decade, domestic violence organizations such as Manavi in New Jersey, Sakhi for South Asian Women in New York, Sewa in Philadelphia, Apna Ghar in Chicago, Saheli in Texas, SNEHA in Connecticut, and Norika and Maitreyi in California, among others, have sprung up. Indeed, while these South Asian domestic violence organizations vary in their commitment to feminist politics, they all share a crucial similarity—they were started mostly by middle-class and professionally employed women or middle-class homemakers.

This is not an essay about Sakhi as much as it is about the way women's organizations begin and develop the fight against domestic violence. The issues raised in this essay could be pursued either as a personal piece (as this one is) or as a collaborative piece written by a group of women from Sakhi. The two methods are both equally important, although they are different projects. In any case, I believe that reflective documentation by individuals with intimate relations with organizations is important. There is not enough documentation of these kinds, although there is much feminist theory and research out there. This is partly due to the fact that such documentation is considered sensitive, and yet, without it, the women's movement cannot grow. Indeed, at this point, when a worldwide women's movement is being widely acknowledged and celebrated even by mainstream forums and we all face the increasing threat of co-optation, it is more important than ever to subject ourselves and our work to an honest and rigorous critique.

We, the group that began Sakhi, like others before and after us, were bourgeois women, politicized by bourgeois feminism. This, in itself, is not necessarily an interesting phenomenon to write about, as the women's movement has too many such stories. However, I am interested in exploring how this affects our abilities to fight violence against women.

Negotiating Class Politics

In Sakhi, we were anxious to be inclusive toward all South Asian women. We described the organization as pluralistic and extended an open invitation to all South Asian women to join. The membership and the default leadership that emerged thus owed more to amorphous factors such as personalities, time commitment, and a general desire to address the problem of domestic violence rather than an explicit commitment to any well-defined political philosophy.

There existed an across-the-board discomfort with ideological discussions that would disrupt this homogeneity. Pluralism, which acknowledges within certain boundaries the role of male power, was considered to be a positive principle. Ironically, pluralism actually made us homogeneous as opposed to all-inclusive (which implies a certain heterogeneity). The result was, on the contrary, not a lack of ideology or a proliferation of many ideologies, but a default one that reflected the lowest common denominator—such as, that wife-beating is wrong. This outcome is not a unique phenomenon to Sakhi.

Sakhi gradually developed to include some of the features that have become common to domestic violence organizations. Some of these are a service line, support groups, training for women who would advocate for individual battered women, educational activities such as presentations, workshops, and leafletting, and coalition work towards legislative reform.

As Sakhi developed, so did certain structural objectives common to women's organizations. Although many organizations unfortunately lose their founding tenets over time, Sakhi had been remarkably successful in maintaining many in spite of its growth. One such objective from the very beginning was to ensure that the organization would be driven by volunteers rather than staff. We wanted to ensure that even if we lost funding there would be a body of women committed to continuing the work. Also, being volunteer-driven would ensure that the direction of the organization was not solely decided by just a few women but by a larger body from whom leadership could emerge. We created decisionmaking forums in which all volunteers, Board, and staff would have equal voice. Although the Board and staff would make many important day-to-day decisions, larger issues such as political direction or organizational policies would be decided by attending active volunteers, Board, and staff at general meetings.

Another objective was to integrate the survivors who call Sakhi during crises into Sakhi's decisionmaking membership. This objective is expressed in our workshops, trainings, and discussions. To this end, we would try to consciously avoid language, processes, and attitudes that would encourage an us-and-them relationship between survivors and the Sakhi women taking their calls. We would avoid hiring staff solely for their professional degrees in counseling and social work and look instead for women with feminist principles similar to those voiced by the organization—women who do not see themselves as distanced from the battered women but as partners.

Still, except for the few instances when survivors have become really involved in the organization, it has been primarily those who are middle-class, educated, and English-speaking who have become involved with Sakhi. This is not uncommon in the battered women's movement.[4]

Within domestic violence programs, class issues come up in subtle ways—such as a battered woman's lack of fluency in English, her inability to pay for public transportation when she comes to support group meetings, and so on. (While a middle-class woman who leaves her husband may face similar difficulties, she has assets such as education, marketable skills, family and friends who can lend money, husbands who can be forced to pay maintenance or alimony, and so on.) The organization's response may be to, say, provide English classes, pay for transportation, and provide translation in support groups. The class difference may thus seem relatively easy to resolve. But this sort of class sensitivity remains at the level of adjustment in services without ever delving into the systemic roots of class exploitation. For most women, a sense of kinship for women in general slides by default into kinship with middle-class women in particular—with a few adjustments for working-class women in terms of services that are provided. Needless to say, such an understanding greatly limits an organization's ability to work towards systemic change for women who are caught in exploitative systems.

How Traditional Domestic Violence Work Is Co-opted

For the first couple of years, Sakhi received offensive letters and phone calls, was the subject of jokes, and was excluded from mainstream community activities.[5] Over time, however, Sakhi has become better known and has begun to be taken seriously by the media, mainstream organizations, and individuals in the community. Sakhi also became more established, with an office, staff, funding, and a growing reputation in the nonprofit world of domestic violence organizations.

Like other domestic violence organizations, as time went on, we gradually began to get financial support from wealthy community members. We began to cultivate this support actively to meet our funding demands and supplement our foundation grants. We were encouraged to do so by other organizations and funders as "diversification of funding" became the catchword for financial security. Our ability to get such financial support, even to a limited extent, reflected our motivation, as professional, middle-class women, to build "professional" operations, as well as the fact that we were able to communicate with the elite in our communities.

That domestic violence organizations are gradually accepted by mainstream society and funders, I believe, owes much to the fact that they do not threaten important principles of straight, bourgeois society: individualism, ideas about privacy, reluctance in naming the oppressor, a belief in the legal system, and a desire for feel-good benevolence.

Domestic violence organizations buttress individualism by focusing on each woman as an individual. For example, a common tenet is that all decisions should be made based on the individual survivor's wishes. Organizations convey this idea in their trainings and outreach activities and cite a good reason for it—they do not want to control or dictate the survivor's life the way her batterer did. But the emphasis on the individual woman creates a disjuncture between the interests of the individual woman and that of collective women, as if the two were always conflictual, and implicitly encourages the individual battered woman to relinquish all responsibility to her larger community of women. This approach has no method for instilling, either in the survivor or in the organization, a belief in the importance or the possibility of taking collective action. This approach is further reinforced by the individualism and uncritical celebration of privacy embedded in broader U.S. culture.

Yet, collective action would greatly alleviate the burden on individual women. For example, when a woman decides to leave her batterer, the burden of her guilt and responsibility could be lightened by a collective show of solidarity from other women. A collective of women could engage in a publicly advertised "strike," whereby they would temporarily or permanently leave their abusive situations together.

Another example of individualism in domestic violence organizations is their heavy use of the Order of Protection (issued by a family court or a criminal court judge to a survivor and her batterer, instructing the latter to cease his violent behavior). The enforcement of these orders is at a dismal low, because the onus is on the woman to singlehandedly hold her batterer accountable—that is, she has to call the police if he violates the order. For many women, this is a tremendous responsibility to bear. Even if a woman is able to call the police, she may find them to be unevenly responsive, further undermining her faith in the order. In contrast is Judith Stevenson's sketch, in which a woman reassures a survivor who is worried over security:

> Best security in the world. Ten to fifteen other women, a couple of baseball bats and a telephone. Those guys don't stand a chance...if we don't face him down surrounded by fifteen allies, what're we gonna do when we're alone in an apartment?...My old man never comes around anymore. Got tired of being harassed by my friends. Tell you the truth, I think he's scared...One thing's for sure—there's a whole lot less guys in this town thinking it's safe to beat up on their women anymore. And we're not their women anymore, either! And they're starting to know it!

As the survivor hesitates over the idea of shelter, the woman on the phone assures her:

> Been to most of them to visit. Or for meetings....It's just a house. Some of them are in old churches; one used to be a warehouse. And up on the North Side, they took over an abandoned house and just refused to give it up. Pretty good, huh?...And last month, a woman...decided she wanted to move back to her own house and turn it into a shelter. Seven women from the shelter moved in with her—and they just took all her old man's stuff and threw it out in the street.[6]

A third example is domestic violence organizations' reliance on judges' issuances of Orders of Maintenance, which order the batterer to financially support the woman and perhaps children. Usually, the batterer defaults and the woman has to go back to court to urge for the order's enforcement. This often means she must miss days at work and hence, lose her pay. A possible collective strategy, in contrast, could be picketing in front of the batterer's place of work and/or home to embarrass him in the community. But such strategies will become viable only if we celebrate them as part of our tradition of resistance, and not if they are considered isolated and freak incidents.

I realize that certain collective solutions may be seen as breaking the law and that there are difficult moral questions about individual rights, especially in the light of abuses against individuals by repressive state machineries. Domestic violence organizations in the United States often balk at the thought of such action, and they base their reluctance on the assertion that the survivor does not want to go public; hence the organization must abide by her wishes. I believe that if public identification and ostracization of such men became a regular part of our work, women would begin to see such strategies as logical. However, battered women often say no to the idea because each woman, if asked at all, is asked individually. These solutions need not become thoughtless vigilantism, but rather should emerge out of rigorous discussions. After all, what is an "ethical dilemma" in a society that condones violence against women? Nandita Gandhi and Nandita Shah describe a collective campaign in India:

> In January 1982, in Delhi there was a demonstration in front of the in-laws' house after a woman had survived an attempt at murder. The pressure created with the participation of neighbors and women's groups forced the in-laws to give back her dowry. It was quite common for a group of women to accompany the

> distressed woman to her home and retrieve her belongings and dowry. Lawyers were quick to note that this would lay the women open to the charge of breaking in and burglary. But, in the absence of any law or speedy method which would give women what was rightfully theirs, women's groups relied on their own credibility and social pressure.[7]

Domestic violence organizations in the United States balk at such methods because, above all, they believe in the bourgeois notion of good citizenship, which means abiding by the law even when written by the oppressor.

Privacy is another principle that guides many domestic violence organizations. Elaborate procedures of confidentiality protect the individual woman through a system of policies aimed at rendering her invisible, supposedly for her own sake, so that the batterer cannot get information about her. I do not mean to dismiss the dangers to survivors from violent men, but this strategy strongly discourages collective action. Thus, the concept of women guarding one another, vilifying batterers so that they cannot dare to harm the woman, and other similar tactics are not even contemplated.

This kind of individualistic, privacy-oriented methodology for resistance is also endemic to an ideology that refuses to name the enemy in material (or concrete) terms. Batterers are not named and confronted as identifiable men living in our communities. Whereas the battered woman takes the risk of naming herself publicly when she escapes her violent life, as her marital family may often try to slander her actions, her oppressors remain unnamed and protected through the shroud of privacy.

Most domestic violence organizations mainly seek recourse through the legal system (such as through orders of protection, divorces, orders of maintenance, and custody) or through the police, both of which have been known to be sexist, racist, anti-immigrant, and anti-poor. The fight comes down to having a good lawyer. Along with this strategy comes a fear of reprisals from the legal system if one engages in unconventional strategies—such as the fear of slander suits being brought against the organization. The idea that this is a fight in which strategies must be developed to counter precisely those fears which keep in place oppressive power-wielders is rarely entertained. Since these organizations are usually allied with one another and rarely with movements that practice collective action to truly challenge bases of power, they get into the habit of congratulating one another on their "growth" in size and cannot critique their fundamental lack of political growth. Gail Sullivan says,

> Another way that funding and social service agencies provide a cooptive influence on battered women's groups is the promotion of a bigger-is-better, quick-growth approach. Battered women's groups began as small, grassroots, primarily volunteer programs. However, services are most respected if they are large, have sizeable staffs and are well-funded.

Sullivan describes the slow and insidious process of co-optation of visions that originally began with a burning desire to see change happen:

> Co-optation, that is the assimilation of something different into the mainstream, is a constant problem for any political movement. It is a natural process in this society, which maintains the status quo by turning radical demands and visions into acceptable, non-threatening changes (i.e. Black, Third World and women's liberation struggles become limited to Affirmative Action programs to make them palatable). Co-optation is not always direct frontal assault: it is often slow, sometimes direct, sometimes indirect; it happens not only as a result of external forces on us, but also as a result of our own choices, as they are influenced by the values with which we have been inculcated.[8]

Belief in the legal system, in individual privilege, and fear of the unforeseen consequences of challenging the status quo are particularly convenient to organizations as they let them off the hook in terms of organizing a grassroots movement. Collective actions will necessarily involve venturing down untrodden paths, unsettling the norm, and organizing a collective movement that works in unison.

"Model Minority" Organizations

Asian American domestic violence organizations have extended the scope of anti-violence work by demanding sensitivity to Asian women. We have asserted the existence of Asian women and refused to be statistically invisible. We have also contributed to extending the definition of immigrants and people of color to include Asians. These achievements are hard-won and very significant.[9]

Like other Asian American activists who highlight the oppression and exploitation in our societies, we have also continually challenged the "model minority" myth surrounding Asian communities. We have pointed out how the myth is generated by mainstream U.S. ideology to divide people of color by appealing to some of them to acquiesce to U.S. standards of success at the cost of building solidarity with other marginalized groups.

However, even as we speak out against this myth with great vigilance, we can often ourselves be trapped in the myth. As "professional" activists, when we go about "establishing" institutions, we often lose sight of the politics that initially drove us, and become involved in establishing the "best" and the most "successful" institutions. We compare our institutions to those which are "successful" and "established," and strive to be the "model minority" of the non-profit world. We become involved in quests for recognition that are often indistinguishable from those existing in a corporation or business. We are encouraged by awards from institutions that should be challenged, we are gratified to be invited to serve on various Boards, we are thrilled by the respect given to us by those whom we see as being in powerful positions, the elite and the wealthy in our communities.

This kind of mindset is ultimately damaging to our ability to form strong alliances with the struggles of people of color in the United States. In our intervention in the debate on racism, for example, we may often limit our analysis to cultural sensitivity, to the serving of "special needs," and at most to a critique of immigration laws. However, without an analysis of racism as a First World nation's project to create a vulnerable underclass of exploitable workers of color, our alliances with the struggles of people of color will remain transitory and shallow. The underclass is created through criminalization of people of color, targeting them through state institutions (such as the police force, the criminal justice system, and immigration authorities), and naming them as the "problem" behind the growing inequalities. An analysis that is attentive to such realities would force domestic violence organizations to problematize their own strategies. Domestic violence organizations might then build alliances with organizations that fight economic servitude, particularly of women of color whose labor is the most exploited. Or, they would ally themselves in the fight against the U.S. government's siege on people of color.

The tragic consequence of a lack of self-critique and rigorous analysis is that organizations become distanced from constituencies they claim to represent and from movements that, due to their confrontational methodology, are less visible in mainstream forums. Organizations that began with some notion to strive for "fundamental social change" become less and less clear about its meaning, although they may continue using the term rhetorically, dimly aware that they indeed had set out to cause such change in the first place.

Towards a Radical Politics/Claiming History

Alliances with other movements allow for exchange of strategies, ideas, and philosophies, thus providing renewed energy and creativity. We can learn from strategies used in other countries which, although they cannot be emulated exactly, can refresh our minds and instill new ideas. In India, for example,

> Some of the most colorful and militant struggles against wife beating have been closely linked to alcoholism. Groups of women belonging to Women's Voices (Bangalore) have confronted the wife-battering husband and have openly threatened him.... In Chattisgarh (Madhya Pradesh), women and union leaders organized a mass pledge at which men had to take an oath that they would not drink or beat their wives, and that they would contribute money for the family....[In Uttar Pradesh] some of the [liquor] dealers were paraded through the village with blackened faces, stripped naked or garlanded with shoes. Similarly in Manipur, there is a long tradition of night patrolling by the women to make their campaign against liquor and drugs more effective. Women guard the streets with lighted torches in their hands and fine those who are found to be drunk or on drugs.[10]

In another instance, anti-domestic violence activists used strategies from another struggle, that against landlord injustice in Bihar, India:

> Many of the villagers were part of the Mazdoor Kisan Sangram Samiti which waged militant struggles against landlord injus-

> tice. But the menace of drinking and wife beating was within each household and had escaped discussion or action. One day, a badly beaten woman's screams and her blood-splattered condition angered all the women of the village. Spontaneously, they decided to go on strike. They refused to perform any household chores, including looking after the children, till the village men promised to stop beating their wives. Politically, they had been taught to use strikes and organized action against their oppressors and they had, unconsciously but effectively, transferred these lessons into their personal lives and against their personal oppressors.[11]

(Their decision to go on strike is also interesting as it forces their community to recognize household work as labor.)

Wenny Kusuma, the Executive Director of La Casa de Las Madres, a battered women's shelter in San Francisco, in her speech at the First National Asian Women's Health Conference in 1995, describes some of the differences between the approaches to domestic violence work in the United States and in China:

> In the U.S., we emphasize immediate separation from the violence itself....The second thing we emphasize is confidentiality, that both the location of the shelter and her identity are confidential. In China...they did not think that shelters were a solution...they were emphasizing public condemnation....When a woman called the crisis line, they had the authority to call the police and to then call the block leader where the family lived. They had the authority to call for a block meeting, a neighborhood meeting...a meeting in a person's trade union, to call a meeting in a person's home neighborhood block, and to confront him....Some of his vacation time may be taken away, and then some of his pay might be taken away from him....Ultimately what they decided to do was to organize what they called "model husband award competition"...wives would nominate based on the good behavior of their spouses....They then went through a seven-step process of interviewing in-laws, children, separate from the man himself. They got quite a bit of publicity, and the man would get an equivalent of a day's pay.[12]

The Domestic Workers Project

In addition to sharing strategies across movements and countries, another way to intervene in an organization's comfortable routinization is to introduce issues that challenge its membership and politics. In Sakhi, in 1994, we decided to initiate a project to organize domestic workers in the South Asian community. Sakhi had received calls from household workers, and we had become aware of this community of workers, their exploitation, and the silence around it. Some of us also wanted to address class exploitation at a systemic level. Although these reasons were not articulated at an organizational level, women in Sakhi were largely in agreement about the importance of addressing the needs of this group of workers. At varying levels of conviction, we also believed that this should be an "organizing" project with the goal of having domestic workers be a part of the leadership of the project, and that it should not be about providing direct services.

Much of Sakhi's membership is drawn from the very class that hires domestic workers. This means that the organization has both workers and potential and actual employers inhabiting it at the same time. This is not a unique phenomenon, as the history of labor organizing shows us. Nevertheless, the project posed the possibility of illuminating divisions that have always existed among the members, but which the membership could perhaps have avoided discussing before. The membership would thus be forced to reckon with its own stated commitment to empowerment, to the interests of working-class women, and to ending exploitation of women.

Domestic workers, many Sakhi volunteers, and those survivors who are part of the Domestic Workers Committee (DWC), describe with sadness and anger the evening when the potential within Sakhi to explore meaningful answers to difficult questions was extinguished. Six women, using the legal power vested in them by the nonprofit laws of the State and taking lightly, one is forced to say, the trust vested in them by hundreds of women who have been a part of Sakhi's history, did away with what has been built over several years.

On April 21, 1997, five of the seven Board members of Sakhi at the time (the others resigned) and the Program Director unilaterally and without any consultation dissolved the DWC and fired its coordinator, who is a survivor of abuse and an ex-domestic worker. There was no prior indication of this move; indeed the DWC coordinator was not permitted to attend the Board meeting, as she normally would do, on the evening when the fate of her job and project was being decided. The decision was communicated to her in an inappropriate manner in front of all the staff. At the same Board meeting, the Steering Committee (the body of staff, Board, and committed volunteers empowered to make broad organizational decisions) was dissolved, thus precluding any organization-wide discussion.

The Board and the Program Director sent out public statements describing their actions. One of their declarations was that the intent of DWC had always been to become independent from the time it was started. Since I was Program Coordinator at Sakhi at the time we began the project, I can testify that this is not the case. Another declaration was that they would encourage DWC to become an independent organization. Ejection without any financal and logistical support or due process, however, has not been an encouraging experience for DWC. The Board and Program Director claim that conflicts within Sakhi due to the presence of DWC were paralyzing the organization, and that due process for deciding on separation would have taken too long. The reality is that the DWC, which was half of Sakhi's work, was far from being in a state of paralysis, and the fact that discussions through due process can take a long time can never be an excuse for abandoning it altogether.

One could go on and on about the events. It is more important to ask why the events happened and what lessons they have for us. Is it possible that the women who have taken decisions so momentous to Sakhi have been insufficiently critical in facing the challenge of doing radical work in a conservative community? Almost half of the volunteer base, all the domestic workers, and some survivors who are members of DWC did challenge the decision. However, it is important to point out that the Board and Program Director's decision has not been without support. Among the rest of the volunteer base, some have voiced discomfort with the process while others have agreed with the Board totally. I fear that rationalizations such as the need to move on to do "real work" and end "ideological debate" have won the day within Sakhi.

The DWC is presently involved in setting up an independent organization called Workers' Awaaz (Workers' Voice) in New York City.

Organizing a Radical Asian Battered Women's Movement

It may be useful to explain my use of the term "organizing" in the title of this essay. I use "organizing," a term that seems to be liberally used to describe political work, with greater deliberation here. It is often loosely equated to such other terms as "advocacy," "community work," "service provision," "community education," and "coalition building," and can therefore also stand for a combination of these terms. "Organizing" exploited and powerless peoples, to me, more accurately means the development of a sense of power among these peoples. In this context, organizing of exploited peoples does not simply mean achieving their presence in an organization in any capacity. Organizing is successful when the leadership is drawn from exploited people, who then make decisions for themselves and the organization.

Rhetorically, the goals of the battered women's movement are to transform power structures that perpetuate violence against women and to build power among women. Women of color have added to this perspective by introducing the particular ways they are oppressed, and their goal is to build power among women of color. The special powerlessness created by economic servitude of women also leads to a recognition of the need to build power among poor, working-class women. Among Asian battered women's organizations, there are several barriers that prevent us from reaching our larger goal of empowering women to overcome oppression, as I've attempted to show in this chapter.

In order for us to practice radical politics through our community work, we need:

1. A clear articulation of the contours of exploitation in as much of its complexity as possible, and a commitment to naming the institutional structures that support these oppressive frameworks.

2. A desire to challenge the foundations of exploitation. The challenge must be more than rhetorical; it must be targeted at actual bodies or peoples, and it must threaten business as usual for powerholders.

3. A well-formed notion of who is most exploited. The exploited, who will benefit the most from the dismantling of identified, complex exploitative frameworks, can be those women who are simultaneously oppressed because of their gender and their economic and cultural powerlessness.

4. A commitment to build collective power among those identified as being exploited.

5. A commitment to use only those means of political action that will serve the above-stated goals and to stay away from all action that does not move towards the above-stated goals.

6. Alliances with organizations and methodologies that move us towards these goals.

As we strive to do our work self-critically, it is crucial for us to be aware of the effects of power outside us as well as inside us. When we build up an understanding of power whereby a clearly identifiable external group is seen as *the* oppressor, it is tempting to perceive liberation to be the end of control by that group. Such an analysis lets us off the hook by not acknowledging our own complicity in exploitation, as the oppressive system is seen as lying outside us. The path to fundamental social change is a slippery one, and the only way to avoid moving in unwanted directions is to remain vigilant about the parameters of our work, both at a personal and at an organizational level. It seems superfluous to emphasize the importance of staying on this path—because if we are not going to do political work that truly threatens business as usual, why are we doing it at all?

Notes

1. My analysis emerges out of my work with Sakhi in New York City, and from talking to allied organizations such as Manavi, Apna Ghar, and New York Asian Women's Center, as well as other non-Asian domestic violence organizations. Since I was part of the group that started Sakhi, I include myself as a subject of the analysis that I offer in this essay. I remained active in Sakhi's projects until the dismantling of the Domestic Workers Committee and have great admiration for many of the women who have put enormous energy into Sakhi in the past. This essay, although a product of several years of interaction with countless women inside and outside Sakhi, is my personal perspective, and I am solely responsible for it.

I am indebted to S. Shankar for thoughtful discussions and helpful comments. I am also grateful to the following individuals for reading versions of this essay and helping me think through my ideas: Cecilia Castelino, Jael Silliman, Yumna Siqqiqui, Mona Sehgal, and Chandana Mathur. I would also like to thank women I have met through Sakhi, as well as numerous other individuals I have worked with in New York City—all of whom have taught me a great deal about community organizing and helped me grow politically.

2. In an earlier essay, I discuss in greater depth some of the complexities behind assuming a South Asian identity. "The Public/Private Mirage: Mapping Homes and Undomesticating Violence Work in the South Asian Immigrant Community." *Feminist Genealogies, Colonial Legacies, Democratic Futures*. Eds. Jacqui Alexander and Chandra Talpade Mohanty. New York: Routledge, 1996.

3. My use of the term "Asian American women" is strategic. It has been used over the years to refer to a very diverse community, and it is fair to say that people of Asian ancestry in the United States use the term with varying degrees of conviction to describe themselves—indeed many do not use it at all. However, because of its historical usage in identifying a significant group and its activities, it is useful for certain arguments in this essay.

4. Wharton, Carol S. "Establishing Shelters for Battered Women: Local Manifestations of a Social Movement." *Qualitative Sociology* 10.2 (Summer 1987): 158.

5. I describe some of these events in an earlier essay, "The Habit of Ex-Nomination: Nation, Women, and the Indian Immigrant Bourgeoisie." *Public Culture* 5.1 (Fall 1992): 19-44.

6. Stevenson, Judith. "Getting Up Off Our Rhetoric to Survive." *Aegis* 34 (1982): 27.

7. Gandhi, Nandita, and Nandita Shah. *The Issues At Stake: Theory and Practice in the Contemporary Women's Movement in India*. New Delhi: Kali for Women, 1993. 58.

8. Sullivan, Gail. "Funny Things Happen on Our Way to Revolution." *Aegis* 34 (1982): 12, 17.

9. More details on these achievements are beyond the scope of this essay, but factors such as the growing number of Asian American community organizations and the increased (although still limited) visibility of Asian American issues in the activist and funding communities indicate the gradual rise in attention paid to the problems of Asian/Asian American communities.

10. Gandhi and Shah 65-66.

11. Gandhi and Shah 66.

12. *Coming Together: Proceedings of the First National Asian Women's Health Conference*. San Francisco: National Asian Women's Health Organization, 1996. 71-72.

Redefining the Home

How Community Elites Silence Feminist Activism

By Purvi Shah

The argument with my uncle starts a few minutes after the "discussion" begins. In this particular conversation, we move beyond his exaltation of Reagan and my ridicule for the jellybean president. We have returned to the battleground where we always clash: women's rights. I sit in my uncle's living room, flanked by four of his male friends, and in their expressions I see how ridiculous I sound. *Marriage is a political and not just a social act.*

While my statement is far from revolutionary, inside this home, I am a heretic. Convinced that marriage is solely a cultural event, the idea of such an institution being "political" is practically blasphemous. Politics is a presidential race, the latest legislative or court decision. Politics does not include all the ways in which power is maintained. In this house, the "private" ceremony of marriage is considered part of "culture," rather than the "public" realm of "politics." Why? Because it involves "tradition," social customs, and intimacy (real or otherwise) between people.

Such dichotomies as politics/culture and public/private make it nearly impossible to show how family structures and institutions such as marriage can perpetuate or promote violence against women. The idea that the home is private, its affairs governed by culture, makes it possible to justify male superiority and domestic violence—they are simply the result of "tradition," "heritage," and culture. The separation of politics from culture is similarly used to silence activist messages, by barring progressive groups from participating in community events and constructing a sanitized version of culture that suits elite interests and power.

Activist Exclusion at the India Day Parade

On August 20, 1995, nearly 100 South Asian activists protested their exclusion from the 15th Annual India Day Parade in New York City. On August 11, parade organizers from the Federation of Indian Associations (FIA) had banned the participation of progressive groups, such as Sakhi for South Asian Women, a social change organization that works with battered South Asian women; the South Asian Lesbian and Gay Association (SALGA); South Asian AIDS Action (SAAA); the Committee Against Anti-Asian Violence's Lease Drivers Coalition; and Yaar (a South Asian civil rights and education organization).

The FIA, which covers the tri-state area of Connecticut, New Jersey, and New York, justified its decision on two bases: these groups were not solely composed of Indians, and they did not represent "traditional Indian values."

The FIA board of directors argued that groups that characterize themselves as South Asian (a category that includes people from Bangladesh, Bhutan, India, Nepal, Pakistan, Sri Lanka, and Tibet) are not strictly Indian and therefore should not be included in Indian community events. According to *Asia Online*, FIA President Nitin Vora said, "We had no other options than to disallow [Sakhi]...purely because they were not an Indian organization."

Yet many Indians are involved in the excluded groups, all of which provide services and/or outreach to the Indian community. Moreover, other South Asian groups, such as Nav Nirman/Queens Child Guidance Center, faced no problems obtaining approval to participate in the parade.

Why did the FIA deem Nav Nirman respectable enough to participate, despite its stated South Asian—not exclusively Indian—focus? In part, the answer lies in the fact that the FIA does not consider the work of Nav Nirman/Queens Child Guidance Center to be social activism. As founder Walter Picardo emphasizes, the center is engaged in "social work. We are not activists."

Clearly, progressive groups were rejected not merely because they include members from outside India, but because they did not represent the FIA's values. "This is the India Day Parade. It has to do with Indian culture, traditional Indian values," the FIA president said to another reporter. Vora explained that while he does not object to homosexuality, carrying placards that advertise sexuality, as SALGA did, is not in accordance with "Indian values."

While Sakhi had marched in the India Day Parade for each of the five years previous to 1995, the FIA has repeatedly attempted to block SALGA from marching. In 1992, the FIA initially denied SALGA permission to march, but intervention from the New York City Human Rights Commission forced the FIA to yield. The next year, the FIA stipulated that SALGA could march only if it did not carry signs; SALGA refused this condition. In 1994, Sakhi invited SALGA to march along with its volunteers. Parade organizers did not appreciate the circumvention, citing this "misbehavior" as another reason Sakhi was disallowed from participating in the next year's parade. SALGA member Priy Sinha explains why the FIA excluded progressive groups: "Part of it was that the FIA was continuing a legacy of antagonism toward SALGA. Definitely this past year, they stressed the history of it. The history of what had happened was one of the reasons for not letting us march." The basic sentiment of the FIA's leaders is summed up quite boldly by board member Kiran Desai, who commented to a *New York Newsday* reporter, "They did not meet our standards of what we want to place in our culture."

Wrapped up in this homophobic denial of Indian lesbians and gays is a rhetoric of nationalism. According to *The India Journal*, FIA Vice-President Ram Suchdev said,

> People who will be marching in the parade will have some affiliation with the Indian cause and culture. South Asian groups are not Indian organizations representing Indian interest mainly related to patriotic and cultural needs for the Indian society.

After the parade he added, "Any Indian who has true feelings towards making this parade successful should consider India's interest first, then their own identity. It seems that those who are trying to protest have made the spirit of the Independence Day celebration secondary. They want to propagate their philosophy and identity as primary objectives." In other words, rather than adhering to the correct "cultural needs," activist groups "propagate their philosophy and identity." That is, the cultural event of the parade is not the place for redefining notions of family and the individual; this political work is considered disrespectful and alien to the culture.

One of the unstated goals of the India Day Parade is to set cultural norms, to determine what counts as Indian—and what does not.

While the FIA unjustly viewed lesbian and gay identities "as subverting Indian identities," Sarita Ahuja from SAAA acknowledges,

> A lot of people who identify as Indian don't identify as South Asian. The nationalism is a fragile nationalism and that's why they're wanting to project a national identity in India rather than [a] regional [one]. Given the history and difficulties that India has staying together as one country, it [a regional identity] is threatening.

Thus, the term "South Asian" also marks a political stance for a younger generation of activists. The term has become an organizing tool for recognizing common concerns and fighting against common injustices beyond national borders and throughout the diaspora. According to Prema Vora, a program coordinator for Sakhi, "I don't think there are any groups in the U.S. who define themselves as South Asian who are from our parents' generations."

Diluting Activist Messages at the Pakistan Day Parade

Some organizers of New York South Asian community events have allowed progressives to participate, but still employ tactics that dilute, if not silence, activists' progressive messages. Sakhi had no problem being allowed to march in the Pakistan Day Parade a week after the India Day Parade protest, but again, SALGA was excluded. Robina Niaz Zaidi, a Sakhi board member, indicates that the Pakistan Day Parade organizers were supportive, saying, "I was told that the organizers were far more helpful than organizers of the India Day Parade. They were very happy that we were participating."

While Sakhi has marched for each of the three years the Pakistan Day Parade has existed, this inclusion signals only a tenuous endorsement of their work. Before the parade began, as Sakhi volunteers set up, men from the crowd and other floats badgered Sakhi members and made threatening comments. In response to explanations that Sakhi fought for women and women's freedom, one man sneered, saying he could show us what freedom was.

The hostile environment impeded Sakhi's effectiveness at the parade. In the streets, women who were approached by Sakhi volunteers reacted guardedly. Women were simultaneously curious and embarrassed to show interest, observes Abira Ashfaq, a Sakhi volunteer. They were often standing next to spouses or other male family members, men who, Abira says, often derided the Sakhi brochures. "I'm sure any mention of a women's resource group that works with victims of domestic violence, or claims to show class interest in regard to domestic workers, will not sit too well with Mr. Pakistani man." She notes:

> You have to remember a lot of adult women didn't come on their own. They were with their sponsors, in most cases their husbands. That is usually their immigration status. Also economically, unless they've been here for a while, they're dependent on their sponsors.

Still, while many women could not react positively to Sakhi's presence, Robina remarks that other women passed by Sakhi volunteers and then came back to pick up literature, often explaining that they needed it for a friend.

Sakhi's ability to project a message of social change was further hindered by inaccurate characterizations by parade organizers. At the parade stand, the announcer referred to Sakhi members as "women who help other women" and women who perform "social work." This depiction muted the activist tone of Sakhi's advocacy work on behalf of survivors of domestic violence and exploited domestic workers. It depoliticized Sakhi's mission to enact social change, as well.

It is true, however, as Robina says, that Sakhi did not give parade organizers a written description of their work, and that they do provide direct services such as court accompaniments and phone counseling. "It's unfair to put the responsibility on the organizers," she comments. Sarita explains that this translation of Sakhi into a social services organization rather than a political advocacy group may simply be a way of making the organization's work more accessible. When she conducts public policy in India, people also describe her as a social worker. "Not all of it is a malicious intent or subversive intent," she says. "It's trying to get across to the community that you're doing good work."

But, according to Abira, "The concept of social services is less threatening because it blames no one, and only seeks to make front-yard repairs....Also, social services can be viewed through the spectacles of economics, charity and giving zakat (alms). Acceptable things." Social work is seen as a service performed in support of the status quo: social workers help the less fortunate become part of mainstream society.

Political activists turn this equation on its head, placing responsibility for unmet needs and injustices on society instead of on individuals. Sakhi's mission is to fight against the structures, mechanisms, and attitudes that allow abuse to continue. Instead of helping women simply to cope, these activists challenge a world that allows—and often condones—batterers and exploitative employers. To describe such work as "social work," Abira comments,

> sounds more like "prosperous helping poor"; it doesn't point at victims and victimizers. Nobody is imbalancing the status quo and nobody seems to be placing blame in societal structure, since poverty and other related issues are "plainly inevitable" and women's misery, even more so.

The Diwali Festival

A similar type of dilution of Sakhi's politics occurred two months after the India Day Parade protest, during the October 15 South Street Seaport Diwali festival, when eight Sakhi volunteers were given the space to perform a *garba-raas* (a Gujarati folk dance). The lyrics to the feminist song they garba-danced to encouraged women to rise up and join the struggle, as event organizers from the Association of Indians in America (AIA) explained before the performance. Not only did the Diwali festival organizers allow Sakhi to dance alongside more conventional troupes, but SAAA and other progressive South Asian groups were given space to distribute materials and conduct outreach.

Nonetheless, the inclusion of progressive South Asian organizations in the Diwali events did not imply unequivocal support. Five years earlier, in 1990, AIA had barred Sakhi from performing a play on domestic violence during the Diwali festival. Anannya Bhattacharjee, who was a Sakhi program coordinator at the time, said that the nature of the performance made a difference to AIA organizers. "When they heard a play, they were okay," she says. "Then when they saw the brochures, they said it [the Diwali festival] was a cultural event and not a political one." Dancing is taken to be a benign activity that does not impinge on the world of politics. Dancing, particularly garba-raas, contains religious overtones; the associations are seen as devotional, not confrontational. "I don't see music as being so explicit. Even though they are feminist songs, it doesn't seem to bother them that much," Bhattacharjee adds. "I think that it being a garba does make a difference. The organization being more established only has so much to do with it."

Constructing Culture to Exclude Activism

The idea that culture and politics are separate is used by community elites alternately to bar progressive organizations from community events and to recast activism as social service that doesn't implicate society. This stance, that what is cultural cannot be political and what is political cannot be cultural, dilutes the impact of political messages, such as the garba's feminist lyrics. Until we are able to show that this division is false, our work will either be denied or reconstructed by community organizers to suit their own needs.

In all of the rhetoric regarding the FIA's decision to exclude progressive groups and the use of such neutral terms as "social work," one thing is clear: community leaders are threatened by the work activist organizations do. FIA President Vora said of the India Day Parade controversy that Sakhi "unnecessarily made it a threatening issue." While part of his acknowledgment of feeling threatened is motivated by a desire to be seen as a victim or on the defensive against an unjust aggressor, it is true that some community leaders are fearful of the destabilization of current norms.

What in particular do FIA leaders and others who minimize activism and social change fear? In terms of the India Day Parade controversy, the notion of patriotism for one's country of origin was thrown into question. Statements made by FIA leaders, as well as the text of the parade brochure, constantly emphasize pride for India, Indian culture, and Indian identity. FIA leaders and people in the general Indian community have asserted that the refusal of progressive groups to carry Indian flags or signs reading "Long Live India" is a denial of the parade's patriotic spirit. Although these groups have carried such signs—SALGA carried a sign that read "SALGA celebrates Indian Independence" in the 1994 parade—Sakhi's refusal to endorse the Hindu nationalism of the parade organizers caused them to step back. (In an interesting play on the issue of allegiance, a SALGA member at the 1995 parade protest sported a banner that read, "Long Live Queer India.")

This concern for national pride and patriotism is not limited to the India Day Parade. One reason that the Pakistan Day Parade crowd was hostile to Sakhi members is that this parade is a space for Islamic followers and Islamic fundamentalists who often support male dominance to solidify their ties to the nation of Pakistan.

The notion of "South Asian" is itself dangerous because it threatens the national-cultural boundaries that these parades attempt to reify. While India Day parade organizers were careful to include a range of India's religions (including floats from the Jesus Society, the International Society for Krishna Consciousness, and the Muslims of India), this show of bypassing cultural differences is possible only within certain borders: the borders of the homeland. Indeed, as a South Asian domestic violence group, Sakhi not only challenges what the home is, but also what the homeland is. While the term "South Asian" can be problematic if it points to a group that is solely Indian and Hindu, it is useful for marking the region's shared histories and cultures. The term "South Asian" is particularly useful in a diasporic context—such as in the United States—because it refers us to a collective homeland. The term "South Asian" allows progressive workers for social change to bypass national allegiances and claim belonging elsewhere. It is hard to admit to the shame of domestic violence, and even harder to see that the homeland may not be the pristine place of one's memory. South Asian groups blur this memory and ask community members to do a hard thing: reach out beyond religious, ethnic, and spatial divides to people once seen as enemies.

Tied up in this fear is a deep-seated anxiety that progressive groups will serve as a model for the next generation. Besides characterizing the India Day Parade as a place to "pay respect to the country of their roots," the *News India-Times* also described how parade Grand Marshal and Bombay film star Rakhee closed the parade by asking the crowd to join her in a chant of "Jai Hind," with participants lifting "thousands of little Tricolors" into the sky, "a lump in their throats." According to the article, Rakhee "appealed to Indian-Americans not to forget their homeland and stressed the need for teaching Indian values and traditions to their younger generations." SALGA's Priy Sinha comments that this appeal to values is one way in which activists, particularly gays and lesbians, are seen as "vectors of this polluting Americanization." Concern for youth morality is another reason for the exclusion of progressive groups. One SALGA sign that FIA leaders constantly refer to as a sign of discarded values read, "Do you know whether your child is gay or lesbian?"

FIA leaders are equally eager to present a particular image of Indians to mainstream America. In the same breath with which Vora dismissed homosexuality as not in accordance with "Indian values," he added, "That is not what we should be showing to the American people." The FIA does not want progressive groups to display what they see as the community's "dirty laundry." The parade brochure provides an interesting example of how the FIA hopes to portray Indian culture to Indians and non-Indians alike. In his history of the FIA's existence, Jhalak Patel describes how the Joint Committee of Indian Organizations, the precursor to the FIA, not only celebrated Indian holidays and assisted people in India, but also "participated in American celebrations which further the acceptance of Indians in America." Other brochure contributors point to Indians as a professional class and stress the need to teach traditional Indian values to young people. Parade organizers maintain the model minority myth in the hopes that white America will leave us alone as long as we go about our business. (We only have to look to new, sweeping anti-immigrant legislation to realize that isolation will not provide security.) FIA leaders promote a vision of India and Indians in the United States as middle- to upper-class, well-behaved, morally upright, and conservative, a snapshot that Indians in our own class, ethnic, religious, sexual, and regional diversity deny through our mere existence.

The Impact on Domestic Violence Work

Although unstated, an assumed definition of culture is operating in all of the previous scenarios: my uncle's home, the India Day Parade, the Pakistan Day Parade, the Diwali festival. In these particular incidents and in the general perpetuation of domestic violence, dichotomies such as politics/culture and public/private do not exist in isolation. Rather, in these contexts, culture is coupled with the private, and politics with the public. Both the home and the homeland become sacred (private) spaces that defy intervention. This understanding of culture and home reflect a masculine approach, in which aggression, nationalism, refusal to compromise, and ownership are valued. These unstated masculine constructions are dangerous not only because the space of culture is limited to exclude progressive ideas and action, but also because these power imbalances allow domestic violence to continue.

One of the first conceptual revolutions we need to enact is the belief that a home in which violence occurs is a public space. Domestic violence must be seen not as a personal (private) problem within the closed arena of a home, but as a political (public) problem influenced by cultural, social, and environmental factors. Through the home and the institutions that embody the home, such as marriage, we must show how the unstated assumptions regarding culture contribute to the perpetuation of violence. Challenging these premises allows domestic violence to be viewed not as a closed family problem, but as a larger social problem.

In the South Asian fight against domestic violence, we must recognize that our resistance transgresses not only personal boundaries, but also cultural boundaries. By making domestic violence a cultural-political problem, we counter the ways in which batterers use "tradition" and "history" to justify their behavior. By moving beyond identity politics, beyond the questions of home and homeland, through remaining dedicated to transnational social change, activists can focus on the ideologies behind domestic violence (or heteronormativity or economic exploitation, etc.) rather than individual incidents to build a framework that allows for community participation and intervention.

Countering Silencing Tactics

Activists can take steps to ensure that the false divide between the cultural and political is not used to marginalize progressive messages:

• For situations like the Pakistan Day Parade, in which activism is described as social work, written descriptions would let activists represent themselves. Sakhi's Prema Vora points out that activists themselves often portray their work as unthreatening. "It's the way we talk," she says. "'We're a group of women helping women' is different from saying that we're a group of women who is fighting against exploitation in all its forms in the South Asian community. People use different words depending on who we're talking to." Of course, this is the smart tactic, to tailor outreach based on audience, but keeping the message of activism and social change strong and clear is one way to avoid being mistaken.

• Gain media support. "The media is a great way for people to know that South Asian gays exist, that South Asian feminists exist, that we're not just a bunch of pencil-twisting nerds," comments

Sinha. Sinha adds, "In terms of gay and lesbian issues, I think the community finds it really easy to ignore us. Most of the South Asian queer organizations are just struggling to have a voice....All of these confrontations are just about getting visible in the South Asian community." Confrontations may not endear us, but they provide vehicles for people to voice their support. Other models of acceptance do exist: northern California's FIA has allowed Trikone, the local South Asian lesbian and gay group, to march since their parade began three years ago.

• Organizations must build up legitimacy in the community and provide ongoing outreach. While the media can counter attempts to silence us, we must still go back to our own communities. SAAA's Sarita Ahuja argues that advocating for social change must go hand-in-hand with providing services. "It's not one or the other. You provide services and while you're doing that you try to change people and have some influence. The legitimacy comes first from having community-based services and then working for social change. Without social service networks, how are you going to access people?" Ahuja admits that people buy into the model minority myth and avoid getting help, but asks, "What is the point of doing all the work if it doesn't change what the community thinks about us?"

Sources

15th India Day Parade - 1995, Federation of Indian Associations.

"Beautiful India Day Parade in New York City." *The Minaret.* 21 August 1995.

"Colorful I-Day Parades Held." *News India-Times.* 25 August 1995: 1, 32.

"Groups Banned from Parade." *India Currents Magazine.* September 1995: 20.

Hassan, Sadat. "Rakhi Gulzar Wins the Hearts at 15th India Day Parade." *Asia Online.* 28 August-3 September 1995: 12.

Pereira, Cynthia. "FIA excludes some groups from India Day Parade." *The India Journal.* 17 August 1995: 1, 4.

Pereira, Cynthia. "India Day Parade Draws Fire." *The India Journal.* 20 August 1995: 1, 4.

Sengupta, Somini. "Indian Parade: Gays Not Allowed." *New York Newsday.* 14 August 1995: A12.

On Asian America, Feminism, and Agenda-Making
A Roundtable Discussion

With Pamela Chiang, Milyoung Cho,
Elaine H. Kim, Meizhu Lui, and Helen Zia
Moderated by Seema Shah

SEEMA: What do you think unifies Asian women in the United States as a group? Does it makes sense to talk about or organize ourselves as Asian American women?

HELEN: Well, I think we do have a lot of things that unify us as a group, even though we are very diverse and have to learn more about each other. But I think what unifies us as Asian women is pretty similar to what unifies us as a community at large. We are basically seen as more or less the same, and we encounter the same sort of problems in the United States, even though we have very different histories and backgrounds. Here in the United States, our political and cultural historical differences are not evident to the public. The other thing is, as Asian American women, we have a lot more in common culturally than we have that separates us. The 100 million women who are missing from the world [due to female infanticide], not so coincidentally, come primarily from Asia: South Asia and East Asia. And there are cultural patriarchal practices here in the United States. Our common understanding of oppression that begins in Asia draws us together.

MEIZHU: Many immigrant women, though, do not see themselves as Asian American. My mother has been here for a very long time and is a U.S. citizen, but she would never call herself Asian American. She's Chinese! The sense of "group" across Asian nationalities is stronger among the U.S.-born generation.

MILYOUNG: We often talk about the diversity of Asian communities as being an obstacle to effective organizing, which it definitely can be. But, interestingly, it is our experiences with dealing with differences that we have in common. If put into practice, this can be a source of strength. Many of us come from poly-generational families—for example, our grandmothers are somewhere in Asia, our mothers immigrated here, and we were born here. We are all dealing with different issues and realities within one family. In many ways, there can be a lot of conflict; but this is also our strength and our tool to survive, especially in this country. Kids are translating for their parents; grandmothers are keeping us tied into the important values of where we came from. If we could just break through the many differences we have, we could capitalize on how we are so used to dealing with so many facets of reality within our lives.

ELAINE: I agree with Milyoung. One of the reasons Asian Immigrant Women Advocates [AIWA] is such a good model for organizing is that it's been able to find those interstices that people stand on. For example, a student in a college class who herself is not a garment worker might know someone who is—her mother or another relative might be. In contrast, in the lettuce boycott, for example, the housewife who is buying the lettuce did not share a space close to the lettuce picker. AIWA's been very successful at getting young, U.S.-born, 1.5 generation Asian American women involved, partly because of their relationships with other Asian women in different situations.

MEIZHU: I was thinking specifically of the question of identity. My mother was in China during the Sino-Japanese war, and she still does not have a particularly fond attitude towards the Japanese. It is quite different from me and my sisters, who do feel we have more in common with Japanese American women than with white women or black women. The stereotypes are the same, whether we are Chinese American or Japanese American. We're trying to identify ourselves in relationship to other groups, including our mothers. I'm interested in how we are constructing a new historical identity.

On the Feminist Movement

SEEMA: This book explores many of the tensions between the feminist movement and Asian American women. For example, some Asian American women make a point of saying they do not ally themselves with feminism. Others do, but they all have significant criticisms of mainstream white feminism and feminist theory. What are your experiences with the U.S. women's movement, within and outside the academy and in the media?

PAMELA: Personally, I feel that a lot of the agenda has been a white, middle-class one. I'm one of the young people here; my generation of coming into this is different, but my personal experience is that their agenda is a little off from what poor women and women of color face. As women of color, we've tended to be potentially more engaged around what poor women in our communities experience. That's a broader perspective that the big national women's organizations have lacked. When I organized with Latina garment workers from Texas, we would approach these national institutions for support. With a little bit of effort, they would wax and wane. But they don't speak to our issues. And this is parallel to the environmental movement—which is why we formed the environmental justice movement, to hit on a few basic things: bottom-up decisionmaking, building a space for those who are impacted by environmental racism, making poor people of color communities be the core leadership.

HELEN: I agree. I understand Pamela's experience. My own experience is as one of those from an older generation. I think when we talk about the white women's movement, it is important to identify what part of the women's movement we mean. Pamela identified the more middle-class, national organizations. The women's movement is so broad, there are so many organizations, including those that cross class lines. The media and political conservatives have tried to split women and label the entire women's movement as a white, middle-class, bourgeois movement. There are, absolutely, large parts of the mainstream movement that are white and middle-class, but that is not to say that it all is.

Having said that, there is a real problem of white privilege and racism that exists in the women's organizations that are predominantly white. An "old girls' network" has evolved. All of us who have worked in coalitions or within programs where the leadership is dominated by white women have encountered it. I've worked within one of the publications that is identified as part of the mainstream white women's movement [*Ms.* Magazine]. Trying to get other races and classes represented within the pages of the magazine took a consistent and conscious struggle.

ELAINE: My experience has been working in the university. About 12 years ago, 98 percent of the tenured faculty at Berkeley were both white and male. In the last half-decade, about 50 percent of the new faculty hires have been women; most of them white. There's been a big change in the distribution of gender. But there are still very few tenured women of color.

One of the big problems is that there is a certain centrality of whiteness that the white women who come into their work situation reinforce, and some have exhibited a maternalistic attitude towards women of color, particularly Asian American women. It's not that they are insensitive to race, but there is the question of misinterpreting matters of cultural style. For example, some women think you have to wear Birkenstocks and have hairy armpits to be considered a feminist.

When affirmative action was under attack, we tried to be unified to defend it. We tried to overlook these insensitive or maternalistic attitudes, but in many cases, many of the white women who benefitted from affirmative action really didn't try to defend against its dismantling. It was disappointing. But people haven't really addressed schisms among women, in the interests of unity.

MEIZHU: Once again, we define our identities through our relationships to other people and groups. We as Asian American women certainly have a different relationship to the dominant white culture than white women, who are still part of it, even though they are not the ones who have the most power. In terms of the feminist movement, I see our work with them as using united-front kinds of tactics. Sometimes we will be in the same struggle, and sometimes we won't be. We can do that: sometimes we are friends, and sometimes we are critical. We're pushing them.

Sometimes they select issues that are not necessarily our issues. I think of abortion rights as one that was not the first priority on our agenda. However, the work that was done did help all of us in a certain way. The thing that I resent is that they come with an agenda of their own and expect everyone to fall in line. That's when I've had problems with them.

MILYOUNG: I agree with you. The main problem is when they claim something they claim represents all women, as if white women are all women. It may have been different in the 1970s, when there were fewer organizing attempts by Asian women. But now there are lots of strong organizing campaigns led by Asian women. It's not a problem that white women are not attempting to organize women of color en masse, because basically if they did, it would smack of missionary work. In a way, the fact that they haven't incorporated us or made a space for us has given us a lot more independence to define our own agendas.

SEEMA: Do you think Asian American women should or can find a place within the established feminist movement?

HELEN: It depends on the issue. There will be times when we can unite and work together, and times when we won't. There will also be women of color, Asian women, who choose to work within mainstream feminist organizations, who find that they can either create their own space, or find space, for them to be empowered and express themselves politically. There's no reason not to.

Affirmative action is a good example. We can't assume that women who have directly benefitted, personally even, from affirmative action and who call themselves feminist will necessarily ally themselves with the interests of communities of color or Asian communities. Because although groups like the National Organization for Women [NOW] have taken a stand in support of affirmative action, many women have not. I've participated in several discussions in which white women who call themselves feminist or were politically aware really didn't get the affirmative action issue. And knowing them, I knew they had also benefitted from it in their lives. The hope is that even though we can't assume unity with white feminists, we can hope that because of their experience with gender oppression we may be able to reach a common understanding. That is the basis for us to try to work together.

MEIZHU: There has been progress in their addressing of race and class. For example, NOW put welfare reform very high on their agenda. That's not something they would have done ten years ago.

PAMELA: In the environmental justice movement, we faced the question very early on in our formation: would we want to place ourselves in the established environmental movement? We realized that we couldn't, because they were part of the problem around racism. We always felt that as people of color we had to build an inclusive movement, an organization that would be multi-issue focused and grassroots in nature. In working towards environmental justice, we would bring along with us other organizations towards a much more progressive vision around sustainability.

The case of the women's movement and Asian American women may be similar. The priority is, we have to do our organizing of Asian women, particularly immigrant women, and develop our visions and leadership. That's the longterm priority.

MILYOUNG: There is always that possibility of co-optation, of being used for purposes that aren't going to further the agendas of our communities. I agree with Pamela that we need to have a clear vision and build leadership to work towards it, before we get swept into something else. But hopefully in the near future there will be room for equal partnership.

ELAINE: One of the issues that keeps coming up is the tightrope walk that Asian Americans do, their relations between the "margins" and mainstream. That's going to be increasingly an issue in the 21st century.

People of my generation were used to segregation. California has changed demographically, and things won't ever be the same as in the past. Increasingly, Asian American women will have to negotiate new positions vis-à-vis the dominant culture. I don't know how I would articulate myself in a white women's organization, and I haven't really had to do it. But I think that my daughter would have to think about that much more than someone my age.

HELEN: That's true, Elaine. I think [Asian American women's organizing options] also vary regionally. In the heartland, as opposed to the coasts, women may not have the option of creating their own community-based organization.

ELAINE: I just came back from visiting some meatpacking plants in a small town—Garden City, Kansas. The workers are all immigrants—Asians and Mexicans who live in a trailer park that looked to me to be completely segregated from the other people who have always lived in that town. All the workers' kids went to the school that served the trailer park.

I used to think that "heartland" meant one Asian face in a group of 30 students. When I thought "meatpacker," I thought, a white man in a labor union. But actually what I saw was really different from my expectations. It is true that all the regions are different, but things are changing so much everywhere. We need to think about how we will achieve this delicate balance, being very rooted in whatever community and having a relationship to the constantly shifting dominant culture.

On the Asian American Movement

SEEMA: Let's talk about the Asian American movement. Several Asian women have criticized the Asian American movement for not including women and women's concerns. The early Yellow Power movement has been criticized for being male-identified. What has been your experience with the Asian American social movements in and outside the academy?

MILYOUNG: I wonder if part of this impression is a result of historical misrepresentation, due to men taking credit for the work of others. I've been involved in community work for ten years, and it is very clear to me that women are at the core of what's going on. Although I wasn't present in the 1970s during the Yellow Power movement, I'm just assuming that there were a lot of women involved. Maybe the issues were framed by the men who may have dominated, but I would assume that women have always been involved. Maybe their voice and perspectives were stifled, and their participation and contributions have been underdocumented. But in terms of involvement, we've always been there.

MEIZHU: It's not clear exactly what you mean by women's concerns. There has been women's leadership, but some of their concerns about power for Asian Americans in general have been [the concerns] of men as well. Speaking out against racism was a women's concern. Chinese women workers in the 1930s wanted to contribute to the nationalist fight against Japan. They organized in order to raise their wages to send money home. That was their concern. Are you stereotyping what a women's concern is?

HELEN: I was thinking about the issue of violence against women—domestic violence, sexual harassment, sexual assault. Asian women have organized around these issues without much involvement of Asian men that I know of.

In those areas of organizing, there may be more linkage between Asian American women and white feminists, though I think that is changing. Over ten or fifteen years of organizing the battered women's movement, Asian women's organizations have made a lot of ties and have a shared organizational history and struggle with the women's movement.

In contrast, the anti-Asian violence movement, like the criminal justice establishment, doesn't consider violence against women "hate crimes." This is a big separation, and is reflected not just within the anti-Asian violence movement, but in the broader hate crimes and violence against women movements. What are your thoughts on that, Milyoung?

MILYOUNG: In many ways, this separation is kind of arbitrary. Violence against women is clearly about power and hate. I remember the board of the Asian Women's Shelter in San Francisco was discussing this about five years ago, when I was working at CAAAV [Committee Against Anti-Asian Violence, in New York City]. In a way, we were just following the protocol of the criminal justice establishment.

HELEN: Actually, the Asian Women's Shelter's discussion about this generated quite a lot of debate and led to the formation of a study group. Elaine's book, *Making More Waves*, describes that particular episode. There was a lot of resistance within the anti-Asian violence movement, which initially said, gender crimes are one thing, hate crimes are another. They were looking at things in a legalistic framework.

MILYOUNG: Let me add something. One of the main reasons CAAAV was formed was to combat one effect of racism as it affects Asians. In the late 1980s when CAAAV first started, the main thrust was to organize against racial violence and racism and how we were being targeted in all these different ways. Because pinpointing how racism affects us was the larger picture, violence against women, which often occurs within our own families, did not fit within CAAAV's original framework. But of course, strategies need to change, and that discussion needs to come up again.

HELEN: But what happens when race and gender overlap? When a woman of color or Asian woman experiences sexual violence or sexual assault, what part of her is being targeted: that she is a woman or that she is Asian? At what point does the anti-Asian violence movement pick it up, versus when the Asian battered women's movement picks it up? Those separations are still very real.

Now there is a federal Violence against Women Act, which describes gender-motivated crimes as hate crimes. That will include hate crimes that are committed against Asian women by Asian men, if they are gender-motivated. As these cases come forward, we will be forced to discuss it.

MEIZHU: Once again, there are some generational issues. With my parents' generation, part of their strategy for survival, as well as part of their culture, was not to let the foreigners know the problems going on within their own communities. Violence against women was one of those things. Our task is to challenge the anti-women aspects of Asian culture, while respecting our mothers' strategies for survival in different historical periods.

ELAINE: In the Yellow Power days, there was the idea—even though I agree with Milyoung that women participated very actively—that the main movement wouldn't be exactly women, although women would be supportive of it. There would be, instead, "women's auxiliaries," which could include something on domestic violence, for example. If women sold rice cakes to raise money, their donation would be considered "the women's contribution" to the nationalist cause. Koreans in the 1980s, when protest movements were so strong, would say, "well, feminist concerns need to be taken care of after we take care of reunification." Among Asian Americans in the Yellow Power days, the guys would be aligned with the Black Panthers, and the women would make some coffee and help out. And they could have their women's meetings, a women's journal, and women's issues, but they would be under the umbrella of the universal movement.

What is interesting is that the women transformed that auxiliary stuff into very cutting-edge social movements. For example, the drive against homophobia in Asian American communities has really been led by Asian American women. Women have redefined violence to be more encompassing and are paying attention to social class, as in the various efforts to organize workers. Also, many Asian American women work on transnational issues, like the maquiladoras over the San Diego-Tijuana border. It is interesting to see that although these organizing efforts might have started out as something some of the men would dismiss as "just" women's issues or women's causes, women have transformed them into the most pressing issues.

MEIZHU: So part of women's exclusion has to do with women naming and claiming the leadership.

ELAINE: By doing what needs to be done and by doing the work.

MEIZHU: And by writing about it and showing how that has been cutting-edge. I like that idea. Some of the stuff that the guys were doing that seemed to be cutting-edge might not have been.

ELAINE: It was important at the time. There's no doubt that even if there was patriarchy in Asian American communities, many women got their first sense of self and subjectivity in a racist society from organizing with Asian American men. And not all violence towards Asian American women comes from Asian men, it comes from the white society as well, so organizing with Asian American men was really empowering in a way. But on the other hand, this "women's auxiliary" thing was condescending and paternalistic.

HELEN: We have nothing to gain from being silent, from keeping a culture of invisibility. That includes the generational issue of keeping our communities' problems to ourselves. Something that I've heard many times over is that when sexual harassment occurs to Asian women by Asian men, Asian women feel they cannot come forward. The community pressure is so great—it would look like they were trying to betray the community. Asian American women are being asked to sacrifice and not seek justice. Those are things that we need to bring some light to.

MEIZHU: Which brings us back to the initial question. It makes a lot of sense to organize ourselves as Asian American women.

On Building Coalitions

SEEMA: Do you think Asian American women have succeeded in participating in other social movements and if so, how?

MILYOUNG: I think a lot of us got our training from other movements. I went to college in the mid-1980s. At that time, for those of us who grew up in areas with very low-visibility Asian communities and who were bent towards progressive politics, some of the most obvious things we could get ourselves involved with were Central America solidarity work, the anti-apartheid movement, corporate divestiture, reproductive rights. These are issues that don't necessarily overlap with the main driving forces of the Asian American movement. But we learned how to cut and frame issues, and about organizing strategies, through working with these other groups.

HELEN: That's true for those of us who were emerging in other times as well. We got our training in other social movements.

MEIZHU: And socialist movements! Many of us came out of left political groupings as well, which was really great training, learning by engaging in anti-racist activities and class struggle.

The most important social movement for us, though, is the movement of African Americans. They have had a much longer history of fighting oppression. We have not only benefitted by participating with them in the civil rights movement and beyond, but we have also learned a great deal about how to think about Asian Americans within the larger context of people of color.

Organizing Immigrant Women Workers

SEEMA: Many Asian American women have been inspired by campaigns organizing Asian women workers, such AIWA's campaign to organize Asian seamstresses and other workers. What do you think is the significance of this kind of work, and what do you think it can mean to Asian American women?

PAMELA: I think this is the cutting-edge work. AIWA's campaign is the kind of thing that really cuts down what we mean around gender, race, class issues. And talking about it in relation to capital, and who benefits and who burns, gets to a transnational nature. It's a necessity in our work at APEN [Asian Pacific Environmental Network] in organizing in Richmond, California, with the Laotian community. We're starting first and foremost with the Laotian community's girls. Some grew up in refugee camps from the Vietnam War, some grew up here, but now most have lived much of their lives in the United States. For us, organizing with them means dealing with poverty, the impacts of welfare reform, and a lot of issues that they face at home and in society as young women—domestic violence, you name it.

At APEN we thought about where we really need to do organizing. It's really the so-called newer communities—immigrant and refugee communities. We really need to start at that place and not simply at the point of Asian glass ceiling issues in corporate America, because we really need to talk about transforming society. I think that the benefit for us in the Asian community is that we have groups like AIWA that really take that on.

ELAINE: I think AIWA is a model for organizing, not only for those reasons, but also because their work complicates the idea of "Asian women." They work with women from vastly different language groups, such as Vietnamese, Chinese, Koreans, and Filipinas, and that's very hard. AIWA puts Asian seamstresses together with Mexican seamstresses, and then provides translations! This is extremely difficult and very important work.

College students may come from the suburbs and the middle class, but they would not all necessarily like to go down the road to yuppiedom, completely divorced from issues that people in the immigrant working class face. What AIWA does is very inclusively make a way for them to participate. On one level, [in relation to AIWA's campaign against fashion designer Jessica McClintock] you could just decide not to buy that prom dress or that bridesmaid's dress from Jessica McClintock. Or on another level, you could draw some graphics for their demonstration, or write press releases, or do some publicity. There are all these different ways AIWA has creatively figured out how to incorporate people from different backgrounds. That kind of inclusiveness is very necessary for the movement for immigrant workers to succeed. What I would hate to see happen would be for people to think that donating $25 now and then would be enough. Or for them to think, "Oh, I really feel sorry for those women who are working there, but that's not me."

Another interesting campaign is that of KIWA [Korean Immigrant Worker Advocates], trying to organize Korean waitresses and Mexican kitchen workers in Korean-owned restaurants in Los Angeles. These are two different genders, two different ethnicities, but they ostensibly have something to share, beyond the Korean nationalism shared by the Korean restaurant owners and the Korean waitresses.

PAMELA: At the core, what these organizations are about is building a leadership and, in that way, an organization for a different kind of leadership. In the future, it won't necessarily be any of us who came out of college enlightened who will be the next leaders; there will be people of different classes as part of the decisionmaking. We sometimes forget how hard that is. Really hard work!

MEIZHU: How do we promote this cutting-edge work in the labor movement? Having suffered so many years of frustrations in the trade union movement as a local union president, I feel we have to connect up with other progressive people that are within labor itself, to really promote the leadership of these new workers, as well as women and people of color. In the unions, I was always fighting not just the bosses, but the white-boy mentality of the union bureaucracy.

HELEN: AIWA and other garment worker activists, and Asian labor activists working with immigrants and migrant workers, have been at the forefront of making links between issues, not only domestically, but globally. They are showing not just what we can do to make social change, but what our role is in the global economy, as residents of the United States and the industrial north. Even if the big labor unions are doing work around class issues, there's still the issue of global class that needs to be addressed.

Towards an Agenda

SEEMA: What do you all think are the most pressing issues for Asian women in the United States today?

MILYOUNG: First, we need to define our vision for the future. An immediate goal would be to make sure that we continue to involve people in the struggle so we don't lose people—to selling out because they can afford to sell out, or to desperation or deportation.

PAMELA: This is nothing that is new, but that ever-rising potential to be used as a buffer, between white privilege and then other people of color and indigenous people. There are the stereotypical Asians in business and financial institutions, and a general perception that that's where all the Asians are—but then we have 25,000 immigrant Asian women seamstresses going off to work in the Bay Area. There will be a greater disparity between those who have made it and those who haven't, as we see the impacts of welfare reform. I can also see a very conscious move on the conservative right to elevate and create a conservative front of people of color. It's not just Clarence Thomas anymore. The right definitely has a strategy around that.

MEIZHU: I think that there are economic issues, certainly, for Asian women. We still are at the bottom of the heap in many ways as immigrants, we're still among the poorest because of our countries of origin and domestic violence and all that. The glass ceiling and attacks on affirmative action still keep us in a fairly low position. Equality issues are still present.

Another issue will be that, as with Clarence Thomas, there will be Asian women who rise to prominence who become mainstream standards. They won't be the people that we progressive Asian women really claim as our models.

Another issue I see is that as we become second-generation, third-generation, fourth-generation, how do we really hold onto our home cultures? How do we shape this Asian American identity in a way that can be lasting, so we don't become integrated and assimilated? That means articulating what activism and leadership mean from the Asian American womanist point of view.

ELAINE: I think language rights are a very pressing issue. The other issue I think is really pressing relates to this being the media age, in which everyone knows who golfer Tiger Woods is and everybody knows who the murderer Andrew Cunanan is. But even if AIWA gets on *60 Minutes,* who is in control of how they get represented, and what gets remembered about them afterwards compared to Tiger Woods? I think that racist representations are still a pressing issue. No matter how many generations an Asian person is here, Asian Americans can still be thought of as not American. The media reinforce that—as they have been doing as they cover the Democratic Party and the "Chinese" campaign contributions controversy.

HELEN: I think all of those are very key issues facing us: being able to take control over our own images and create our images and our identity, to represent what we want to represent, and get the role we play and the issues that we are concerned about out there, framed in a way that we want them framed.

ELAINE: And that's what this book is attempting to do.

II. An Agenda for Change

Sakhi demonstration against domestic violence

Asian Women's Health

Organizing a Movement

By Sia Nowrojee and Jael Silliman

Over the last decade, several pan-Asian organizations have been established. Many address the particular needs of women and girls. These include the National Asian Women's Health Organization (NAWHO), Asian Immigrant Women Advocates (AIWA), the Committee Against Anti-Asian Violence (CAAAV), Asian American Pacific Islanders in Philanthropy (AAPIP), Asian AIDS Project, National Asian Pacific American Legal Consortium (NAPALC), Congressional Asian Pacific American Caucus Institute, Asian American Health Forum, and Asian American AIDS Foundation, as well as the Asian Women's Shelter in San Francisco. Pan-Asian organizations have challenged the "model minority" myth which has been perpetuated, albeit with different intentions, by both "successful Asians" and the mainstream culture. The myth masks the economic disparities and ethnic differences among Asian Americans.[1] Moreover, it exacerbates tensions between Asian communities and other communities of color, who are often compared perjoratively with this model minority. Asian Americans are often scapegoated by low-income whites and other minority groups who claim they take away educational and job opportunities.

The model minority myth perpetuates the false notion that Asian American communities are generally wealthy, with broad access to health and other social services. This false assumption translates into little funding for services earmarked for Asian communities. Asian women's health needs, in particular, have not been identified as research priorities in any advocacy or policy arena.[2] Improving Asian women's health requires organizing for change both within and outside of our communities, with an understanding of the global forces that impact our health.

Despite our growing numbers, most national research projects still identify Asian populations as "statistically insignificant." This makes it difficult to access even basic epidemiological information on Asian communities. A lack of knowledge of the immense diversity that exists within Asian America, in terms of cultural and ethnic background, language, immigration and/or refugee status, degree of assimilation, and socioeconomic and health status, have resulted in a lack of understanding about the kinds of interventions that would be most effective in reaching different Asian populations. As a result, health programs to assess and respond to the health risks and needs of Asian women and girls have been limited.

What we do know about the health of Asian women and girls is not promising. Though they are the most likely among women of color to have health insurance, selected subpopulations of Asians lack coverage. Asian American women are the least likely to have had a gynecological exam or pap smear in the last year, often because they lack knowledge about risk factors and believe that cancer is inevitably fatal.[3] A 1996 NAWHO survey examined the use of reproductive health technologies by Asian American women in six California counties with significant populations of Asian Americans. It found that half of the women had not visited a healthcare provider within the last year for reproductive or sexual health services. Moreover, one fourth had never received any reproductive or sexual health information in their lives.[4] Another study involving Chinese American women found that only 18 percent had annual pelvic examinations.[5] At least one third of Vietnamese, Laotian, and Cambodian women in the United States receive no first-trimester prenatal care; nearly half of Cambodian and Laotian American women consequently have higher-risk births.[6]

Rates of cervical cancer are higher among Chinese and Southeast Asian women than among their European American counterparts.[7] The national breast cancer rates of Asian American women are still the lowest of all women in the United States; however, as women move to the United States from Asian countries, their chances of getting breast cancer increase; the risk of breast cancer in successive generations increases, as well. This increased risk is presumably related to the loss of protective factors from low-incidence Asian countries and greater risk for breast cancer associated with residence in the United States.[8] Over half of the 600 Asian Americans responding to a 1995 national Asian American sex survey reported that they did not regularly use contraception or protection against sexually transmitted diseases (STDs).[9] Respondents also reported that sexual violence, sexual stereotypes, and shame impeded their sexual health. In another national reproductive health poll, one third of Asian American women respondents did not know where to obtain an abortion.[10] The poll also found that Asian American women are the least likely of all women of color to receive information about HIV/AIDS, and the most likely to believe that they are not at risk for HIV/AIDS.[11]

Rates of STDs in Asian communities may currently be severely underestimated. In 1992, the state of California reported just 32 cases of syphilis among Asians, compared to 420 Hispanic and 781 African American cases. There were 482 cases of gonorrhea among Asians, compared to almost 6,000 Hispanic and over 16,000 African American cases. These disproportionate statistics strongly suggest the likelihood of underreporting of STDs within Asian communities.[12]

The First National Asian Women's Conference, organized by NAWHO in November 1995, brought over 500 Asian American women together to discuss the health risks confronting them and to outline priorities for action and research. A broad cross-section of the Asian American community attended this historic event, including government officials, health professionals and advocates, and community leaders. Over 12 states were represented, girls and women ranging from ages 13 to 65 participated, and translation was provided in two Asian languages.

The topics addressed in the conference shattered the silence of the Asian American community on a broad spectrum of issues.[13] They challenge the notion of a "model minority" community that does not need resources, research, services, or advocacy on health and socioeconomic issues. Participants unequivocally identified sexism, racism, homophobia, and violence—from within their communities, mainstream society, and the state—among the key threats to Asian women's health. This analysis demands a community and a feminist response to challenge the multiple oppressive structures that affect

Asian American women's health, in contrast to an individual or self-help approach.

Conference participants noted that Asian women perceive health broadly to encompass mental, physical, emotional, social, and sexual well-being. Spirituality, which includes the performance of rituals, ceremonies, meditations, and the use of traditional medicines and consultations with traditional leaders is often considered an important aspect of maintaining one's health. Many Asian American women report using traditional health practices and medicines. There is a high rate of non-compliance with Western prescriptions among them, perhaps in deference to traditional treatments. In addition, research on Korean American women found that many avoid going to U.S. physicians because of "communication difficulties" and because they are "treated disrespectfully" by "impatient doctors and nurses."[14]

While many progressive Asian American organizations do not make health their central concern, they include health issues in their advocacy, organizing, and analysis. Thus there is a great diversity in the ways in which Asian organizations are approaching health concerns.

Asian Women's Roles and Health

Asian American women's notions of health are shaped by the ways in which our roles are constructed in our families and communities, as well as by mainstream socioeconomic, political, and cultural structures. As in most cultures, Asian families often place women in the taxing role of primary caregiver. Selfless devotion to the needs of other family members is held up as an ideal. This concept of selfless devotion can prevent Asian women from viewing their own health needs as legitimate and worthy of attention. Both community-specific cultural norms and the mainstream economy and culture reinforce these gender-based expectations. For example, economic pressures often require women to work outside the home. However, there is little public support for working mothers, and Asian communities often do not recognize or acknowledge the central role women play in family maintenance and survival. Thus, both the household and caregiving work of Asian American women is invisible within Asian American communities and in mainstream U.S. society.

Notions of sexuality and body image imposed by both Asian culture and the dominant culture also affect the ways in which Asian women think about themselves and their health. The silences within Asian communities regarding women's sexuality are based on several assumptions: that sex only occurs within the confines of heterosexual marital relationships, primarily for the goal of reproduction, that sex is another duty that women should perform for their husbands, and that there are different standards of sexual conduct for men and women. These assumptions often deny the spectrum of sexual relationships among Asian American women, which include consensual and pleasurable sex between partners, both heterosexual and homosexual, as well as the prevalence of violent, coerced sex; infection; unwanted pregnancy; incest; and unsafe abortions.

Issues relating to sexuality are extremely difficult for Asian American women and girls to discuss openly among family members, partners, or within the community. The recent NAWHO survey of Asians in California confirmed that one third of the 734 person sample never discussed pregnancy, STDs, birth control, or sexuality in their households. More than half were uncomfortable discussing reproductive health with their mothers and were even more uncomfortable discussing these concerns with their fathers and brothers.[15] Lesbian and bisexual women face particular challenges in finding supportive and safe environments to discuss their relationships and health concerns. As one South Asian lesbian activist states, "Because most teenagers are assumed to be heterosexual, it is common to feel that your sexuality just 'happened' without any sense of active participation in sexual choice and behavior."[16] The Asian Lesbian and Bisexual Women's health project reports that "sexuality is often not discussed in Asian households....This lack of knowledge silences Asian lesbian and bisexual women, not only in terms of discussing their sexuality, but by preventing them from recognizing symptoms of disease or dysfunction and seeking appropriate healthcare services."[17]

There are direct health consequences stemming from the ways in which Asian women's roles and relationships have been defined by others, be they from within or outside of our communities. A NAWHO assessment of Asian women's use of reproductive and sexual health services found that there is a tendency among Asian American women to view gynecological ailments as important and legitimate only when they concern reproductive functions. This narrow view of reproductive and sexual health often prevents Asian women from seeking proper medical help when they experience symptoms unrelated to pregnancy. This has particular consequences for women who are either not likely to become pregnant, or do not perceive that they are, such as young or menopausal women, users of contraceptives, and lesbians. The assumption that women's sexual health is only linked to reproduction translates into Asian women's failure to seek out broader health information and services for STDs, including HIV/AIDS, basic gynecological care, and sexuality education.

The Commodification of Asian Women's Sexuality and Bodies

The history of immigration in the United States has played a role in the construction of Asian women's sexuality. In the 1800s, Chinese immigrants to the United States found their sexual interactions both within and beyond their community tightly controlled through immigration and segregation laws. Chinese women were not allowed to migrate to the United States, and Chinese men in the United States were prohibited from having sexual relations with white women.[18] The stereotype of Asian male asexuality that developed then persists today. In direct contrast, the stereotype of Asian women as being cheap, submissive, accessible sexual objects also pervades U.S. culture. The exponential growth in the global trafficking of women, particularly Asian women and girls, for industrial, domestic, and sexual work contributes to the view of Asian women as commodities rather than individuals with rights. The Western pornography industry, with its interpretations of the *Kama Sutra*, its specialized marketing of Asian women as passive yet artful and willing to please, and tourism in Asian countries, all contribute to the objectification of Asian women.

Asian women's sexuality—both in this country and abroad—cannot be disengaged from its global context. Economic forces and militarism have defined and exploited Asian women's sexuality for profit and as the spoils of war. U.S. servicemen abroad have worn T-shirts that describe Asian women as "Little Brown Fucking Machines." The potential consequences of these views were brought to the fore by the rape of a 12-year-old girl by U.S. soldiers in Okinawa in September 1995.

For Asian American and other immigrant women in the United States, these images and stereotypes have an immediate impact on health and self-esteem. One national sexuality survey found that 17 percent of Asian women have been forced to perform sexual acts against their will. In another survey, one respondent whose mother had been raped by a white Amêrican GI said, "A lot of Vietnamese American women and/or our mothers have experienced rape, so that's how we learn about sex."[19]

Many Asian American women work in the sex industry, where they are advertised as "exotic." Their workplaces may be massage parlors, strip joints, bars, informal brothels, or, for mail-order brides, their homes. These women face poverty, imprisonment, deportation, racist and sexist violence, rape, isolation, degradation, and lack of access to information, as well as other health hazards. The Asian AIDS Project, which provides health education and support services to women in the massage parlors of San Francisco, finds that sex workers often do not have even the most basic information on how to protect themselves against work-related health risks.

CAAAV, through its Community Courts Project, conducts outreach to women workers in massage parlors in New York City. It provides health education in different Asian languages and works with women to organize for better working conditions. For example, CAAAV has discussed how women can resist customer and police violence on the job, and has begun a self-education program on the issues that affect Asian women sex workers. CAAAV also links sex workers with organizations that provide health services for STDs, tuberculosis testing, drug use, and gynecological care, as well as immigration services. Still, much more work needs to be done to improve not only the health and working conditions of Asian American sex workers, but the larger economic and social conditions that enable their exploitation.

Immigration and Health

Many recent immigrants, particularly women, find themselves isolated in their new homes. For instance, in 1992, 42 percent of the Vietnamese American population five years of age and older lived in linguistically isolated households—that is, a household in which no person aged 14 years or older speaks only English, and no person aged 14 years or older who speaks another language speaks English "very well."[20] Linguistic isolation severely limits access to healthcare. Many immigrants have left extensive support networks in their home countries, and there is little in U.S. culture that replicates these connections. These factors exacerbate their sense of isolation and heighten stress. The NAWHO South Asian women's health project found that while many young women follow traditional behavioral norms in their homes and with their families, they try to assimilate into mainstream U.S. culture outside. This creates a cultural schizophrenia that causes unique stress conditions. Additionally, many immigrant and refugee women bring with them health histories rooted in their countries of origin. For example, for many Southeast Asian refugee women, the trauma of dislocation and resettlement results in medical conditions such as the psychosomatic or non-organic blindness reported among Cambodian women 40 years of age and older. Even when they seek care, language barriers make these conditions difficult to diagnose and treat. Their stress and trauma are compounded as they resettle in violent, inner-city environments.[21]

Increasing rates of HIV infection in many Asian countries make STD and HIV screening and treatment, as well as support services for immigrant Asian women, particularly important. Yet, these services are few and far between. Fear of communicating, coupled with shame and guilt regarding stigmatized conditions such as HIV/AIDS, deters Asian Americans from seeking healthcare. In fact, many refugee and immigrant women are at increased risk of both interpersonal and institutional abuse by virtue of their vulnerable immigration status. Current federal health proposals seek to further reduce even basic healthcare services for immigrants.

Asian women's residency in the United States is particularly vulnerable due to existing and pending immigration legislation that reflects both labor needs and heterosexist assumptions.[22] Most Asian women come to the United States as spouses of male immigrants. Men have the right to confer or withhold legal status for their wives, just as a U.S. citizen does for a mail-order bride. Mail-order brides who are allowed into the United States on 90-day fiancée visas can be sent back to their home countries if they do not meet with "customers'" approval. The undocumented status of many Asian women immigrants makes their health needs invisible.

Asian women are beginning to question the gender- and class-biased assumptions of U.S. citizenship laws. Immigration policies currently favor professional males as the "desired" or "right" kind of immigrants. This devalues the labor of women in the domestic and service sectors. While there is a high demand in the United States for domestic workers, they are not considered a priority for receiving immigration status. Thus many domestic workers are undocumented, making them even more vulnerable to exploitation and abuse from their employers. Similarly, sex workers are criminalized, even as the sex industry makes huge profits. The large number of undocumented male and female Asian workers in the hotel, restaurant, garment, and sex industries are subject to unfair labor practices as well as severe occupational health risks with little access to healthcare.

Domestic Violence

Asian American households are often intergenerational; older Asian women live with their sons, daughters, and other relatives, documented or undocumented, but remain invisible outside the family and community. Linguistic and educational barriers often prevent their integration into U.S. society. Moreover, many elderly Asians are extremely poor and financially dependent on their children, who are often their only connection with the outside world. The mainstream U.S. concept of the household as a nuclear unit ignores the needs of these extended family members. It masks their poverty and lack of access to resources, even within what appear to be privileged or comfortable households. Women in extended family households often experience abuse from other household members. Wives and domestic workers are particularly subject to abuse, more so when they are undocumented. Their "illegal" status translates into fear of public institutions. They are denied or deny themselves support services and forego legal challenges even in deeply abusive relationships or situations.

It is noteworthy, therefore, that for many Asian American women, organizing around social change has begun with organizing in response to violence against women in the forms of elder and spouse abuse. This is particularly evident in South Asian communities, where domestic violence organizations such as Sakhi, Apna Ghar, and Manavi reflect the extent of violence in these communities and the capacity of women to form effective organizations to counter violence. There have also been attempts by activists within Sakhi and

Workers' Awaaz to address employer violence towards domestic workers in their homes.

In addition to community-specific organizations, pan-Asian organizations such as the Asian Women's Shelter in New York City, work across Asian communities to counter violence. The establishment and growth of these organizations explodes the myths that "Asians take care of their own" or that "Asian women do not experience violence." These organizations have sought to advocate on behalf of Asian women in the court system, where they are greatly disadvantaged. Many states, for example, do not require interpreters for victims of domestic violence. Consequently, many Asian women have lost custody of their children. Many organizations have also worked against the use of the cultural defense, which purports to "explain" abusive behavior as acceptable practice in Asian cultures and therefore beyond the pale of U.S. law. However, the mental, emotional, and physical health of many Asian women is seriously undermined by violence in their homes.

The sensitivity and familiarity required to work across Asian communities at the level of service provision is demonstrated by the Asian Women's Shelter. A group of Asian women formed the shelter in 1988 to create a "safe" space for Asian women. As Beckie Masaki, Executive Director and co-founder of the shelter puts it, "a sense of safety does not only mean having locks on the doors and a secret location." It means a place where women feel safe, surrounded by what is familiar to them. To create a nurturing and safe environment, the Asian Women's Shelter provides its clients with language-appropriate services, as well as five kinds of rice, because each Asian community has its own way of preparing rice and knows its rice is the best! Also, familiarity with the culture makes the shelter staff aware of the fact that for many Asians, rice is a source of survival and nurturance that will help women heal.

Complexity of the Healthcare System

A range of structural barriers, such as anti-immigrant sentiment, linguistic differences, and budget cuts, affect Asian women's access to and use of existing healthcare services. The increasing complexity of the healthcare system, driven by market forces and increased privatization, have only exacerbated these barriers. Abuse and violence within the healthcare industry towards poor women, especially those who cannot speak English, further fuels Asian women's distrust of the healthcare system. A 1986 national survey found that 81 percent of women who are forced by court orders to undergo Caesarean sections are African American, Latina, or Asian. Twenty-four percent of those Asian and Latina women did not speak English as their first language. Even those Asian women who can speak and read English avoid services that are culturally alien at best, and inappropriate at worst. Lack of outreach by existing community services to women who are often unaware of their existence further contributes to underuse of services, feeding the stereotype that Asian communities do not need public, easily accessible health and social services.

Organizing an Asian Women's Health Movement

Asian American women organizing together—both within and across our communities—is important now, perhaps more than ever. Anti-poor legislation is having an increasingly detrimental effect on the poorer sectors of Asian American communities. Asian Americans are the fastest growing group of welfare recipients, and they are not all single mothers. This negates the much-bandied notion that it is women's licentiousness that is the cause of poverty in the United States. In 1975, only 0.5 percent of parents receiving Aid to Families with Dependent Children (AFDC) were Asians, but by 1990 the percentage had grown to 2.8 percent. In 1979, 14,020 Asians received AFDC in California, comprising 2.6 percent of the total AFDC population; by 1992 the number of Asians on AFDC jumped over 480 percent to 82,177—approximately 9.5 percent of the state's total AFDC population. Southeast Asians, whose welfare dependency rates reach over 50 percent, have the highest dependency rates of any ethnic or racial group nationwide. In California, they comprise 87 percent of the total Asian welfare population and constitute the largest group of Asians on AFDC.[23] Many refugees from Laos, Cambodia, and Vietnam with no formal education or English proficiency have been channeled into welfare programs as part of a national strategy to facilitate their economic assimilation.[24]

Welfare cuts hit these immigrants particularly hard. Welfare cuts also seriously impact those Asians who work in low-security, high-risk jobs, such as those in sweatshops, canneries, and the sex industry, as well as in taxicab and kiosk management. Welfare reform is having a devastating impact on poor women, and even legal immigrants are denied social security, food stamps, cash assistance, and other social services. Immigration restrictions—and the fear of them—have serious implications for both the availability and use of health and other social services. In the days after Proposition 187, an anti-immigrant bill, was passed in California, crisis calls to the Asian Women's Shelter in San Francisco dropped by 38 percent. School attendance by Asian and Latino children also dropped in several counties of California, and use of health clinics serving Asians in Los Angeles declined. For primarily immigrant communities, fear of Proposition 187 diminished their access to potentially life-saving services.

In this hostile external environment, Asian American organizations must be committed to real power-sharing and equal representation within their ranks. Asian American organizations need to share information about existing resources, in spite of competition for funds. Established leaders must be prepared to serve as mentors to less-established activists, providing guidance as well as the willingness and opportunities to act on new ideas using new methodologies. In particular, Asian organizations must be especially careful not to claim to be pan-Asian if in fact they are not, either in services or representation. Pan-Asian organizations must allow time for their memberships to learn about the historical differences and stereotypes regarding country of origin, ethnicity, age, educational level, socioeconomic class, and political affiliation among Asian communities. The need to be open and honest about differences is critical. The need to organize within different communities is still essential, while advocacy efforts can be more broad-based or pan-Asian in scope.

NAWHO: A Case Study

NAWHO provides an interesting model from which to examine health advocacy for and by Asian Americans. It is a nonprofit, community-based health advocacy organization committed to improving the overall health of Asian women and girls. Formed in 1993, it is representative of the new wave of pan-Asian organizing that has developed over the last decade. From its inception, NAWHO has organized across a broad cross-section of Asian women with the understanding that the needs and concerns of women of Asian descent are at the same time specific and diverse. NAWHO is aware of the incredible diversity embedded in the term "Asian." However, it has made a conscious decision to work under this banner with a clear understanding of the strengths and pitfalls of doing so. The category "Asian" carries a political weight and strength that individual ethnic or national groups cannot garner. Moreover, working under this rubric may counteract the isolation of Asian women and has the potential for forging creative political partnerships across ethnicities and nationalities (NAWHO does not claim to represent Pacific Islanders, while it is committed to supporting their work).

Through an informal affirmative action policy, NAWHO has hired staff and recruited volunteers and board members who represent a range of Asian communities, immigration status, ages, and education levels. The staff currently includes a Korean immigrant, a Japanese American sansei, a first-generation Indian American, and a Laotian immigrant. NAWHO develops projects that focus on specific communities while addressing cross-cutting concerns. In so doing, it has emphasized the need for conducting outreach and advocacy in specific communities because language, cultural differences, and immigration status and histories make meaningful grassroots work across Asian communities close to impossible.

NAWHO's South Asian women's health project and the Southeast Asian reproductive health education project are both geared toward eliciting and sharing much-needed information on health issues within these different communities while involving them in their own advocacy. In contrast, NAWHO's assessment of the factors influencing Asian American women's use of reproductive and sexual health services and its Asian lesbian and bisexual women's health report were not community-specific. Women from a range of communities were included, based on an understanding that Asian women face similar issues, albeit in different ways, and that developing common advocacy strategies can be very effective.

While underlining the need to be inclusive and to work across Asian communities, NAWHO has committed itself from the outset to working with other women of color. Women of color activists serve on the board of directors and advisors, and NAWHO works with established women of color health organizations, such as the National Black Women's Health Project and the National Latina Health Organization.

Racism both within and beyond the Asian community has led many Asians to distance themselves from or deny that they are in fact people of color; this, in spite of the racism these communities face daily. So while Black and Latino communities, in spite of their differences, have established both internal and external recognition of the value of collective organizing of people of color, Asian organizations have little history of organizing in this manner. It is therefore significant that NAWHO is a founding member and current Secretariat of the Women of Color Coalition for Reproductive Health Rights. The process of coalition-building across communities of color is not without its challenges, particularly for Asian women. As newcomers to this arena, Asian women have the difficult task of representing the diverse Asian community, often to communities who, if they are not in fact more homogeneous, at least have a longer tradition of identifying as one community with one common language.

NAWHO worked with the Women of Color Coalition to participate in the 1994 International Conference on Population and Development in Cairo and the 1995 Fourth World Conference on Women in Beijing. At both conferences, NAWHO played a critical role in ensuring that U.S. women of color were heard in both domestic and global negotiations, and that Asian American women and organizations, such as AIWA and Asian Health Project, were represented. For the first time, Asian American perspectives on immigration, reproductive and sexual health and rights, violence against women, community organizing, and sustainable development were represented in national and international policy dialogues.

In its second biennial health conference in May 1997, NAWHO focused on creating a political presence and voice for Asian American women to advocate for improving the quality of their lives. Local, state, and national leaders heard directly from Asian women about their key health concerns and aspirations. Since then, NAWHO has provided an educational forum for Congressional members and their staff, government agencies, and women's health organizations, focusing on gaps in breast cancer prevention efforts for Asian American women.

The emerging Asian American women's health movement has begun the process of deconstructing the stereotypes and structural barriers that have prevented Asian women from realizing good health. With careful strategizing that includes a vision of respect both for diversity and pan-Asian strength, Asian women are laying the foundation for empowering themselves and improving their health while building stronger and safer communities.

Notes

NAWHO's efforts to organize stem from its feminist orientation; it is part of the transnational women's health movement. We would like to acknowledge the critical suggestions, comments, and information provided by Mary Chung, Priya Jaganathan, and Anannya Bhattacharjee.

1. Although only 15 percent of all Asian and Pacific Islanders and only 29 percent of all households headed by Asian and Pacific Islander females reported incomes below the poverty level in 1995, there is great variation among subpopulations. For instance, 6 percent of Japanese Americans, compared to 60 percent of Laotians, were below the poverty level in 1990. The proportion of Vietnamese families reporting incomes below the poverty level was more than three times greater than that of Asian Indian families in 1990. Leigh, Wilhelmina A., and Melinda Lindquist. *Women of Color Data Book*. Draft. 1997 National Institute of Health, Office of Research on Women's Health, 55.

2. Chen, M.S., and B.L. Hawks "A Debunking of the Myth of Healthy Asian Americans and Pacific Islanders." *American Journal of Health Promotion* 9.4 (March/April 1994): 261-268.

3. Communications Consortium Media Center (CCMC) and the National Council of Negro Women (NCNW). *The 1991-1992 Women of Color Reproductive Health Poll*. Washington, DC: CCMC and NCNW, n.d., Leigh and Lindquist, 55.

4. National Asian Women's Health Organization (NAWHO). *Expanding Options: A Reproductive and Sexual Health Survey of Asian American Women*. San Francisco: NAWHO, 1997.8.

5. Mo, B. "Modesty, Sexuality, and Breast Health in Chinese-American Women." *Western Journal of Medicine* 157.3 (1992).

6. Leigh and Lindquist 55. Zane, N., D. Takeuchi, and K. Young, eds. *Confronting Critical Health Issues of Asian Pacific Islander Americans*. Thousand Oaks, CA: Sage Publications, 1994.

7. Jenkins, C., and M. Kagawa-Singer. *Confronting Critical Health Issues of Asian Pacific Islander Americans*. Eds. N. Zane, D. Takeuchi, and K. Young. Thousand Oaks, CA: Sage Publications, 1994. 105-147.

8. National Asian Women's Health Organization (NAWHO). *National Plan of Action on Asian American Women and Breast Cancer*. San Francisco: NAWHO, May 1997. 4.

9. "1995 Asian American Sex Survey." *A. Magazine: Inside Asian America* August-September 1995.

10. CCMC and NCNW, op cit.

11. op cit, Nowrojee, Sia. *Perceptions of Risk: An Assessment of the Factors Influencing Use of Reproductive and Sexual Health Services by Asian American Women*. San Francisco: NAWHO, 1995.

12. Nowrojee, Sia. "Asian Women's Sexual Health: A Framework for Advocacy," Keynote address. Coming Together, Moving Strong: Mobilizing an Asian Women's Health Movement Conference. San Francisco. November 1995.

13. Conference sessions addressed the overall status of Asian women's health; environmental and occupational health; reproductive and sexual health, including the needs of Asian lesbians and bisexual women; violence against women; cancer prevention and treatment; breast health; substance abuse; HIV/AIDS; holistic approaches to wellness; alternative medicine and nutrition; mental health issues; the implications of managed care for the Asian American community; and the need for aggressive political advocacy in defending a progressive policy agenda.

14. Duluquisen, E.M., K.M. Groessl, and N.H. Puttkammer. *The Health and Well-Being of Asian and Pacific Islander Women*. Oakland, CA: Asian and Pacific Islanders for Reproductive Health, 1995.

15. NAWHO, *Expanding Options* 10-11.

16. Bannerji, K. "No Apologies." *A Lotus of Another Color: An Unfolding of the South Asian Gay and Lesbian Experience*. Ed. R. Ratti. Boston: Alyson Publications, 1993.

17. National Asian Women's Health Organization (NAWHO). Asian Lesbian and Bisexual Women's Health Project. San Francisco: NAWHO, Spring 1996.

18. Takaki, R. *Strangers from a Different Shore*. Boston: Little Brown & Company, 1989.

19. Nowrojee, Sia, Crystal Jang, Dawn Pessaffo, Cianna Steward, and Jennifer Lee. "A Frank Conversation about Sex." Nowrojee, Sia "Asian Women's Sexual Health: A Framework for Advocacy." Keynote Address. Coming Together, Moving Strong: Mobilizing an Asian Women's Health Movement Conference. National Asian Women's Health Organization. San Francisco. November 1995.

20. Martin, J.A. "Birth Characteristics for Asian or Pacific Islander Subgroups, 1992." Supplement *Monthly Vital Statistics Report* 43.10 (1995). Supplement.

21. Rozee, P.D., and G. Van Boemel. "The Psychological Effects of War Trauma and Abuse on Older Cambodian Refugee Women." *Women and Therapy* 8.4 (1989): 23-50; Frye, B.A., and C.D. Avanzo. "Cultural Themes in Family Stress and Violence Among Cambodian Refugee Women in the Inner City." *Adv. Nurs. Sci.* 16.3. (1994): 64-77.

22. Masaki, Beckie, Anannya Bhattacharjee, and Karen Narasaki. "Violence Against Women: A Public Health Issue." Coming Together, Moving Strong: Mobilizing an Asian Women's Health Movement Conference. National Asian Women's Health Organization. San Francisco. November 1995.

23. Ong, Paul, and Evelyn Blumenberg, eds. "Welfare and Work Among Southeast Asians." *The State of Asian Pacific America: Economic Diversity, Issues, and Policies*. Los Angeles: LEAP, 1994.

24. NAWHO. *Welfare Reform Information Packet: Why This Packet Is Important to Asian Americans*. San Francisco: NAWHO, 1995.

Expanding Environmental Justice

Asian American Feminists' Contribution

By Julie Sze

An Asian American feminist movement for environmental justice is critical for both expanding the scope of environmental justice and for realizing a radical Asian women's politics and vision.[1] Among the social injustices that affect large numbers of Asian women in the United States and around the world are occupational health hazards, labor exploitation due to economic globalization, and anti-immigrant policies. Each of these poses an obstacle to the creation and protection of a healthy environment for Asian women.

A diversity of Asian American communities face environmental risks such as high rates of lead poisoning on the job, lack of open space, elevated exposure to military toxics, and health hazards from fish consumption.[2] A draft position paper on Asian environmental justice issues in the United States circulating within the Environmental Protection Agency (EPA) reflects a growing recognition of Asian environmental justice issues, according to Angela Chung, an environmental protection specialist from the EPA's Office of Environmental Justice.[3]

Asian women's organizing shares a number of similarities with environmental justice organizing. These similarities need to be recognized and built on to further the common goals of both movements.

The Environmental Justice Movement

Environmental justice is a social movement led by and for people of color that views environmental issues as having social, public health, economic, political, and ideological components. It thus seeks not only environmental justice but also economic, political, and cultural justice, both in the United States[4] and abroad.[5]

Early catalyzing events for environmental justice include nonviolent direct action in 1982 against the proposed siting of a hazardous waste landfill in the predominantly African American community of Warren County, North Carolina, and the 1987 publication of *Toxic Wastes and Race* by the United Church of Christ Commission for Racial Justice, which documented the disproportionate location of toxic waste sites in communities of color. Environmental justice first came to prominence when advocates documented that people of color suffer from disproportionately high effects of environmental pollution, as well as unequal protection from the state. According to the Commission on Racial Justice, three fifths of African and Hispanic Americans live in communities with uncontrolled toxic waste sites, and approximately half of all Asian/Pacific Islanders and Native Americans live in communities with uncontrolled toxic waste sites.[6] In one study, the EPA took 20 percent longer to identify Superfund sites in minority communities, and pollution in those neighborhoods resulted in fines only half as high as those in white neighborhoods.[7] Environmental justice activists attempt to remediate environmental damage and at the same time educate people of color about how power, knowledge, science, and authority are constructed.

Environmental justice repudiates elitist, racist, and classist wilderness/preservationist conceptions of the environment as being equal to "nature"—typically characterized as pristine, green space devoid of people.[8] Such conceptions often regard nature as being threatened by the sustaining activities of people in "underdeveloped" countries. Environmental justice foregrounds social categories and shifts the concept of the environment to include not just natural resources such as air, water, and land, but also public and human health concerns.

In a span of roughly 15 years, the environmental justice movement has succeeded in changing what environmentalism means. In February 1994, President Clinton signed the Executive Order on Environmental Justice, provoked by the organizing of people of color, most notably at the historic 1991 People of Color Environmental Leadership Summit, at which the Principles of Environmental Justice[9] were introduced and adopted.

One of the key contributions of the environmental justice movement has been to challenge long-held assumptions about risks and hazards. Rather than considering risks and hazards to human health and the environment in isolation, environmental justice advocates consider cumulative risks—the combination and accumulation of hazards. While individual polluting sources may not pose fatal health hazards, their cumulative effect might. Consideration of cumulative risks is particularly important in urban settings: in rural areas, toxic sites are often the result of single, egregious polluters, whereas in an urban environment, toxic pollution is more often a problem of cumulative hazards.

Environmental Justice and Asian American Women

> I live in San Jose [California]. I assemble electronics parts and boards at my company. I've been there for ten years. I was a housewife in Korea....We got very little training about health and safety. I have headaches, nausea, dizziness, shoulder aches, backaches....I see everyone with the same problems in my department. Some women have Carpal Tunnel Syndrome, high blood pressure, and kidney problems. It's difficult to learn about safety at work....we lose our health.[10]
>
> —Korean electronics worker

A number of initiatives by Asian American women have connected workers' rights and occupational health with environmental justice concerns. According to Pam Tau Lee of the University of California at Berkeley Labor Occupational Health Program, immigrant Asian women are disproportionately employed in hazardous industries such as the garment and the electronics/semiconductor industries. The hazards they face include exposure to toxic materials, low wages, and institutional neglect by the government, unions, employers, and consumers.[11]

Fifty-three percent of all textile workers and apparel workers in the United States are Asian women.[12] Garment workers face increased exposure to fiber particles, dyes, formaldehydes, and arsenic, leading to high rates of byssinosis and respiratory illness. Asian Americans—primarily women—comprise 43 percent of electronics workers in assembly line and operative jobs in Silicon Valley.[13] Asian and Latina immigrant women in the electronics/semiconductor industry suffer from "damage to the central nervous system, and possibly the reproductive system, as a result of using dangerous solvents to clean electronic components, as well as exposure to other chemicals," according to Lee. They suffer occupational illness at triple the rate of workers in general manufacturing.

The Asian Pacific Environmental Network (APEN) is the most prominent Asian environmental justice organization in the United States. Other organizations that work on Asian environmental justice issues include Asian Immigrant Women Advocates (AIWA), which organizes and empowers immigrant Asian garment and electronic workers, "so they can improve their living and working conditions," according to Helen Kim, an organizer from AIWA.[14]

Young Hi Shin, AIWA's executive director, gave one of two major papers presented by an Asian woman at the first People of Color Environmental Leadership Summit (the other was given by Pam Tau Lee). It is no accident that its focus was also occupational health issues—many activists argue that occupational health is the number one environmental justice concern for Asian Americans.

Both Lee and Shin helped create innovative models to educate immigrant Asian women about occupational and environmental hazards, for example, by including political education in English classes. In these classes, immigrant women practice their English by translating warning information about chemicals they are routinely exposed to at work.[15] Lee explains how trainers in the Labor Occupational Health Program use graphics and risk-mapping—which enable workers to identify health hazards through visual means—to reach diverse linguistic communities.[16]

Environmental Justice Abroad

Internationally, economic globalization necessitates further strategic alliances between radical Asian feminist, labor, and environmental justice movements. According to Lee,

> You will find women in the Philippines, Malaysia, and Japan and other parts of Asia working very hard to stop deforestation, organizing around military toxics, organizing around issues of health and safety....Environmental justice efforts do not confine themselves to local efforts or national ones. Environmental justice activists also work in solidarity with those in Asia, Africa, Mexico, Central and Latin America against corporate greed and profits.[17]

Poor people and people of color both here and abroad have suffered from economic globalization orchestrated by governments and corporations and supported by mainstream environmental organizations in the United States. The World Wildlife Fund, Natural Resources Defense Council, National Audubon Society, and Environmental Defense Fund all supported the North American Free Trade Agreement (NAFTA), to the outrage of labor and social justice organizations.[18] While NAFTA claims to emphasize protection of natural resources, it encourages the degradation of human life by driving down wages and work standards to maximize corporate profit.

The links between occupational health and environmental justice will become increasingly relevant as more multinational corporations move their factories to countries with little or no worker or environmental protections. Asian countries such as Indonesia, Singapore, Vietnam, South Korea, Taiwan, Thailand, and China are low-wage countries where legions of workers—mostly women—face slave-like working conditions. One of the more egregious work situations led to the deaths of 188 workers who were trapped in a fire at the Kader toy factory in Thailand in 1993.[19]

One of the leading theorists of the links between the exploitation of women, labor, and natural resources in an international development matrix is the Indian environmentalist, Vandana Shiva, a leading spokesperson for radical Asian politics and environmental justice. Shiva, a physicist, philosopher, Science and Environment Advisor with the Third World Network, and Director of the Research Foundation for Science, Technology and Natural Resource Policy in Dehra Dun, India, has researched, written, and spoken extensively about how Third World women are particularly targeted in the logic of "maldevelopment" that exploits both women and nature as commodities.[20] According to Shiva,

> You really can't separate issues of ecology from feminism or from human rights or from development or from issues of ethnic and cultural diversity....to me, the choice...is between environmental justice and green imperialism, between a common future for all or continued economic and environmental apartheid.[21]

Shiva is also an activist with the International Forum on Globalization and with the Chipko movement, a women's movement in the Himalayas that successfully resisted World Bank deforestation projects. The "Chipko andolan" translates literally into "hugging movement."[22] In the United States, "tree hugger" is generally a pejorative term (used by people from across the political spectrum) to describe environmentalists who care more about trees than about people. People of color often level this charge of elitism against mainstream environmental organizers. Their critique is entirely valid and necessary, but the fact that many environmental justice advocates in the United States do not know the history of this term, which emerged from an integrated struggle for both human dignity and preservation of natural resources, suggests that the links and histories of environmental justice struggles in other countries need to be highlighted.

The Anti-Immigration Assault on Asian Women

Shiva's critique of macro-level economic policies and their impact on individuals is reinforced by Cathi Tactaquin, Executive Director of the National Network for Immigrant and Refugee Rights. According to Tactaquin, in the United States, immigrants and refugees are scapegoated for various social ills, such as "stealing" jobs or "ruining" the environment. Tactaquin points out that the real global threat is from "neo-liberalism—the globalization of poverty imposed by United States policies and by international financial institutions."[23]

Environmentally based anti-immigration and zero-population movements pose a serious threat to Asian and Asian American women. A growing number of anti-immigrant and zero-population advocates argue that immigration should be limited because of environmental degradation. This argument—most developed in California—is another version of the "limited resource" argument that convinced voters in California to pass Proposition 187, an anti-immigration bill, in the fall of 1994. The "limited resource" perspective argues that finite resources—whether financial or environmental—are wasted on immigrants generally, and illegal immigrants specifically, who are purely a resource drain and make no contribution to their adopted society (regardless of the fact that they provide low-wage labor that is much used—and abused). Therefore, proponents conclude, the answer to a multitude of social and environmental problems is to reduce immigration.

For these activists, "environmentalism" is used to justify severe, punitive, and regressive calls for immigration moratoriums and changes in national immigration legislation. In 1995, Population Environment Balance, Californians for Population Stabilization, and Carrying Capacity Network called for a five-year immigration moratorium with a ceiling for all countries of 100,000 immigrants. Negative Population Growth placed advertisements in environmental magazines such as *E* and *Natural History* calling for an immigration moratorium.[24]

Anti-immigrant and zero-population advocates fuel a political and social atmosphere of hate and misinformation by pandering to the white electorate's fears of "Third World-ification" by Latinos and Asians. The fundamental assumptions that ground this argument are:

- More immigrants mean more environmental degradation and a lower quality of life.
- Population growth is the primary cause of environmental degradation, and high population density leads to ecological devastation.
- A rising population, fueled by immigration, is the cause of water quality and scarcity problems.
- Immigrants not only have higher rates of population growth, but quickly adopt resource-intensive lifestyles.
- The world's people of color cause overpopulation—birth rates for people of European descent are under control.[25]

On the contrary, the nation's single largest environmental polluter is the U.S. military. Rich people consume more resources than poor people. The United States has 5 percent of the world's population and uses 36 percent of the world's resources. The average American uses energy at the rate of 3 Japanese, or 6 Mexicans, or 12 Chinese, or 33 Indians, or 147 Bangladeshis, or 422 Ethiopians.[26] Rather than reducing wasteful consumption of natural resources by rich people generally, and of Americans specifically, these xenophobic "environmentalists" want to reduce human populations—specifically immigrants of color, even though immigrants are not the primary (nor for that matter, a significant) cause of environmental degradation.

Anti-immigration environmentalists' dangerous arguments have been absorbed by mainstream politicians. For example, Senator Reid from Nevada described the Immigration Stabilization Act of 1994—which called for more limits on and fewer benefits for illegal immigration and refugees—as "one of the most important bills for protecting the environment." According to Reid,

> As you know, our environment is beset from all sides by the

> problems of the gravest and most intractable kind: vanishing ecosystems, acid rain, global warming, groundwater pollution, air pollution, and dwindling wetlands and farmlands. All of these problems have one root cause—too many people. If we have any hope of slowing our country's population growth, immigration must be reduced.[27]

The Political Ecology Group is a multiracial social justice organization based in San Francisco that fights anti-immigration and zero-population policies. It creates and disseminates factsheets that outline the myths and facts on immigration, population, and the environment.[28] The Political Ecology Group researches anti-immigration groups and other allied groups, such as the Federation for American Immigration Reform, to publicize their scapegoating statements and funding links to right-wing eugenicist foundations.

We need to expand our efforts to educate and mobilize Asian women to assert our right to live and work safely and productively wherever we choose.

Conclusion

Since Asian women are disproportionately affected by environmental and social injustice, we are also uniquely positioned to lead insurgent movements for justice. Our efforts pave the road for stronger domestic and international resistance against corporate and political agendas that exploit Asian women, our labor, and the natural environment.

Radical Asian women must continue to theorize about and organize around a wide range of issues, including: labor exploitation, healthcare, institutional violence, domestic violence, and cultural discrimination. Radical Asian women's movements, like environmental justice, envision multiracial, multiethnic, international/national movements for progressive social change.

International workers' rights and environmental justice movements need to share information, make organizational links, and coordinate campaigns against wage and environmental exploitation. Radical Asian women as labor organizers and environmental justice advocates need to organize across borders and recognize our common visions for justice, community-based self-determination, and a safe and healthy environment.

Notes

The ideas in this essay are my own, and do not necessarily reflect the views or position of the New York City Environmental Justice Alliance, for whom I work. I'd like to thank my Executive Director Michelle DePass, Asian Immigrant Women Advocates, Asian Pacific Environmental Network, the Political Ecology Group, EDGE: Alliance of Ethnic and Environmental Organizations, Pam Tau Lee, Lilly Lee, Angela Chung, and others for their assistance with this essay.

1. Though I reject the notion that any static or essential Asian feminist perspective exists, I believe that race- and gender-specific analysis is critical. See, for example, Anthony, Carl. "Why Blacks Should Be Environmentalists." *Call to Action.* Ed. Brad Erickson. San Francisco: Sierra Club Books, 1990.

2. Schaffer, Gwen. "Asian Americans Organize for Justice." *Environmental Action.* Winter 1994.

3. Telephone interview with Angela Chung.

4. Bullard, Robert. *Dumping in Dixie.* Boulder: Westview Press, 1994; Bullard, Robert, ed. *Confronting Environmental Racism.* Boston: South End Press, 1993, and *Environmental Justice and Communities of Color.* San Francisco: Sierra Club Books, 1994; Richard Hofrichter, ed. *Toxic Struggles: The Theory and Practice of Environmental Justice.* Philadelphia: New Society-Publishers, 1993; Lavelle, Marianne, and Marcia Coyle. "Unequal Protection: The Racial Divide in Environmental Law" in Hofrichter, ed., *Toxic Struggles.*

5. "The Global Connection: Exploitation of Developing Countries" in Hofrichter, ed. *Toxic Struggles.*

6. United Church of Christ, Commission for Racial Justice. *Toxic Wastes and Race in the United States: A National Report on the Racial and Socio-Economic Characteristics of Communities With Hazardous Waste Sites.* 1987.

7. Lavelle and Coyle, op cit.

8. Darnovsky, Marcy. "Stories Less Told: Histories of U.S. Environmentalism." *Socialist Review* (October-December 1992): 9214.

9. "Principles of Environmental Justice." Proceedings from the First National People of Color Environmental Leadership Summit. United Church of Christ, Commission for Racial Justice, 1992.

10. *Working Healthy.* Asian Immigrant Women Advocates brochure, 7.

11. Proceedings from the First National People of Color Environmental Leadership Summit. United Church of Christ, Commission for Racial Justice, 1992. Lee is a former labor organizer and a board member of the Washington Office on Environmental Justice, the National Environmental Justice Advi-

sory Council, and Asian Pacific Environmental Network.

12. Saika, Peggy. "APEN Brings Asian Pacific Perspective to Environmental Justice." Washington Office on Environmental Justice Newsletter, Summer 1995.

13. Schaffer, op cit.

14. Telephone interview with Helen Kim, 13 September 1996.

15. Schaffer, op cit.

16. Swanson, Sandra. "Can We Balance the Scales of Environmental Justice?" *Safety + Health* (October 1995).

17. Interview with Pam Tau Lee, 21 August 1996.

18. Athanasiou, Tom. *Divided Planet.* Boston: Little Brown & Co., 1996. 191.

19. Zuckoff, Mitchell. "Trapped by Poverty, Killed by Neglect." *Boston Globe* (10 July 1994).

20. Shiva, Vandana. "Women & Nature." *Environmental Ethics: Divergence & Convergence*. Ed. Armstrong and Botzler. New York: McGraw Hill, 1993, and "Development, Ecology & Women." *Healing the Wounds: The Promise of Ecofeminism*. Ed. Plant. Philadelphia: New Society Publishers, 1989.

21. Ethnic News Watch. *India Currents* 6.4 (July 31, 1992): M15.

22. Shiva, Vandana. *Staying Alive: Women, Ecology, and Development.* London: Zed Books, 1989. 67-77.

23. National Network For Immigrant and Refugee Rights. *Network News*, Summer 1996.

24. Loh, Penn. "Creating an Environment of Blame: Anti-Immigration Forces Seek to Woo Environmentalists." *RESIST* newsletter (December 1995): 4.

25. Political Ecology Group Immigration and Environment Campaign Organizer's Kit.

26. *Environmental Action* (Summer 1994): 15.

27. *Environmental Action* (Summer 1994): 23.

28. Political Ecology Group Immigration and Environment Campaign Organizer's Kit.

Empowering Women
SNEHA's Multifaceted Activism

By Bandana Purkayastha, Shyamala Raman, and Kshiteeja Bhide

The main strand of feminist research has usually been based primarily on white, middle-class, feminist experience and has usually been limited to activism associated with the assertion of women's rights and the expansion of women's roles. Yet all over the world, women have been active within their communities, often in their roles as mothers, sisters, aunts, and daughters. Women have nurtured relationships, resisted oppression, and played a crucial part in upholding the rights of communities to determine their own future. As women from South Asia, we are aware of these forms of activism among our mothers, grandmothers, and great-grandmothers. The history of their activism, which was sustained by their roles and networks within the community, is finally starting to be written.[1]

SNEHA[2] is both a continuation and an innovation of the South Asian traditions of activism we have carried with us to the United States. A different historical and geographic context alters the specific form of our work, but we, like previous generations of South Asian women, are dedicated to empowering women. We, too, realize that our class, racial/ethnic background, generation, and gender affect the nature of our specific experiences. The story of our organizing and ongoing work exemplifies this belief.

Our activism in the United States was the culmination of a number of experiences. As immigrants to the United States, we were not able to draw as heavily on our extended families, friends, and communities for our identities and well-being as before, nor had we become totally assimilated to the ways of our larger society. Many of us faced an age-related dilemma as well. What roles remained for us when we had fulfilled our roles as mothers and wives? We were also very aware of the ongoing emphasis on maintaining the reputation of the family. As women, we were the "keepers" of this reputation. Our conduct, our apparel, and our skill in family maintenance were all yardsticks by which this reputation was measured. Seeking outside help transgressed this norm. All of this placed a very heavy burden on us. Who could we turn to? Who would understand our cultural and emotional anchors?

SNEHA was formed as a collective to address these needs by providing support and information to South Asian women. The brainchild of Vijaya Bapat and Shyamala Raman, it grew out of a meeting in November 1983 of 11 original members. Our current core membership profile is varied. Some of us work at home, others work outside the home for pay. However, we all have organizing experience, usually from our countries of origin. Thus we bring unique skills and perspectives to our collective understanding of each issue.[3]

Our activism draws on the model of the extended family that is prevalent in South Asia.[4] Such a model is comprised of relatives, close friends, and neighbors. Some non-kin are accorded a status equivalent to family members because of daily interaction. An "aunt" could be a blood relative or the mother of a very close friend. These types of relationships have deep roots in the South Asian ethos. In times of family crises, it is often a relative or friend who serves as an empathetic listener. The confidant is usually a person who does not have a stake in maintaining the status quo. The socially recognized position of older women as keepers of relationships often gives them sufficient leverage to initiate needed changes.

SNEHA's activities are inspired by extended families. We are available to listen unconditionally; if required, we provide information about mainstream agencies and begin a referral process. We are both of the community and harbingers of change. Our objective is to serve with respect and affection—we try to ensure that women who come to us do not become more vulnerable. We view our work as a collective process of empowerment.

Some examples illustrate the varied nature of our involvement.

A 52-year-old woman[5] calls SNEHA. She has devoted her life to her family, keeping house, and bringing up the children while her husband was busy with his career, in hopes of achieving the American dream. She feels she has achieved her family goals. The children are away at Ivy League colleges, well-positioned for elite careers of their own. At this point in time, her husband makes it clear that he no longer thinks they are compatible—she certainly does not fit the image of a successful professional's wife. It is difficult for her to figure out what to do. She is proud, and she does not want to become the subject of conversation at various social gatherings within her immediate circle. She has some knowledge about services available in the larger community, but she is not sure how to access them. She remembers her one encounter with a service organization and how embarrassed she was at the odd looks she got because of her brown skin, her clothes, and her accent, which appeared to make people think she was poor—not an educated, upper-middle-class homemaker. At one level, she hopes things will somehow work out with her husband; at another level, she realizes her life is getting worse every day. Initially she simply needs to talk. Later she is ready to access services.

Rumi is a young woman with an extended family of in-laws. She has negotiated being able to go to school for an advanced degree by arranging to have her infant cared for by her in-laws. When the child is hospitalized a few times with recurring symptoms, the doctors at the hospital are suspicious. The system swings into action. Rumi is arrested, and a very high bail is set. She is automatically treated as a criminal, and her parental responsibilities are evaluated based on the norms of a nuclear family.

Sumi was a very bright student and had begun a successful career in India when she met Rishi, a postdoctoral researcher in the United States. They got married and moved here. Once in the States, however, things don't work out. Rishi expects Sumi to cook, clean, and be a model housewife like the women he knew when he was growing up. In addition, he often expresses frustration about how he is treated at work and how his potential is not recognized. Sumi sympathizes—her few attempts at finding some academic pursuit worthy of her expertise have been futile. Yet she is also reluctant to fit into the role that Rishi expects of her. She has a sense of who she is and what her potential is, even though she has not been able to locate the proper arena for herself in the United States. They quarrel almost constantly. She feels stifled, frustrated, and in despair. She seeks counseling. The counselor seems to suggest that she leave her husband. For Sumi, this is an unacceptable solution. There are not just two individuals but two families involved in this marriage. The repercussions of her walking out on Rishi are likely to touch people back in India. Moreover, her prospects of making it on her own in U.S. society are not very encouraging. This is when she calls SNEHA. Both she and her husband are more willing to jointly discuss matters with someone who understands where they are coming from.

Aisha came to the United States 15 years ago through the sponsorship of her brother. She then brought her husband, Sood, to this country. Aisha works hard to help Sood set up a small business. As they become more established, Sood spends increasing amounts of time drinking. He stops providing for her and frequently abuses her physically. First Aisha tries to "cope" by maintaining that all is well. Later, she becomes increasingly desperate. She calls a mainstream agency and asks them to speak to her brother to get him to intervene. Puzzled by her reasoning, the agency calls SNEHA.

In contemporary U.S. society, there is an ongoing danger of Asians and other immigrants being labeled deviants simply because they have acted in accordance with their cultural understandings. Furthermore, because of the increasing fragmentation of social services, there is always a chance that no one person (or group) will monitor an evolving situation. The expectation that a husband would change his behavior because of the reactions of his wife's brother, even after a 35-year-long marriage, resonates among South Asians. Yet it could be dismissed by outsiders as delusional. Similarly, the position of a daughter-in-law in an extended family or the dilemma of a young wife whose behavior impacts her family in her home country require cultural sensitivity.

Negotiating these situations requires both understanding the symbolic meanings of people's behavior and at the same time refusing to condone the ongoing subjugation or abuse of women (which, ironically, has often been excused as merely the expression of a cultural difference rather than as an outrage that is unacceptable in any society). It requires understanding that while individuals within a family may need help, they also frequently need some family-like support to shield them from the effects of the larger society, particularly when they are at their most vulnerable. For SNEHA, this requires working for small changes on the individual level while insisting on broader institutional change, but in such a way that the whole structure does not crash down, further injuring the individual seeking help, who is caught in the middle.

While the focus is on individuals, this ongoing work aims at creating a climate of change within the group as well. Through our work we try to point out that problems of women, which could often be resolved within the extended families in the South Asian context, simply remain unaddressed in the absence of similar networks in the United States. The group that suffers disproportionately in trying to maintain family honor against all odds is women. Thus we try to build networks which work like the extended family. At the same time, such activism asserts the group's (and the South Asian community's) right to participate in institutional decisionmaking in the United States. Thus SNEHA concentrates on empowering both the individual and the group.

Between Communities

Another facet of our activism involves forming bridges between our communities. As women volunteers who come from different parts of South Asia, we have forged, and continue to forge, bonds across our diverse religion- and language-based groups. As the U.S. South Asian community has grown in size, there has been a corresponding increase in its linguistic, religious, ethnic, and caste diversity. Many of these groups are often eager to maintain their distinctiveness from the others, and dredge up outdated practices that are then described as traditional and authentic. Women, of course, are expected to be the symbols and bearers of these "authentic traditions." The role of women in creating these traditions in the first place is often overlooked, as are the socio-historical contexts in which these traditions were practiced, which differ vastly from the current context. The work of SNEHA and many other similar groups is a challenge to those who would maintain static traditions.

In order to keep a spirit of unity in diversity alive, we organize events that bring people together on the basis of their commonality. One such ongoing activity is our annual Golden Social, where we bring together senior South Asian residents to enjoy an afternoon with their peers. Similarly we have organized workshops on health—based on the understanding that health is not just a body issue, but requires an understanding of the mind and its socio-cultural anchors as well—raising adolescents, and planning finances from an immigrant perspective.

We have carved our space as a recognized group among the web of groups in U.S. society. Thus we are able to resist the efforts of outside "experts" to redefine, stereotype, or even minimize our issues by draining them of cultural significance. As vocal, confident, and visible volunteers, our presence is also a challenge to the myth of the subjugated Asian woman. This is another facet of our collective empowerment.

The Unseen Activism

Not all of our activities are carried out so visibly. We also organize and provide the space for women (of all races and ethnicities) to come together to read and discuss a variety of literature on social, cultural, and historical issues that affect our lives at present or have affected the trajectories of immigrants at other times. These efforts help increase our awareness of who we are and how we are situated at multiple and changing intersections of inequalities. This is part of our unobtrusive mobilization. It helps us to become aware of social symbols, myths, and processes of control, and to understand how to take charge of our lives. It also alerts us to the struggles undertaken by others and how they designed their solutions. This is a process of collective learning. It equips us to become effective activists. The organization of these reading sessions helps us to establish connections with different groups of people. More importantly, it helps us in the process of creating and disseminating images of our community.

The notion of upholding communities currently faces two kinds of criticism. First, such activism is seen as limited because it leads to the creation of boundaries between those who are in the group and those who are outside it. Yet when we work within our community, we do not close off the boundaries between ourselves and others. Instead, we try to shield the most vulnerable members from being stereotyped by others, and, at the same time, we actively seek commonalities with other groups that contend with similar issues.

Second, we are often criticized for maintaining specific cultural ideals that contradict Western notions of women's rights. Yet when we uphold our traditions, we uphold them in a manner that is empowering to us as women. We draw on our deep historical memories of strong, active women, whatever their occupation, who have frequently been successful in sanctioning those who treat our sisters or aunts or mothers as lesser human beings.

Our activism includes resistance against oppressions, empowerment of individuals and groups, and an ongoing, conscious effort to try to understand who we are within our rapidly changing circumstances. Our politics consist of legitimating our right to define issues as well as to use or control the resources of society.[6]

Our task, at present, is beset with many hurdles. There are innumerable people in the larger society who do not believe Asian women can be anything but ignorant, poor, tradition-bound, powerless, domestic types.[7] There are outside experts who would deny our rights to define who we are. Since SNEHA does not run shelters or help with financial resources, we are not seen as doing anything concrete for people in distress. There are also people within our community who see us as "family breakers."

Our ongoing internal concern is to avoid becoming a large, bureaucratically set up organization. Remaining small yet effective enough to take on larger, more organized, more powerful structures is an ongoing issue. Raising sufficient funds to support our activism is another ongoing concern.

While much has been written about the largest and most visible elements of activist organizations, there has been little recognition of numerous vital, effective, small organizations like ours, which make a difference on a variety of vital levels. Our model of activism transcends the racial, ethnic, and class dichotomies that appear to affect many other organizations. Our presence is a reminder that not all women of color share the experience of economic marginality. We share black feminists' ambivalence about making public the issues of the community, because there is the real ongoing concern that these dysfunctional images will be used to describe the normal life of the entire group. At the same time, we share with middle-class feminists, both white and black, the need to break out of the culture of domesticity. We also explode the myth of the anti-family feminists, and at the same time we are a challenge to the fact that all families are functional. As we parley our influence within our communities, we challenge the myth that the notion of empowering women is derived from the work of white feminists alone. Through our specific insistence on maintaining a tradition of homosocial networks, which we then see as strengthening heterosexual ones, we publicly disagree with those women who would break away from society to form true women's communities. There is an increasing tendency in the United States to reduce all adult homo- and heterosocial relationships to sexual terms alone. Our activism includes challenging such simplistic definitions. Our presence testifies to the need for a more nuanced understanding of political activism.

Notes

1. See Kumar, Radha. *A History of Doing.* London: Verso, 1993; and Chattopadhyay, Kamaladevi. *Indian Women's Battle for Freedom.* Delhi: Abhinav, 1982.

2. The word SNEHA denotes a loving relationship. This name reflects our ethos.

3. We have professional counselors and medical personnel among our members, as well as people experienced in social service and in organizational skills.

4. South Asia refers to people from India, Pakistan, Bangladesh, Sri Lanka, Nepal, Bhutan, and Afghanistan.

5. The specific details of the following cases have been altered to maintain the confidentiality of the people who sought our help.

6. This notion of empowerment has been discussed by a number of people, including Basu, A. "Indigenous Feminism, Tribal Radicalism and Grass Roots Mobilization in India." *Dialectical Anthropology* 15 (1990): 193-209; Basu, A. *Two Faces of Protest: Contrasting Modes of Women's Activism in India.* Berkeley: University of California Press, 1992; Bookman, A., and S. Morgan. *Women and the Politics of Empowerment.* Philadelphia: Temple University Press, 1988; Ray, R. "Public Agendas and Women's Interests: Organizing Women in Two Indian Cities." Diss. Madison: University of Wisconsin, 1994.

7. Chandra Mohanty discusses these issues in "Under Western Eyes: Feminist Scholarship and Colonial Discourses." *Third World Women and the Politics of Feminism.* Mohanty, C., A. Russo, and L. Torres. Bloomington, IN: Indiana University Press, 1993.

Building Shelter

Asian Women and Domestic Violence

By Cheng Imm Tan

In 1981, as a volunteer for the Legal Ministry, a project of the Unitarian Universalist Urban Ministry (UUUM) that provided free legal counsel and assistance to the poor in Boston, I researched the legal needs of the burgeoning Asian population in Massachusetts. Unanimously, resettlement agencies serving Asian immigrants and refugees identified domestic violence and the corresponding lack of appropriate resources as the key issue facing Asian communities. Despite the fact that Asians were the fastest growing minority group in Massachusetts, no attention had been given to domestic violence in these communities.

In 1982, I started working as a student intern at Renewal House, a battered women's shelter that was also a project of the UUUM. Between 1982 and 1986, I remember only two Asian women who sought shelter at Renewal House, which provides safe shelter to approximately 35 families annually.

By 1986, the Asian community made up 2.4 percent of the state's population, mainly due to the large influx of Asian immigrants and refugees whose first language was not English. Isolated by linguistic and cultural barriers, Asian battered women from these communities were not even aware that outside assistance was available. Shelters, police, and the courts were also unaware of the particular needs of Asian battered women and children, and lacked the multicultural and multilingual skills needed to reach out and serve Asian battered families effectively.

The story of Ling (not her real name) is an example of these particular needs. One evening while she was cleaning fish, Ling's husband, who had been repeatedly abusive to her over the past eight years, began to pick a fight, accusing her of being a bad wife. When Ling did not answer any of his accusations, he became even angrier and picked up a chair to strike her. As he lunged at her with the chair, she screamed at him to stop and tried to ward him off, still holding the knife. The chair missed her, and he tried to wrestle the knife from her. In doing so, he cut himself, yet he continued to attack Ling. She managed to escape and ran to a nearby store to call the police. When the police came, her husband, who spoke good English, accused her of attacking him. She was arrested and put in jail with bail set at $2,500.

Then there was the case of Thuy (not her real name), who, in desperation to get away from her abusive husband, sought the safety of a battered women's shelter with her child. One day while she was in the bathroom, her child fell down and cut himself on the forehead. She was admonished by shelter staff for leaving the child on his own. A few days later, while she was cooking supper and another woman in the shelter was watching her child, he got into a fight with other shelter kids. Again, Thuy was reprimanded for neglecting her child. Not knowing enough English, she could not explain what had happened. A child abuse/neglect complaint was filed against her, and she was investigated by the Department of Social Services. For Thuy, it was yet another traumatic experience in a system that she does not comprehend and that does not understand her.

Another Asian woman and her family were unable to eat the Western food served at a local shelter. When the woman cooked her own food, a child at the shelter spat at her food because it looked "weird." Another child made fun of the way she spoke, imitating her, and making funny noises. Others teased her by switching her bedroom lights off and on while she was inside.

Another Asian woman who had been advised by shelter staff to get a restraining order was asked to meet a legal advocate at court, but did not show up. When she was asked why she did not keep the appointment, she only shook her head and cried. The shelter staff finally decided that she was uncooperative and asked her to leave. What the staff did not know and what she could not explain with her few words of English was that she was terrified to get a restraining order. Her batterer belonged to a gang and had threatened that if she went to the police he would send a gang member to find her and kill her.

In 1986, I wrote a proposal to the Department of Public Health requesting a small grant to fund the publication of a resource booklet on domestic violence that would be translated into Khmer, Vietnamese, and Chinese in an attempt to reach the largest Asian communities in the state. At that time, I was the only full-time Asian bilingual staff member at a shelter, although there were over 30 battered women shelters across Massachusetts. The only other shelter that had Asian staff was Harbor Me, a battered women's program in Chelsea, which had a part-time Vietnamese advocate. I worked with Harbor Me to write the booklet, which featured the stories of Asian women who had struggled with violence in their lives and had been helped by a shelter. The booklet included a section on women's legal rights, how to access the police and courts, and how to get a restraining order.

It took a year to complete the project. Finally, in 1987, "Violence Against Women is a Crime" was available in Chinese, Vietnamese, and Khmer. However, several issues still needed to be addressed. If Asian battered women read these booklets and decided they wanted to get help, who could they call? How could they access shelters or police and legal resources when these resources did not have multilingual staff or information?

We decided to reach out and recruit community organizations that served Asian families to help create a grassroots movement to address domestic violence. We listed these community organizations as resources in the booklet. We then organized a domestic violence training for the bilingual staff of these groups to help them understand the dynamics of domestic violence and the legal rights of victims, as well as to familiarize them with shelter resources. The training also covered common myths about domestic violence, taught how to identify and approach potential victims, and provided national and state statistics on battered women. Our hope was to be able to train community workers to take domestic violence seriously and be able to help battered Asian families access the available resources.

The Southeast Asian Task Force against Domestic Violence

On a cold wintry day in 1987, a group of over 20 Asian refugee and immigrant service workers and community activists, mostly Southeast Asians, gathered for the training on domestic violence. At the end of the training, they became very vocal about the seriousness of domestic violence in Asian communities. Asian families, they said, were being torn apart by domestic violence. They had witnessed Asian refugee and immigrant women suffering in silence, not knowing what help was available. These women were afraid to tell their stories, afraid to seek outside help, afraid of being blamed, afraid of suffering more violence, and afraid of community censure. For some, the only way out was suicide.

By the end of the day, this group of community workers and activists had formed itself into the Southeast Asian Task Force against Domestic Violence. The task force identified three main goals: extensive outreach and education within Asian communities to break the silence and create an environment of intolerance of domestic violence; fundraising; and advocating for the creation of appropriate resources to provide immediate assistance to battered Asian families. The task force began meeting monthly.

There were many challenges that faced the task force. According to task force members, few Asians were aware that domestic violence is a crime, nor were Asian battered women aware of their rights. Many battered Asian women feared and distrusted government and authorities, and expected discrimination and unfair treatment.

For example, a Chinese woman whom I helped to get a restraining order was in such terror of the court system that she crouched in a corner of the courtroom, unable to move until she was called to be heard. I stayed close to her and tried to support her the best I could. At first I thought that she was afraid because she would see her batterer. In fact, she was afraid of her batterer, but she was even more fearful that the judge would not believe her story and would blame her for the violence, just as her batterer had. Her distrust and fear of the court system were so strong that she almost left several times while we waited for her case to be heard.

The task force also faced internal challenges. Within Asian communities, domestic violence is often viewed as a "private family matter." When the task force first started to hold forums, trainings, and talks about domestic violence for Asian communities, we were often accused of meddling and of breaking up Asian families that had already lost so much as a result of war and other hardships. Staff were harassed and threatened by batterers. Their car tires were slashed, and one staff member was threatened with the kidnapping of her son. The

Asian communities in Boston were small enough that often the advocates knew both the survivor and the batterer. Some community members feared that bringing domestic violence into the open would only confirm negative stereotypes about Asians and further fuel the fires of racism against us. Often, battered women were encouraged to endure the violence to "save face" in the community.

The mother of one woman who had been shot and killed by her husband (against whom she had a restraining order) lamented in a *Boston Globe* interview, "I did not want my daughter to go through a divorce because a divorce is not easily acceptable in the community.…I did not sense the danger [she was in] because I was so focused on the shame my daughter's actions would bring in the Cambodian community."

Battered Asian women who dare to look for outside help, file reports of abuse, or get a restraining order often suffer scorn and blame from the community. A woman who leaves her batterer often faces loss of respect and ostracism from her community, and thus her connection to whatever support system her community offers. For the refugee immigrant woman, the choice to leave her partner is particularly difficult; it often means leaving the only person familiar to her.

For women who have faced the odds and decided to leave, economic concerns present yet another obstacle. Language barriers, lack of childcare, and lack of marketable skills make survival an extremely challenging task. For many refugee and immigrant families who do not speak or read English, simple tasks such as taking the subway, using a pay phone, asking for directions, finding housing, enrolling children in school, and getting a job are major challenges. At the same time, long waiting lists for English as a second language (ESL) classes keep women from getting the language education they seek. For example, in Boston's Chinatown, the average wait for a free ESL class is two years. Other women who may have skills and language abilities cannot find the childcare necessary to live independent lives.

In response to some of these challenges, the task force stressed that ending domestic violence is not about wrecking homes or cultural traditions, but about attacking learned behaviors and attitudes that destroy hopes, dreams, and lives. We pointed out that all Asian families deserve violence-free lives—particularly those who have already gone through much suffering and struggle as refugees and immigrants in search of a better life.

I quickly learned that the feminist rhetoric I had learned in the battered women's movement, which often casts the issue of domestic violence exclusively as a gender issue, was not useful in Asian communities. To say that domestic violence is the result of sexism and the accumulation of power and control in the hands of men gave the impression that all men were the "enemy," and prompted defensiveness and resistance. To link ending domestic violence with the promotion of women's rights provoked resistance even from some women, who tended to support the idea of promoting the common good of the family and community above the self. Feminist language served only to polarize the community and to create suspicion and mistrust. But once people could hear the message and understand domestic violence, their resistance decreased. And as trust and relationships began to be established, they began to work with us.

We did not wait for battered women and their families to come to us, but went to places where the community gathered, such as temples, festivals, grocery stores, restaurants, community agencies, and healthcare centers. We did home visits. Outreach to communities that were larger, more organized, and concentrated in particular areas, such as the Chinese, Cambodian, and Vietnamese communities, was easier than to those communities that were smaller or more dispersed, such as the Laotian, Korean, Japanese, and Filipino communities. The task force tried to recruit board members and volunteers from these various communities.

It was vital for us to recruit the support of elders and leaders in communities that held them in respect. We organized radio shows and community events in which community leaders and elders spoke publicly against domestic violence in order to begin creating a climate of intolerance of violence in the home. We also brought community leaders together to write and sign a public statement against domestic violence at a well-attended public event.

The task force was underfunded and understaffed. It was a coalition of individuals and organizations who already had their hands full with their own commitments. The task force operated with no funds of its own, but depended on the support of its participating organizational members to assist with mailing, printing, food, and other costs. Limited staff time was provided by the participating organizations whose staff were on the task force. As a minister of the UUUM, which is committed to serving refugee immigrant communities, I was very fortunate that I was able to undertake this project as part of my ministry, allowing me to put in the time required to move things forward despite the lack of funds and staff.

But by 1989, the task force was beginning to lose momentum. Without clear direction and leadership, the task force was in danger of collapse. Task force meetings had dwindled to about four core people. For the task force to survive, clear leadership was needed. I recommended that we work on developing a clear organizational structure and plan of operation. We created a steering committee. I was voted in as the chairperson and assumed leadership of the task force. We established working subcommittees, and policies for membership and participation, and worked with the few core members left to recruit new members and identify achievable goals and priorities.

Because not everyone in the Asian refugee and immigrant communities could read and write, the task force's first outreach and education objective was to create a pictorial and multilingual poster on domestic violence. The pictures in the poster depicted several scenes of domestic violence followed by a picture of one woman calling another for help. To cover the cost of printing the poster, the task force invited several community agencies to be co-sponsors. The task force unveiled the poster at a celebratory event and press conference held at Boston City Hall in October 1990. That same year, the task force developed curriculum materials on domestic violence for ESL programs and distributed these materials widely to ESL teachers in the greater Boston area. Steps at incorporation as a private, nonprofit organization were also taken, and the task force changed its name to the Asian Task Force against Domestic Violence to be inclusive of all Asian communities.

Regalvanizing the Movement

Renewal House and Harbor Me responded to the task force's call for multilingual direct services to battered Asian families by creating a collaborative two-year project called the Southeast Asian Advocacy and Outreach Project in 1989. The program was designed to provide immediate assistance to Cambodian, Vietnamese, and Chinese battered families and to point the way toward providing effective services for all Asian battered families. Both shelters hired a Cambodian and a Vietnamese woman to reach out to and assist battered families, while I worked with Chinese families.

At the end of the two years, in 1991, Harbor Me decided to hire only Cambodian bilingual staff as a part of its program. Harbor Me hired two Cambodian staff to serve Cambodian families and to provide peer support for each other. I left Renewal House to create an independent project under the UUUM called the Asian Women's Project, which continued to provide outreach and advocacy, but no shelter, to Vietnamese, Cambodian, and Chinese battered families.

The Asian Women's Project also created an Empowerment Program to equip Asian battered women with the necessary skills needed to live in the urban United States. The Empowerment Program consisted of English language tutoring and a food-catering program called "Bamboo Shoots," which offered a Cambodian and Vietnamese lunch and dinner menu to other nonprofits and to many UU churches. All the profits of Bamboo Shoots went to the cooks, who were Asian battered women trying to maintain independent lives.

1991 was a sad year. An Asian woman who had worked closely with the task force was stabbed 18 times and then burned to death by her batterer, who also killed himself. We were shocked and saddened, and it galvanized and inspired us to work even harder to bring attention and resources to address domestic violence in Asian communities. That year, I began keeping statistics of domestic violence fatalities for the first time. In 1991, over 13 percent of the women and children killed as a result of domestic violence in Massachusetts were Asian, even though Asians constituted only 2.4 percent of the state's population.

The task force responded to these deaths with increased organizing and public speakouts. In December 1991, the task force organized the first conference on domestic violence in Asian communities. Over 200 people attended the conference. We had expected only about 150 people, and the place was jammed. The task force then organized follow-up discussions with Asian community organizations and battered women's shelter groups. Also that year, task force members met with Asian community workers in Lowell, Massachusetts. As a result, an independent coalition, Southeast Asian Families against Domestic Violence, was formed.

In 1992, the task force was presented with a leadership award at an "Asian Unity Dinner." The struggle to get domestic violence recognized as a serious issue by Asian communities had finally begun to take root. The task force then began organizing to create the Asian Shelter and Advocacy Project (ASAP), the first Asian battered women's shelter with multilingual services and resources.

Building the Shelter

In 1993, the task force hired its first paid staffperson, Carmen Chan. We held several fundraisers for ASAP, created a large advisory committee to assist in fundraising, and recruited many volunteers to assist us in our efforts.

By September 1993, ASAP had been established with the support of the city of Boston, the state of Massachusetts, and the Asian and mainstream communities. The Asian Women's Project at UUUM was dissolved, and the staff of the Asian Women's Project became the staff of ASAP. In July 1994, only a little over a year after the task force launched its campaign to create the ASAP, a festive celebration was held to commemorate ASAP's opening.

Conclusion

Today, ASAP is able to provide shelter and support for approximately 25 families at a time and to work with another 25 families who are staying on their own or at other shelters. ASAP has Vietnamese, Cambodian, and Chinese full-time advocates who do outreach to bring information and resources to Asian families and work with those who need emergency help, shelter, housing assistance, court advocacy, medical assistance, and referrals.

The work is, of course, far from finished. In many ways we have just begun. ASAP, which has been providing safe shelter and support to battered Asian families since 1994, is already overwhelmed by the demand for its services.

It is important that the Task Force does not remain the only resource for Asian battered families. The Asian refugee and immigrant communities represent a diversity of cultures and languages in different geographical areas. It is impossible to expect that one shelter with limited resources can fulfill the needs of this large and diverse community.

The establishment of the Task Force should not mean that the rest of the domestic violence movement can wash its hands of addressing the needs of Asian refugee and immigrant communities, and of other disenfranchised groups whose voices have yet to be heard and whose needs continue to be overlooked. Bilingual interpreters in courts and hospitals are still largely unavailable. There is still inadequate Asian representation on the police forces that patrol Asian neighborhoods. Many domestic violence resources and services, law enforcement agencies, and courts still lack sensitivity to the particular needs of Asian battered families.

Before long, domestic violence will cease to be a "hot" issue. But this will not mean that it has been eliminated. The vitality and success of our families and our communities depend on us continuing to take steps to make a difference. Ultimately, no one is safe unless all of us are safe from violence in the home.

III. Global Perspectives

AIWA protest against Jessica McClintock, Inc.
Photograph by John Anner

Breaking the Cycle

Women Workers Confront Corporate Greed Globally

By Miriam Ching Louie

As organizers we descended on the 1995 United Nations Fourth World Conference on Women in Beijing and the Non-Governmental Organization (NGO) Forum in Huairou, China, dog-tired and ravenously hungry. Hungry to discover just what was propelling so many women from their homelands to this side of the Pacific. Hungry to finally connect with the women whose newsletters and emergency response alerts we had exchanged over the years.

In face-to-face meetings with sister organizations we felt just how tightly the global economy entwines the lives of women workers of the South with migrant women from the South working in the North. When Filipina, Indonesian, Zambian, and South African migrant domestic workers testified about abuse suffered at the hands of employers in Singapore, the Middle East, and Europe, we thought of the thousands of Latina migrants raising babies, cooking, and cleaning for other families across white America. When Hong Kong seamstresses and Korean shoe factory workers choked back tears telling how they had lost their jobs to young, rural women in China, Indonesia, and Guatemala, we remembered how the jobs of Mexicana seamstresses at Levi-Strauss in San Antonio, Chinese seamstresses at Koret in San Francisco, and Mexican cannery workers at Jolly Green Giant in Watsonville ran away to Costa Rica, Guatemala, and Iraputo, Mexico.

Experiences shared between women workers at the United Nations gathering in China are the direct result of the penetration of capitalist relations into every corner of the globe—greased by Western-dominated financial institutions, structural adjustment policies, transnational corporations, and neoconservative social agendas. With the collapse of socialism in the Soviet Union and eastern Europe, and the heralding of free-market capitalism as the only model of economic development, women increasingly find themselves being the first contributors and the first victims of economic restructuring schemes around the world. Women are often the "first hired and first fired" in development policies, exploited through the "feminization of labor" and the "feminization of migration."

The Feminization of Labor

The globalization of the economy and women's human rights were the two main overarching themes at the NGO gathering in China. Women of the South excoriated the structural adjustment policies holding their countries economic hostage to international lending institutions. The policies foisted on developing countries—of devaluing currency, cutting government budget deficits and spending, eliminating price controls and subsidies, restraining wages, privatizing public services, and changing tax systems—obviously share much in common with the pro-corporate, anti-people thrust of Reaganomics and the Contract on America, as well as the neoconservative government agendas of the other G-7 countries.

The Beijing gathering drew many Asian women workers' organizations, who chronicled the path of destruction economic restructuring programs have cut through their lives. The Committee for Asian Women (CAW), a pan-Asian network of 28 women workers' organizations, organized a workshop and distributed its new book, *Silk and Steel: Asian Women Workers Confront Challenges of Industrial Restructuring*, featuring analyses based on women workers' experiences. The workers' stories revealed several trends.

First, through the "feminization of labor," i.e., the super-exploitation of growing numbers of women producing for the world market, countries sweat out the start-up capital and foreign exchange to finance economic development. But as development proceeds, capitalists invest in other ventures and lay off the women workers who started their empires for them. Women reap nothing for their cheap labor in dangerous, subhuman conditions, while the wealthy profit even more. For women, it's the Industrial Revolution repeated over and over again, relocated from the Triangle Shirtwaist Factory fire that burned workers to death in 19th-century America to South Korea's cramped chicken-coop sweatshops, Mexico's toxic maquiladoras, and China's Special Economic Zone workers' dormitories of today.

Choi Myung Ae of Korean Women Workers Associations United is a laid-off shoe factory worker who still suffers foot pains from work. At the NGO Forum, she described how 50,000 women who had made shoes for 20 years for the likes of Nike, Adidas, and L.A. Gear have lost their jobs to younger women, who often make less than a dollar a day working in Indonesia and Central America, where companies have relocated for even larger profits. Similarly, Tong Lai Chi, a laid-off seamstress with the Hong Kong Women Workers' Association, recalled, "in the early '80s the nightmare beg[an]" as factories moved to China, leaving behind a trail of devastated seamstresses who, in their 40s, were considered too old for jobs as domestic workers in rich women's homes.

Meanwhile, China's economic reform program, introduced in 1979, also draws heavily on the exploitation of young, rural women. The *Unofficial Report: Women Workers in China,* produced by the Hong Kong-based China Labor Education & Information Centre, was secretly circulated outside a forum workshop on labor law and protections for women workers, organized by the government-affiliated All-China Federation of Trade Unions. The report states that 53 million women are working in Chinese urban areas, with an additional 50 million in foreign-investment and township-and-village enterprises. Women workers in these shoe, clothing, toy, kitchenware, and other manufacturing enterprises often receive wages that are far below the legally mandated minimum; typically work for six to seven days a week, 10 to 20 hours a day, in dangerous, abusive conditions without vacations, pensions, or sick leave; and are subjected to bogus wage penalties if they fail to keep up with the awful pace. In flagrant violation of Chinese labor regulations, many of these workers are denied the right to organize in order to entice foreign investors. Organizers who formed independent groups, such as the Workers' Autonomous Federations and Protection of the Rights of Working People, have been arrested. Several remain in prison.

CAW members also drew attention to a new division of labor within Asia, where capital and jobs move from industrialized subregions to developing subregions. A simple North-South, metropole-periphery analysis is no longer sufficient to understand many regions of the South. Newly industrialized countries, such as Korea, Hong Kong, Singapore, and Taiwan, together with Japan and other G-7 countries, now control capital, technology, and the markets, while developing countries provide land, resources, and low-paid workers. Less developed countries, under pressure from the World Bank and International Monetary Fund, are opening their economies to foreign capital investment in export-processing industries, undermining traditional agrarian economies.

Irene Xavier of Persatuan of Sahabat Wanita (Friends of Women Organization) explained the consequences of development in Malaysia, a small country that, after 25 years of welcoming foreign investment and immigrants, now has ten free trade zones and is the world's largest producer of silicon microchips. "Now our women are dying of all kinds of cancers and suffering from spontaneous abortions and health afflictions. Nothing is done. No one can stand up to the transnational corporations, not even the government, which already destroyed all the independent militant trade unions." She warned that although Malaysia is touted as the economic miracle of the region, it's the women and poor communities on the bottom who have paid the highest price for development. She added that women in India, Bangladesh, and Indonesia will soon have the kinds of problems Malaysian women are experiencing, who can in turn expect to suffer the problems of women workers in Japan, Hong Kong, and Korea in the future. Xavier's observation echoed the stories of hardship and struggle shared by workers from the Friends of Women Foundation in Thailand, Karmojibi Nari in Bangladesh, and the Self-Employed Women's Association (SEWA) in India.

As competition between low-wage women workers intensifies, employers can institute more part-time, temporary, contingent, and contract jobs; speedups; and discrimination on the basis of age and marital status. Women will also suffer more unemployment and underemployment.

Feminization of Migration

The globalization of capitalist development is also accelerating women's migration within and across borders. Like capital, women are migrating in search of new economic opportunities. In developing countries, young women are recruited from the countryside to work in the export processing zones, urban factories, and homes of the wealthy.

Braving the cold drizzle and mud-soaked pathways of the NGO

gathering in Huairou, migrant women workers' groups beat drums and held up prison bars as they marched, chanting, "Migrant rights are human rights!" Initiated by the International Migrant Rights Watch Committee and Migrant Forum of Asia, the march featured testimony from migrant women workers such as an Indonesian migrant domestic worker whose Kuwaiti employer abused her and refused to use her name, simply calling her "slave."

The organizations criticized the sending governments for failing to provide decent-paying jobs for women at home, and criticized the receiving countries for denying migrants' legal status and human rights. They decried transnational corporations for using and discarding migrant women workers in the name of profit, declaring in their joint statement, "We hold the 'free market system,' promoted and expanded by GATT [General Agreement on Trade and Tariffs] and the WTO [World Trade Organization], responsible for maintaining the social and economic inequalities within countries and between countries."

Immigrant women workers' organizations exposed the abuse of migrant workers in low-paid manufacturing and service jobs such as in the garment and electronics industries and agriculture, as well as the hospital, hotel, restaurant, and nursing home industries. They noted how formerly immigrant-sending countries such as South Korea, Hong Kong, southern Italy, and Japan have become immigrant-receiving countries, with segmented labor markets that exploit migrant women to replace native-born workers.

The exploitation of migrant women workers is often critical to the economic development strategies of sending countries, because these women generate foreign exchange that lines the pockets of politicians, recruitment and licensing agencies, and crime syndicates. Filipinas, many with long years of experience organizing against the Marcos dictatorship, have formed organizations and networks in defense of migrant workers. According to the Kanlungan Center Foundation's Center for Migrant Workers in the Philippines, five to six million Filipinos are estimated to be working and residing in over 140 countries worldwide. Sixty percent of those deployed abroad by the government are women, the majority of whom are in the fields of domestic work, entertainment, and medicine. NGOs estimate that remittances sent home by Filipina overseas workers run between six and seven billion U.S. dollars a year.

Sex trafficking is a primary way in which women's labor is exploited for economic development. Sexual exploitation is an international industry that capitalizes on class and colonial oppression of women, as seen on U.S. military bases in South Korea, Okinawa, and the Philippines, where troops are on the prowl for "R & R" (rest and recreation). The economies in Vietnam, Hong Kong, and Thailand also depend heavily on the sex industry. Friends of Thai Women Workers works to educate and assist Thai women facing the perils of overseas jobs in the "entertainment industry" before they leave home. According to Toru Takahashi of Kalabaw-no-kai in Yokohama, Japan, 80 percent of foreign women in Japan work in the sex industry. Her organization joined together with 14 others also involved in counseling, relief, and rescue operations of women migrant workers in Japan to forge the Migrant Women Worker's Research and Action Committee, which organized activities and lobbying efforts in Beijing.

At the international level, activists launched the Global Alliance Against Traffic in Women (GAATW) in 1994 to coordinate action to empower women rather than treat them as victims. GAATW is working to improve practical support and advocacy and to build alliances between international organizations. It has working groups in Germany, the Netherlands, the Philippines, and Thailand.

Sisterhood is Global

In countless exchanges, grassroots organizations shared the many methods used to defend the rights of women workers. During a roundtable co-convened by the Toronto Organization for Domestic Workers' Rights and Asian Immigrant Women Advocates, Lee Kyong Suk of Korean Women Workers' Associations United described how women workers organized against the closure of Sumida, a Japanese-owned electronics factory, by taking their story to Japan and alerting workers at other companies. Although the factory did relocate, the women succeeded in organizing a solidarity campaign in Korea and Japan. The group continues to organize women in trade unions, conduct education, involve women in ongoing activism, and participate in a nationwide association that includes branches from other industrialized regions of Korea.

Julia Quinones de Gonzales of the Comite Fronteriza de Mujer, Mexico, permanently injured her back while working in a maquiladora, or manufacturing plant, in Mexico. She began working as a seamstress at a maquiladora when she was only 15 years old. Her organization was formed to help support workers like her. The committee teaches women about their rights, based on the federal laws that exist in Mexico. Through workshops and training sessions, women learn how to protect themselves at work. Workers discuss salaries and benefits, profit-sharing, and other constitutional rights. The committee supported women workers who gave birth to children with disabilities because of toxic chemical poisoning, winning the families one million U.S. dollars in compensation.

Maitet Ledesma of the Commission of Filipino Migrant Workers in Europe described how the Commission has centers in England, Italy, and Greece, as well as an international office in the Netherlands and over 50 partners among Filipino migrant umbrella organizations in 14 European countries. The commission's programs include education and leadership training for organizing; curricula in lobbying, campaign work, fundraising, and anti-racism; a migrant women's program; and campaigns for the undocumented and for migrant women workers' rights (such as the Campaign to Save the Life of Flor Contemplacion, the Filipina domestic worker who was hanged in Singapore for the unexplained death of her employer's child). The group also belongs to the Migrants Forum in Europe, which is the lobbying advocacy group representing the majority of migrant organizations in Europe.

Masumi Azu of Solidarity Center for Migrants (formerly Solidarity with Foreigners) in Japan works with the rising number of female migrant workers, the majority of whom are undocumented, in the sex-related, domestic work, and manufacturing industries. The group has three organizing desks, for Filipinos, Koreans, and Latin American migrants, and counsels battered and raped women.

The Asian Migrant Centre (AMC) in Hong Kong provides orientation and education programs for migrant workers about their rights in the country of destination, networking and coalition-building with other organizations to make migrant issues more visible, crisis intervention and counseling for migrant women, and advocacy and lobbying, and helps migrants re-enter and repatriate should they voluntarily decide to return home. AMC also works in the Migrant Forum in Asia, which includes 50 migrant and support organizations, and in the

International Migrant Rights Watch Committee (IMRWC). IMRWC was formed in 1994 with support from the World Council of Churches to help organizations advance migrant workers' interests and press for ratification of the 1990 UN Convention for the Protection of All Migrant Workers and Members of Their Families, which only the Philippines, Egypt, Morocco, Sri Lanka, the Seychelles, Uganda, Colombia, and Bosnia-Herzegovina have signed. AMC's Mayan Villalba demands, "Why have none of the countries of the so-called civilized world signed this convention?"

From Global to Local

Asian Immigrant Women Advocates (AIWA) is a community-based group in California that organizes immigrant women working in the garment, electronics, hotel, restaurant, nursing home, janitorial, and other low-waged industries in the San Francisco Bay Area and Santa Clara County's "Silicon Valley." Chai Fen, an AIWA volunteer, tells of Asian immigrant seamstresses in the United States slaving 10 to 14 hours a day, six to seven days a week. Hailing from Guangdong Province in China, Chai Fen followed the flow of immigrant women into sewing sweatshops in the United States, where she made only one dollar an hour at piece rates. She says AIWA helped her overcome the extreme isolation she felt as a new immigrant who knew no English and slaved in a sweatshop for 10 hours a day before returning home, exhausted, to raise her kids.

Launched in 1983, AIWA uses different methods and projects to build a base of trust, membership, and leadership among local women workers. Currently, AIWA pursues an organizing process with three intersecting components: education and analysis, leadership development and skills building, and collective action for change.

Popular Education for Transformation

Like many of AIWA's members, Chai Fen says, "I first came to AIWA to learn English and improve myself. AIWA's Workplace Literacy Classes teach us survival English and our rights in the U.S." Arranged on Sundays or after working hours, the classes use popular education methods to draw out and connect women's stories to larger structures of oppression. For example, before coming to AIWA, many women workers knew nothing about their right to a minimum wage. Now they demand to know why they're not getting it. When workers expressed fear about coming to evening classes, teachers drew out a discussion about why. Subsequent curriculum covered violence and sexual assault against women and what could be done to help women protect themselves. Curriculum drawn from an early Korean immigrant woman's life and celebrating civil rights leader Martin Luther King, Jr., enabled new immigrants to both connect their experiences with those of previous immigrants and racial minorities, and learn how their struggles improved the lives of subsequent generations.

In 1995, AIWA started citizenship classes in response to escalating anti-immigrant attacks in the United States. After the passage in 1996 of punitive immigration and welfare-reform legislation, the demand for the classes grew. As workers prepare to take the citizenship test, which covers U.S. history, the Constitution, and the Bill of Rights, they can analyze the United States' history of expansionism and racialized labor exploitation. Increasingly, workers graduating from the Workplace Literacy and Citizenship classes have been recruited as teachers of classes for new groups of women.

Leadership and Skills Development

Workers' leadership and skills have developed such that the Membership Board and Project Committees organized by Chai Fen and other garment, electronics, hotel, and nursing home workers now plan and implement many of AIWA's projects. The four Project Committees—Outreach, Education, Events, and Fundraising—conduct outreach, provide bilingual services, participate in developing and teaching Workplace Literacy class curriculum, organize educational field trips and events for women and their families, run Leadership Development training sessions, help write grant proposals, and raise donations for AIWA's work. The Membership Board also assists workers in resolving problems with their bosses. The women have also begun to write and produce editions of the workers' newsletter in Chinese and Korean.

Collective Action for Accountability

AIWA encourages workers to organize and act collectively for social change. These actions take place at big and small levels, from the unprecedented act of circulating petitions against anti-immigrant bills inside garment sweatshops to writing letters to a convalescent care home that was abusing workers and patients. Workers have pressured electronics plants to provide first-aid kits and better ventilation and have organized to change the work process to lessen repetitive stress injuries. AIWA also runs a Garment Workers Organizing Project and an Environmental Health and Safety Project for electronics assemblers.

Through three-and-a-half years of organizing the Garment Workers Justice Campaign, workers recently set an historic precedent by winning a corporate responsibility case. The case first arose when 12 women were left holding bad paychecks when the sweatshop where they worked went belly-up. Garment manufacturer Jessica McClintock had ended business relations with the contractor without taking responsibility for paying the workers who sew her expensive evening wear. In March 1996, McClintock and AIWA reached a settlement that included an education fund for garment workers to learn about their rights, a scholarship fund for garment workers and their children, and a bilingual hotline for workers to report any violations of their rights in shops contracted with McClintock. Additionally, the stiffed workers received an undisclosed cash amount, and both sides agreed to make efforts to improve conditions within the garment industry. Workers and AIWA also initiated campaign support committees in cities across the United States, thus creating an infrastructure of support for future organizing. AIWA is now asking other manufacturers to "do the right thing" and show corporate responsibility by signing agreements to protect workers' rights.

AIWA is trying to bring the three elements of its organizing process closer together. Chai Fen says,

> To change a problem that has built up for over a century is not easy. Let us stand up and speak up before it is too late. We want corporations to show responsibility and compassion for the workers who made them rich, whether or not those workers are directly employed by the company, or indirectly employed through subcontractors. We want protection for the workers and the environment in trade agreements so that corporate profits do not come at the expense of workers' lives and the environment. We want the government and the politicians to stop blaming and attacking immigrant workers and their families.

Platform for Action

Beijing has brought home the depth and breadth of the globalization of capitalism and the destructive consequences of structural adjustment, feminization of labor, and feminization of migration for women workers around the world. But Beijing was also a magnet for NGOs to gather and strategize, a thorn in the side of governments, finance institutions, and corporations, and a gauge to measure just how much women and migrant worker organizations have also become features of the global economy's landscape. Bucking conventional wisdom and superior corporate firepower, NGOs are busily organizing in support of women workers' struggles for justice in defiance of capitalist development models financed by women's blood, sweat, and tears. In her critique of the wages of corporate sins in Malaysia, Irene Xavier gave voice to what we already knew: "It's a vicious cycle. Wherever we are, we must struggle to break it."

Sources

For more information, contact: Committee for Asian Women, 57 Peking Road, 4th Floor, Room 403, Metropole Building, Kowloon, Hong Kong, and AIWA, 310 Eighth St., Suite 301, Oakland CA 94607, Tel: (510) 268-0192, Fax: (510) 268-0194, e-mail: aiwa@igc.apc.org.

The Global Trade in Filipina Workers

By Grace Chang

Since the 1980s, the World Bank, the International Monetary Fund, and other international lending institutions based in the North have routinely prescribed structural adjustment policies (SAPs) to the governments of indebted countries of the South as pre-conditions for loans. These prescriptions have included cutting government expenditures on social programs, slashing wages, liberalizing imports, opening markets to foreign investment, expanding exports, devaluing local currency, and privatizing state enterprises. While SAPs are ostensibly intended to promote efficiency and sustained economic growth in the "adjusting" country, in reality they function to open up developing nations' economies and peoples to imperialist exploitation.

SAPs strike women in these nations the hardest and render them most vulnerable to exploitation both at home and in the global labor market. When wages and food subsidies are cut, wives and mothers must adjust household budgets, often at the expense of their own and their children's nutrition. As public healthcare and education vanishes, women suffer from a lack of prenatal care and become nurses to ill family members at home, while girls are the first to be kept from school to help at home or go to work. When export-oriented agriculture is encouraged, indeed coerced, peasant families are evicted from their lands to make room for corporate farms, and women become seasonal workers in the fields or in processing areas. Many women are forced to find work in the service industry, in manufacturing, or in home work, producing garments for export.[1]

When women take on these extra burdens and are still unable to sustain their families, many have no other viable option but to leave their families and migrate in search of work. Asian women migrate by the millions each year to work as servants, service workers, and sex workers in the United States, Canada, Europe, the Middle East, and Japan. Not coincidentally, the demand for service workers, and especially for private household caregivers and domestic workers, is exploding in wealthy nations of the First World undergoing their own versions of adjustment.

For example, in the United States, domestic forms of structural adjustment, including cutbacks in healthcare and the continued lack of subsidized childcare, contribute to an expanded demand among dual-career, middle-class households for workers in childcare, eldercare, and housekeeping. The slashing of benefits and social services under "welfare reform" helps to guarantee that this demand is met by eager migrant women workers. The dismantling of public supports in the United States in general, and the denial of benefits and services to immigrants in particular, act in tandem with structural adjustment abroad to force migrant women into low-wage labor in the United States. Migrant women workers from indebted nations are kept pliable not only by the dependence of their home countries and families on remittances, but also by stringent restrictions on immigrant access to almost all forms of assistance in the United States. Their vulnerability is further reinforced by U.S. immigration policies, designed to recruit migrant women as contract laborers or temporary workers who are ineligible for the protections and rights afforded to citizens.[2]

Both in their indebted home countries and abroad, women suffer the most from the dismantling of social programs under structural adjustment. In the Third World, women absorb the costs of cuts in food subsidies and healthcare by going hungry and foregoing proper medical care. Ironically, these same women continue to take up the slack for vanishing social supports in the First World, by nursing the elderly parents and young children of their employers for extremely low wages. Thus, there is a transfer of costs from the governments of both sending and receiving countries to migrant women workers from indebted nations. In both their home and "host" countries, and for both their own and their employers' families, these women pay most dearly for "adjustment."

Testimonies of Women Living under SAPs

At the 1995 Women's NGO Forum in China, women from the Third World gave first-hand testimony on the impact of SAPs on their daily lives and struggles for survival. The phenomenon consistently reported is that overall standards of living, and conditions for women and girls in particular, have deteriorated dramatically since the onset of SAPs. Often this has occurred after periods of marked improvement in women's employment, health, education, and nutrition following national independence movements prior to the institution of SAPs.

In a workshop on the impact of SAPs on women, an organizer from rural India spoke of the particular hardships women face, as those most affected by cuts in social programs and those first displaced from their farm lands. She reported that lands in India formerly used to produce rice have been rapidly converted to shrimp farms and orange orchards. While rice has always been a staple for local consumption, shrimp are purely cash crops for export to Japan, and the oranges are for export to the United States for orange juice. In her community, peasant women ran in front of bulldozers to try to prevent these lands from being taken over, but to no avail.[3]

Women from many other Third World countries reported similar conditions. An organizer from Malaysia observed, "We are adjusting with no limits to capital mobilizing everywhere. Malaysia has used all of the SAP principles, including privatization of services and deregulation of land acquisition." This woman reported that in Malaysia, land once held by small farmers has also been shifted to shrimp cultivation, while in Sri Lanka, peasants see their lands being taken up to cultivate strawberries for export to other countries.[4] Similarly, peasant women from the Philippines testified that, under SAPs, they have had to relinquish all the profits of their labor to landlords, and that lands once used to grow rice, corn, and coffee have been converted to growing orchids and "other exotic flowers that you can't eat" for export.[5]

In each of these countries, women bear the brunt of SAP-induced poverty daily through lack of healthcare, housing, and food.[6] Filipina rural women have reported going without power for four to eight hours each day and coping with little or no water.[7] Urban women from the Philippines reported working an average of 18 hours a day doing domestic work, laundry work outside their homes, and begging, while men face increasing unemployment. Their children are most often on the street rather than in school, and many families are becoming homeless with the high price of housing and the demolition of houses under development. Families may eat only once or twice a day because they can't afford more, and most go without any healthcare as the public hospitals demand payment up front and prescription medicines become prohibitively expensive.[8] Similarly, one rural organizer from India reported that prices for essential medicines have gone up 600 percent since the onset of SAPs, severely reducing Indian women's access to proper healthcare.[9]

Consistently, women from around the Third World testified that, as women have been displaced from their lands and homes under structural adjustment, women who were once small farmers have been forced to do home work, to migrate to the cities to work in manufacturing and the electronic industry, or to migrate overseas to do nursing, domestic work, sex work, and "entertainment."[10] The women's testimony demonstrates their clear recognition that they bear the brunt of hardships under structural adjustment, while their nations' governments and elites reap fat rewards in the form of women's cheap or unpaid labor and remittances from migrant women workers abroad. Commentary of women organizing in countries affected by SAPs reflects an acute awareness of the ways in which the governments and economic elites of their countries and First World countries profit at the expense of women's labor conditions, education, nutrition, health, and safety. As one labor organizer from India remarked:

> Our governments are surrendering to these multinational corporations and Western agencies. These magnate and mafias, in the name of globalization, want to exploit our workers and resources. Our real concerns are food, water, clean sanitary conditions, health, shelter, and no exploitation. These are the human rights we want. All these governments are telling us to talk about human rights. What are they doing?[11]

Exporting Women: The "New Heroes"

Each day, thousands of Filipinas leave their homes and families in search of work abroad. The Philippine government estimates that more than 4 percent of the country's total population are contract workers overseas. About 700,000 Filipinas/os were deployed through a government agency, the Philippine Overseas Employment Administration (POEA), in each of the past two years.[12] In 1991, women constituted a larger proportion of the country's overseas workforce

(41 percent) than its domestic workforce (36 percent). Of those overseas, approximately 70 percent are women working as domestic servants in middle- and upper-class homes in the United States, Britain, Europe, Japan, and the Middle East. Many of the others work as nurses, sex workers, and entertainers.[13] Such massive migrations of women have led to public charges that the Philippines government is selling or trafficking in women.

Indeed, this massive migration is no mere coincidence of individual women's choices to leave the Philippines. The Philippines government receives huge sums of remittances from its overseas workers each year. "Host" country governments and private employers welcome the migrant women workers for the cheap labor they provide. These governments and employers save money not only by paying abominably low wages, but by failing to provide public benefits or social services to these temporary workers. Finally, recruiting agencies and other entrepreneurs on each end of the trade route reap tremendous profits for providing employers in "host" countries with ready and willing service workers and caregivers of all kinds.

In 1994, the Central Bank of the Philippines recorded the receipt of USD $2.9 billion in remittances by overseas workers. Remittances through informal channels have been estimated at six to seven billion U.S. dollars each year. These remittances are the country's largest source of foreign exchange—surpassing income from either sugar or minerals—and provide currency for payments towards the country's USD $46 billion debt. In 1993, overseas contract workers' remittances were estimated at 3.4 percent of the gross domestic product, which is the equivalent of 30 percent of the trade deficit or of the entire sum of interest payments on the country's foreign debt. These estimates are based on official figures alone and do not include moneys that enter through informal channels. As the Freedom from Debt Coalition (FDC), an organization working to counter SAPs, has put it: "What the country cannot achieve through export of goods, it compensates for through the export of human resources."[14]

Of less importance to the Philippine government but certainly significant in explaining the continued massive migration of women workers are estimates that approximately 30 to 50 percent of the entire Filipino population are dependent on migrant worker remittances.[15] Furthermore, it has been found that women migrant workers send home a larger proportion of their wages than their male counterparts do, even though they tend to earn less than men.[16] Such contributions led one ambassador from the Philippines to Canada to proclaim: "The migrant workers are our heroes because they sustain our economy."[17]

"Host" countries are eager to receive these female mercenaries, as they bolster their economies, too. As many countries of the North undergo downsizing and the dismantling of public supports, migrant women workers offer the perfect solution. The steady flow of migrant women provides an ideal source of cheap, highly exploitable labor. These women are channeled directly into the service sector, where they do every form of care work for a pittance and no benefits. Ironically, immigrant domestic workers, nannies, in-home caregivers, and nurses pick up the slack for cuts in government services and supports that pervade the North as well as the South. Overseas, they provide care for the ill, elderly, and children, while their own families forego this care because of the economic restructuring that drives them overseas.

Filipina Nurses and Homecare Workers

Currently, there are 100,000 registered nurses in the Philippines, but almost none actually reside in the country. Similarly, 90 percent of all Filipino/a medical school graduates do not live in the Philippines. Since the 1970s, the United States has imported women from the Philippines to work as nurses, ostensibly in response to domestic shortages in trained nurses. This importation system became institutionalized with the H-1 nursing visa, which enables a hospital or nursing home to sponsor or bring a nurse with a professional license from abroad to work in the United States for two years.

Under the H-1 program, a migrant woman must take the U.S. nurses' licensing exam. If she passes, she can gain permanent residency after two years. During those two years, she is almost captive to her original sponsoring employer. If she fails the exams she loses her sponsorship, and technically she must leave the country. More often, such women go underground until they can take the exam again. Sometimes, they work in nursing homes where they are underpaid at five dollars an hour. Others buy green-card marriages.

In 1988, the Filipina Nurses Organization fought for the Nursing Relief Act, which has provided some rights and stability to H-1 nurses in the last decade. The law grants nurses permanent residency after five years of living in the United States and working in the nursing profession. Prior to this act's passage, H-1 nurses had to go home after five years and could return after one year's residence in their home countries. Only after this period of absence could they apply to have their H-1 visas renewed. This system kept nurses in low-wage, temporary positions, forcing them to begin again and again at entry level with no seniority or benefits. The Immigration and Naturalization Service routinely conducted raids at hospitals to ensure that this turnover of temporary workers occurred.

Mayee Crispin, a Filipina nurse, organizes foreign nurse graduates (FNGs) at St. Bernard's Hospital on the south side of Chicago. At St. Bernard's, 80 percent of the nurses are single Filipina women on H-1. The starting wage at St. Bernard's is $14 an hour, in contrast to $16 an hour at other hospitals, and the ratio of patients to nurses is high. But many of the FNGs are reluctant to organize, fearful of losing their jobs or their employers' immigration sponsorship if they are identified as being pro-union. Many are sending remittances to their families at home and struggling to pay off their debts from migration.

Crispin proposes that importing nurses from the Philippines is a money-making venture for hospitals and the nursing recruiters they contract. According to Crispin, a hospital typically get workers from overseas by making an official certification that they cannot find U.S. workers to fill its nursing positions. (This is usually because the hospital offers wages that no U.S. worker is willing to accept.) The hospital is then free to contract a recruiter to go to the Philippines in search of nurses. An FNG must pay, on average, between USD $7,000 and $9,000 to the recruiter. Ostensibly, a portion of this fee goes to the recruiter's salary, and a portion goes to a lawyer to arrange the woman's visa. Often both are employed by the hospital, which also gets a cut of the fee. Since most women cannot afford this fee, they agree to have it deducted from their wages. After paying off such fees and sending roughly 25 to 30 percent of their wages to their families at home, their monthly wages quickly disappear. In essence, most of these women live in a situation much like indentured servitude or debt bondage for at least two years. Crispin says that hospitals, by hiring FNGs, not only get cheap labor, they also get a workforce that is extremely vulnerable, fearful, uninformed of their rights, and thus likely to resist unionization.

Ninotschka Rosca of Gabriela Network USA observes the ironic history of Filipina nurses in the United States. In the 1980s, the nursing profession was extremely low-paying, with salaries at about $20,000 a year in the United States, so the country experienced a drastic shortage of nurses. With few U.S. citizens going into the field or willing to do nursing at such low wages, many Jamaican and Filipina women migrated here to do this work. With the downsizing in healthcare, many of the migrant nurses who have been here for over a decade are now finding themselves just as vulnerable as new migrants. Hospitals are attempting to reduce costs by firing their most experienced, and thus highest-paid, nurses. Rosca suggests that U.S. hospitals and the healthcare industry would collapse without Filipina nurses. "We take care of everybody else's weaker members of society, while we let our own society go to hell."[18]

Homecare Workers

Home healthcare is another industry in which immigrant women are highly concentrated and fall prey to both profit-seeking agencies and the cost-cutting U.S. government. Many homecare workers are employees of the state, under a state-funded program called "in-home support services" (IHSS). Some of these women are registered nurses, while others are not trained as nurses at all. The program provides no training, no regulations, and no monitoring of the work, which includes everything from performing medical procedures, preparing meals, and cleaning to helping elderly, frail, or ill clients go to the toilet, bathe, and move about. To keep costs down, the state pays workers a minimum wage of $4.50 an hour and provides no benefits, including no sick leave, family leave, overtime pay, compensation for injuries on the job, or reimbursement for bus fares or gasoline used to run errands for patients or to take them to the doctor.[19] In California, there are 170,000 of these workers statewide, of which approximately 80 percent are women, 60 to 70 percent are people of color, and 40 percent are immigrants.

Josie Camacho is an organizer with Service Employees International Union. Camacho points out that, particularly with the restructuring of hospitals under the ongoing privatization of healthcare, patients are being sent home too early and thus homecare workers are having to provide what should be trained nursing care, often without any formal training. For example, routine duties can include giving enemas and insulin shots, changing bandages, and hooking up dialysis machines.[20] In addition to the gruelling work and low pay, immigrant workers in particular frequently report sexual harassment and other forms of abuse from their clients, including threats of deportation and general treatment as slaves. One worker was ordered to clean the bathroom with a toothbrush.[21]

The union is demanding the workers' rights to dignity and respect, to proper training in health and safety procedures, and to better wages. Camacho explains that these demands are aimed not only at improving the standard of living and rights for the workers, but at improving the quality of care provided to clients. Patients are typically Supplementary Security Income (SSI) recipients and must have assets under $2,000 to qualify for care under the state program. Thus, the government is relying on the weak positions of both impoverished patients, who have no control over the quality of care offered them, and low-wage workers, who have little recourse to fight these low wages and highly exploitative conditions.

Employing an IHSS worker saves taxpayers approximately $30,000 a year, the difference between the cost of keeping a patient in a nursing home and the typical salary of $7,000 a year earned by an IHSS worker who works 30 hours a week. This savings is reaped by the state, county, and (through Medicaid) federal governments, which all share the program's annual cost. Robert Barton, manager of the adult services branch of the California Department of Social Services overseeing the program, commented: "It's a good deal for the government." The union's director of organizing in Washington, D.C., David Snapp, retorts: "It's a scam."[22] The IHSS program provides perhaps the best illustration available of the tremendous savings to local, state, and federal governments through the low-wage labor of migrant care workers. Other savings to the state and employers have not been measured, such as those reaped from not providing public benefits, services, and protections to these workers.

In the private sector, the situation is no better. Agencies and companies turn a profit from placing these workers, just as the state saves money by underpaying workers. Homecare agencies, just like hospitals, make huge profits from recruiting and placing homecare workers. For example, an agency will typically contract out a live-in caregiver to a client for $120 to $200 a day, while the worker herself receives only $80 of that daily rate.

Domestic Workers and Nannies

The majority of migrant Filipina workers are domestic workers and nannies. Many of them work in Canada, which has had a "live-in caregiver program" since 1992 to facilitate the importation of these migrants. Through this program, a Canadian employer (either an individual or employment agency) may apply through the Canadian Employment Office for a prospective employee. The employer must show that it has first tried to find a Canadian to do the job. The prospective employee must have six months of formal training or 12 months' experience in caregiving work and be in good health. If approved, the employee can gain temporary employment authorization for one year, and this can be extended for an additional year. A nanny must undergo a personal interview with Canadian consular officials and obtain security clearance. Once matched with an employer, she must notify the Ministry of Citizenship and Immigration if she wishes to change employers. After two years of live-in work, a nanny can apply for landed-immigrant status. She can then sponsor immediate family members to join her if they can prove they have a source of steady income. Three years after applying for landed-immigrant status, she can become a Canadian citizen.[23]

The film, *Brown Women, Blonde Babies*, produced by Marie Boti, documents the conditions for Filipina migrant women working as domestics and nannies in Canada. Typically, women work around the clock, from 7 a.m. to 10 p.m. and beyond, and are always considered on call. They earn an average of $130 a month after taxes. Women who wish to leave their employers must persuade an immigration officer to let them. In response to one woman's pleas for release from an employer, one immigration officer coldly responded, "You didn't come here to be happy."

In stark contrast to the conditions revealed in this documentary, employers of domestic workers and nannies in Canada romanticize the work and the "opportunities" they offer to immigrant women. For example, *The Globe and Mail*, a Toronto newspaper, boasted that

Canada is the first-choice destination for Filipina migrant workers, claiming:

> For the women themselves, improving their economic status helps them challenge the Philippines' traditional stereotype of women as submissive homemakers who need to rely on their husbands, fathers, or brothers to survive. The huge exodus of female contract workers from the country in the past decade has created a generation of women who are more confident and independent about their role in a society that has now been forced to ask some hard questions about many of its traditional paternalistic attitudes.[24]

Clearly, if Filipina women's roles in their society are subservient, as this statement implies, then those roles are not overturned but reinforced when migrant women are forced to serve as low-wage workers overseas instead of homemakers. The only difference is that they provide domestic services to employers in the North instead of their own families, while servicing their government's foreign debt at the same time.

According to the Kanlungan Foundation Centre, an advocacy group for Filipina migrant workers,

> We do not migrate as totally free and independent individuals. At times, we have no choice but to migrate, to brave the odds....Even from the very start, we are already victims of illegal recruitment, victims of our government's active marketing of our cheap labor,...and suffering the backlash of states that fail to provide adequate support for childcare services, we enter first world countries that seek to preserve patriarchal ideology.[25]

This statement reflects migrant women workers' clear understanding that they are being used to maintain patriarchy in the First World, as governments in these wealthy nations cut social supports.

Just as employers try to justify exploiting servants by romanticizing the "opportunities" they provide these women, the Philippine government attempts to rationalize the trade in women by glorifying its migrant women exports: In 1988, on a state visit to Hong Kong, President Aquino declared migrant women the new heroes of the Philippine economy.[26] Since then, many officials have taken this up as the party line in justifying the trade in women. In response, the FDC states: "Because of their economic contributions, migrant workers are hailed by the administration as the new heroes, and labor export is elevated into a national policy, the appalling social costs and the prevalence of abuses notwithstanding."[27]

Women's Resistance

In July of 1994, Sarah Balagaban, a 15-year-old Filipina working as a maid in the United Arab Emirates (UAE), was raped at knifepoint by her employer. In self-defense, Balagaban stabbed and killed her rapist/employer and was sentenced to seven years in prison. In response to protests, Balagaban was retried, but was then sentenced to death. In outrage, many overseas Filipinas joined protests staged by Gabriela Network USA in front of the UAE mission and the Philippine government consulate in the United States. Again, Balagaban's sentence was revised. This time, she was sentenced to one year in prison and 100 lashes, and ordered to pay her deceased employer's family 150,000 dirhams, the equivalent of USD $41,995. Gabriela's Ninotschka Rosca speculates that the main reason the UAE government rescinded the death sentence was for fear of a walkout by the approximately 75,000 Filipina/os working in the UAE—a walkout that would paralyze the country.

Protests continued after this last sentence, with objections that 100 lashes could actually kill Balagaban. The Philippine government agreed to the final sentence over these protests, reinforcing outrage that the Philippine government refuses to protect its overseas workers and is clearly willing to sacrifice women's lives to maintain good relations with its chief trade partners. Many Filipinas working in the UAE have collected a scholarship fund for Balagaban to complete her education once she finishes her prison sentence. She had quit school in order to work in the UAE to support her parents and to help pay for her brother's education. Balagaban has since become a symbol for overseas Filipinas fighting for their rights.[28]

Teresita Tristan is a widow who left two children behind in the Philippines for a job in Britain as a domestic worker. Before leaving, she had been promised a salary of $400 a month, but when she arrived, her employers took her passport and informed her she would be paid $108 a month. On her first day in the country, she was taken for a medical exam, given medicine to clean her stomach, and was instructed to take a bath and not to touch the dishes with her bare hands until five days had passed. Her daily work consisted of cleaning the entire house, taking the children to school, and preparing the family's meals, while she ate leftovers. She was not allowed to eat from plates or glasses or to use the toilet inside the house. When her employer kept making sexual advances and asking her to go to the guest house with him, she asked to be released so she could return home. Instead, she was transferred to her employers' daughter's home, where she was likewise treated badly.[29]

One day Tristan went to the park and met an Englishwoman who took her phone number and called the police for her. The Commission for Filipina Migrant Workers helped her to leave her employer's home and find shelter. For many weeks, she feared that her employer would come to find her. Now, Tristan belongs to an organization of unauthorized workers fighting for migrant worker rights.

Tristan's story is typical of that of migrant workers, according to Kalayaan, an organization working for justice for overseas domestic workers in Britain. Between January 1992 and December 1994, Kalayaan interviewed 755 migrant domestic workers who had left their employers. The results of these interviews revealed widespread abuses of migrant domestic workers from the Philippines, Sri Lanka, India, Ghana, Nigeria, Colombia, and Brazil. Eighty-eight percent had experienced psychological abuse, including name-calling, threats, and insults, and 38 percent had endured physical abuse of some form. Eleven percent had experienced attempted, threatened, or actual sexual assault or rape. A full 60 percent had received no regular meals, 42 percent had no bed, and 51 percent had no bedroom and were forced to sleep in a hallway, kitchen, bathroom, or storeroom. Thirty-one percent reported being imprisoned or not being allowed to leave the house. Ninety-one percent reported working for an average of 17 hours a day with no time off. Fifty-five percent were not paid regularly, and 81 percent were paid less than was agreed upon in their contracts, with an average monthly wage of USD $105.

A spokeswoman from Kalayaan says that these widespread abuses are made possible by British immigration law. In 1979, the British government abolished work permits for overseas domestic workers but continued to allow overseas employers and returning British residents to bring domestic workers into the country. This concession was granted to wealthy people returning from traveling abroad with employees. As Maria Gonzalez of the Commission on Filipina Overseas Domestic Workers puts it: "In the United Kingdom, migrant women are brought into the country like the baggage of their employers."[30] Migrant women enter with their employers' names stamped on their passports, and they cannot change employers after entering. Even in the rare case that a woman negotiates a contract with her employer, she has no bargaining power or legal recourse if the employer violates it.

Migrant workers have mobilized worldwide to expose these abuses and to fight for protection of their rights. Women in many "host" countries, including Canada, Japan, Britain, and the United States have organized grassroots organizations to offer support and legal advocacy, and to lobby for the protection of Filipina and other migrant workers abroad. Kalayaan lobbies to change British law to allow migrant workers to receive permits directly, to change employers freely, and to stay and work in the country while pursuing legal action against former employers.

INTERCEDE is a similar organization, based in Toronto, that conducts research and advocacy for Filipina and Caribbean migrant domestic worker rights. It provides direct services, such as individual counseling on labor and immigration rights and educational meetings and social activities to aid settlement, and lobbies the Canadian government. In 1981, INTERCEDE succeeded in convincing the Canadian Parliament to grant the rights of Canadian citizens under labor laws to foreign domestic workers on temporary visas.[31] Currently, INTERCEDE is pressuring the government to recognize domestic work as an occupation, to do away with the live-in requirement, and to allow immigrants to gain "landed-immigrant" status immediately upon entering Canada, instead of having to wait two years.

In the United States, healthcare workers (many of whom are migrant women) are the fastest-growing service workers. As some of the most exploited and, until recently, least organized workers, they are a prime target for labor organizers.[32] A recent victory by SEIU against the California government represents the fruits of a five-year struggle by the union on behalf of over 50,000 homecare workers in the state. In the summer of 1990, the California legislature and Governor Pete Wilson failed to reach an agreement on a budget, and the state stopped issuing paychecks. IHSS homecare workers were the first to feel the impact of the budget crisis—some workers' paychecks were delayed up to two months. During the budget impasse of 1992, workers suffered the same series of events.

SEIU brought a class-action suit against the State of California on behalf of more than 10,000 IHSS workers. SEIU argued that the workers suffered extreme hardship because of the delayed payments, including having electricity turned off in their homes and not having enough money for food, among other necessities. A U.S. District Court judge ruled on March 17, 1994, that the delayed payments violated the Fair Labor Standards Act. A settlement reached in May 1995 awarded damages of four million dollars, to be divided among the approximately 50,000 workers who joined the action.[33] This SEIU struggle represents a dramatic victory.

Josie Camacho points to the ongoing challenges of organizing homecare workers: First, there is no central workplace, with workers scattered among as many as 6,000 different worksites in a county. Second, some immigrant workers feel indebted to their employers and are reluctant to join the union. They are afraid and don't know their rights. This has challenged the union to recruit organizers who are multilingual and able to inform workers of their rights. Third, no party is willing to admit responsiblity for, or can be held accountable for, the rights and protection of these workers. All parties, including both the sending and receiving countries' governments, employers, and employment agencies, evade or completely deny responsibility. Yet all benefit immensely from these workers' labor, extracting foreign currency, profits, savings, and care services.

Groups such as Kalayaan, INTERCEDE, and SEIU focus on organizing migrant workers and providing direct services to them in "host" countries while lobbying these "host" governments to change oppressive immigration and labor policies. Other organizations have a different emphasis, putting pressure on the Philippine government to recognize the impact of SAPs on poor women of the Third World at home and abroad. They aim to expose how the Philippine government facilitates the exportation of women migrant workers, sacrificing women in the futile effort to keep up with debt payments. Finally, they pressure the Philippine government to redirect expenditures away from debt servicing, to institute protections for migrant workers abroad, and to stop the export of women from the Philippines and other impoverished countries.

While many organizations focus on fighting for protections for migrant workers overseas, others propose that ultimately the global trafficking in women must stop. Gabriela Network has led the fight against the trade in Filipina and other migrant women. Gabriela accused the Philippine government of feeding young Filipinas into the sex industry in Japan after the Philippine government's policy prohibiting women under 23-years-old from migrating to Japan to work as entertainers was found to have been violated 35 times within a four-month period. Gabriela found that the government made exceptions to the policy for four "favored" recruitment agencies.[34] Gabriela has called for the government to stop labor exportation as its chief economic strategy. The Philippine government denies that it participates in such a trade.[35]

Mainstream U.S. feminist responses to the trade in women have been lukewarm at best. When Gabriela called on women's organizations around the world to put the issue of global trafficking of women on their agendas, the National Organization for Women (NOW) declined to do so, stating that it does not deal with international issues.[36] The real issue may be that privileged women of the First World, even self-avowed feminists, are some of the primary consumers and beneficiaries in this trade. Middle- and upper-class professional women generally have not joined efforts to improve wages or conditions for care workers in the United States, since they have historically relied on the "affordability" of women of color and migrant women working in their homes, daycare centers, and nursing homes. As Cynthia Enloe observes:

> Politically active maids have not always found feminists in the host countries to be reliable allies. Too often local feminist groups in countries importing maids either from overseas or from the poor regions of their own countries were led by women of precisely the social class that hired domestic workers.[37]

Major U.S. women's groups were conspicuously silent during the Zoe Baird controversy, when Baird, the nominee for attorney general, was found to have employed two undocumented migrant workers as a babysitter and gardener. Shortly after the Baird scandal, proposals for a "homecare worker" or "nanny" visa, modelled after the Canadian

Live-in Caregiver program, were discussed at the Immigration Reform Commission hearings. Only a few individuals from NOW attended the hearings, but they were not representing NOW.

Even among grassroots organizations fighting for justice for migrant women workers, it may prove difficult to develop a unified position or strategy. The effectiveness and viability of one strategy, imposing a ban on recruitment of Filipinas for migrant work, has been debated since such a ban was imposed by the Aquino administration in 1988. A coalition of 22 migrant worker groups in Hong Kong formed to press the Aquino government to repeal the ban, arguing that it hindered Filipinas' ability to secure employment, actually debilitating rather than protecting them.[38]

Almost ten years later, debate over the efficacy of the ban continues. Felicita Villasin, executive director of INTERCEDE and executive board member of the National Action Committee on the Status of Women (NAC) in Canada, says that a ban on migrant workers will only drive women to face greater danger and abuses as illegal migrants. Instead, she calls for structural changes in the Philippine economy that will make migration a choice and not a necessity. At least on this last point, Villasin asserts, there seems to be consensus among the women's groups involved in Filipina migrant worker struggles.

Asian/Pacific Islander and other women of color feminists in the First World would do well to take the lead from groups like INTERCEDE and many of our Third World sisters who have been mobilizing around the issues of SAPs and the traffic in women for years now. At the NGO Forum, many First World women remarked that they were the least well-informed or organized on global economic issues. Many First World feminists of color came home from the Forum resolved to undertake or redouble efforts to understand and expose the links between economic restructuring in the First World, SAPs in the Third World, and the global trade in women.

In Canada, NAC and the Canadian Labour Congress co-sponsored a month-long, nationwide Women's March Against Poverty in May and June of 1996. The march culminated in a rally at the nation's capital to bring to Parliament demands for measures to redress women's poverty in Canada and globally. Its call to action included the need to strengthen employment conditions and opportunities for women, to reinforce social services, and to adopt "as a foreign policy objective" the elimination of women's poverty.[39]

In the United States, Miriam Ching Louie and Linda Burnham of the Women of Color Resource Center returned from the NGO Forum committed to designing a popular education project, Women's Education in the Global Economy (WEdGE). The project includes a curriculum and set of trainings focused on a broad range of global economic issues and trends affecting women: the global assemblyline; SAPs; women's unpaid, contingent, and informal work; welfare; environmental justice; women's human rights, sex trafficking, and migration; and organizing around these issues.[40]

SAPs and other economic restructuring policies affect Third World women in similar ways the world over, making survival more precarious, making women's unpaid labor burdens heavier, and exacerbating women's exploitation as low-wage workers both at home and abroad. First World variations of structural adjustment bring consequences that are less well-known but no less insidious. Walden Bello describes the effects of "welfare reform" as the domestic version of SAPs in the United States: In 1992, by the end of the Republicans' assault on social welfare programs, the living standards of many Americans had deteriorated to Third World levels. Approximately 20 million U.S. residents lived in hunger, and infant mortality rates among African Americans reached rates higher than those of countries such as Jamaica, Trinidad, and Cuba.[41]

Bello says that the original intentions of SAPs were: first, to resubordinate the Third World—particularly those nations threatening to become developed—by crippling the authority of their governments and, second, to repress labor globally in order to free corporate capital from any hindrances to maximum profits. Clearly SAPs in the Philippines have been an uncontested success by these measures. The Philippine government has been unable to protect its own female citizens abroad and apparently has given up any intention of doing so. The trade in women from the Philippines has proven immensely profitable to the Philippine government and entrepreneurs, and highly "economical" to the governments that recruit them and the elites who employ them. Yet the struggles and triumphs of women like Balagaban and Tristan, and groups such as Kalayaan, INTERCEDE,

Gabriela, and SEIU stand as testament to the ability of women to resist this global assault on Third World women workers.

Notes

This article is extracted from a chapter in my forthcoming book, *Gatekeeping and Housekeeping*. I would like to thank Luisa Blue, Josie Camacho, Mayee Crispin, Ninotchka Rosca, Carole Salmon, and Felicita Villasin for sharing their great insights, expertise, and time in interviews. I am also indebted to Miriam Ching Louie and Linda Burnham for bravely leading the Women of Color Resource Center delegation to Huairou, and for their pioneering work on Women's Education in the Global Economy. I am grateful to Nathaniel Silva for his insights and comments in developing this piece.

1. Sparr, Pamela. *Mortgaging Women's Lives: Feminist Critiques of Structural Adjustment*. London: Zed Books, 1994.

2. Chang, Grace. "Disposable Nannies: Women's Work and the Politics of Latina Immigration." *Radical America* 26. 2 (October 1996): 5-20.

3. Testimony of Fatima. Workshop on the impact of SAPs, NGO Forum, September 2, 1995.

4. Testimony of Eileen Fernandez. Workshop on the impact of SAPs, NGO forum, September 2, 1995.

5. Gabriela Workshop, NGO forum, September 3, 1995.

6. The "official" figures corroborate these first-hand testimonies of women in countries under structural adjustment: Between 1969 and 1985, per capita food production declined in 51 out of 94 developing countries. Simultaneously, access to food has been severely limited by increased food prices with the devaluation of local currencies under SAPs. Expenditures on education in all poor developing countries except India and China declined from 21 percent of national budgets in 1972 to 9 percent in 1988. Healthcare expenditures were also reduced from 5.5 percent to 2.8 percent of national budgets during this period. See UNICEF report cited by Peter Lurie, Percy Hintzen, and Robert A. Lowe, "Socioeconomic Obstacles to HIV Prevention and Treatment in Developing Countries: The Roles of the International Monetary Fund and the World Bank." *AIDS* 9(6): 542-543.

7. Testimony of Merceditas Cruz. Workshop on Migration and the Globalizing Economy, NGO forum, September 6, 1995.

8. Testimony of Carmen. Organization of Free & United Women under Gabriela, NGO forum.

9. Workshop on the Impacts of SAPs, NGO forum, September 2, 1995.

10. Testimony of representative from International Organization of Prostitutes. Gabriela Workshop, NGO Forum, September 3, 1995.

11. Plenary on Globalization, NGO Forum, September 3, 1995.

12. This number does not include women who are trafficked or illegally recruited, those who migrate for marriage, students, or tourists who eventually become undocumented workers. Compiled by Kanlungan Center Foundation from Philippine Overseas Employment Administration (POEA) and Department of Labor and Employment (DOLE) statistics.

13. Vincent, Isabel. "Canada Beckons Cream of Nannies: Much-sought Filipinas Prefer Work Conditions." *The Globe and Mail.* 20 January 1996: A1, A6. Other authors address more extensively trafficking in women for the sex work, entertainment, and mail-order bride industries. See Rosca, Ninotchka. "The Philippines' Shameful Export." *The Nation.* 17 April 1995: 523-525; Kim, Elaine. "Sex Tourism in Asia: A Reflection of Political and Economic Equality." *Critical Perspectives of Third World America* 2.1 (Fall 1984): 215-231; *Sisters and Daughters Betrayed: The Trafficking of Women and Girls and the Fight to End It.* Video. Prod. Chela Blitt. Global Fund for Women.

14. "Flor Contemplacion: Victim of Mismanaged Economy." Editorial. *PAID! (People Against Immoral Debt).* Newsletter of Freedom from Debt Coalition, April 1995: 7.

15. Kanlungan Center Foundation, Inc. fact sheet prepared for the 1995 UN Conference on Women.

16. Freedom from Debt Coalition, based on DOLE figures.

17. *Brown Women, Blonde Babies.* Film. Prod. Marie Boti. Multimonde Productions.

18. Rosca, Ninotchka. Personal interview. 29 April 1996.

19. Kilborn, Peter T. "Union Gets the Lowly to Sign Up: Home Care Aides Are Fresh Target." *New York Times.* 21 November 1995.

20. Ibid.

21. Camacho, Josie. Personal interview. 18 April 1996.

22. Kilborn. op cit.

23. Ms. Greenhill of the Canadian Consulate in Los Angeles, CA. Personal interview. December 1993; Vincent A1.

24. Vincent A6.

25. *A Framework on Women and Migration.* Kanlungan Center Foundation, prepared for the NGO Forum of 1995.

26. Rosca, Ninotchka. Personal interview. 29 April 1996.

27. Freedom from Debt Coalition, statement prepared for NGO Forum, 1995.

28. *Kapihan Sa Kanlungan: A Quarterly Digest of Migration News*, newsletter produced by Kanlungan Center Foundation. April-June 1995; Rosca, Ninotchka. Personal interview. 29 April 1996; Vincent A6.

29. Testimony, Workshop on Violence and Migration, NGO Forum, 1995.

30. Ibid.

31. Enloe, Cynthia. *Bananas, Beaches and Bases: Making Feminist Sense of International Politics*. Berkeley: University of California Press, 1989. 190.

32. Kilborn, op cit.

33. "Delayed Payment Case for Home Care Workers Settled with State for $4 Million." SEIU press release. May 30, 1995.

34. Press conference. National Press Club in Manila, Philippines, 23 March 1994; "Gabriela Accuses Philippine Government of Pimping." *Gabriela International Update*. August 1995.

35. Rosca, Ninotchka. Personal interview. 29 April 1996.

36. Ibid.

37. Enloe 194.

38. Enloe 188. Slowly, the Aquino government exempted one government after another from its requirements, and by 1989, 22 countries enjoyed exemption from the ban.

39. NAC bulletins on the March.

40. For information, contact: Women of Color Resource Center, 2288 Fulton Street, Suite 103, Berkeley, CA 94704.

41. Bello, Walden, Shea Cunningham, and Bill Rau, *Dark Victory: The United States, Structural Adjustment and Global Poverty*. London: Pluto Press and Food First and Transnational Institute, 1994.

Lost in Translation

Western Feminism and Asian Women

By Delia D. Aguilar

Not too long after the inception of second-wave feminism, U.S. women of color and Third World women called attention to and repeatedly challenged exclusionary tendencies in feminist theory and practice. Now understood as the problem of universalization or essentialism, this ahistorical approach examines white, middle-class women's lives through the singular prism of gender and extends its findings to all womankind. It should be observed, however, that, racist as its effects undoubtedly were, essentialism had currency at a time when "progressive politics" meant, above all else, having a vision of an alternative society. Thus, women's subordination was contextualized in social formations whose relations of production were made explicit—capitalist, socialist, welfare state, feudal, etc.—and changes in gender relations situated within larger transformational agendas.

With the neoconservatism of the Reagan/Bush era, followed by the collapse of the Soviet Union and the establishment of a globalized order premised on capitalist triumphalism, progressives began to lose ground and vision. No longer certain about the tenability of socialist alternatives, not a few have turned to fashionable postmodern conceptualizations that reject perspectives striving to grasp the nature of society in its wholeness or totality. It is in this setting that essentialism has acquired something of the status of a bogey to be shooed away upon detection.

Displacing universalization is the postmodernist notion of "difference," where the formerly invisible "other" emerges and now speaks, presumably with a unified voice—a problematic formulation in that the Western self is thought to have become fragmentary and dislocated.[1] Now, this is not to diminish the importance of the space within which specificities of the lives and identities of Asian American and other women of color are today accorded recognition. Indeed, with "difference feminism," women of color are now able to speak as they had not before. Bell hooks, for example, views the process of coming to voice as an act of resistance and a metaphor for self-transformation.[2]

Perhaps here the key word is "self-transformation," for it must be noted that postmodern celebrations of difference and coming to voice transpire in the absence of an encompassing frame capable of revealing relations of power, particularly those rooted in the political economy.[3] Consequently change, if it occurs at all, is discursive, cultural, and individual. With materially grounded politics effectively abolished, the "other" is either romanticized or seen as very different from the self, so as to preclude any possibility of genuine equality or even dialogue.

Identity or difference feminism, then, has the paradoxical effect of ostensibly recognizing the "other" at the same time that it conceals the material conditions underpinning that marginality. Refusing to name the real world of capital/labor relations in a globalized economy, much less to analyze it, what can the effect of such a feminist politics be on Asian American women? Is it enough that we are now seen in our tremendous diversity so that we can celebrate equally those among us who are in possession of property and those who are not? What sorts of struggles are made possible by this kind of politics, detached as it is from material reality? Who benefits? Who loses?

Teaching Feminism to Asian/Pacific Women

With this feminist politics in mind, let me now turn to my experience teaching feminism to a group of Asian/Pacific women in Manila, Philippines, in 1992. Titled "Intercultural Course on Women and Society," this intensive program was offered by the Institute of Women's Studies in St. Scholastica's College. Seventeen women attended; they represented 13 countries, two of which fall outside the Asian/Pacific region. One woman came from Zambia, and two from the United States. Each year the Institute designates a few slots for women from the "First World" who must pay their own way. The rest of the women are on full scholarships, including travel and living expenses. While a requirement for admission calls for work experience with women, only two students (the ones from the United States) had taken classes in women's studies.

The objectives of the program can best be described as practical in thrust, with the enhancement of existing social movements as a major goal. Learning was not to be conducted solely for learning's sake. The women themselves, at the outset, declared their status as community workers in search of knowledge, skills, and strategies that they could utilize upon return to their home countries. By providing a place where women could live and study together, the Institute sought to develop a critical understanding of women's condition and to forge a sense of solidarity among Asian/Pacific women, with the hope of "exploring cooperative actions" in the context of "working toward a more just and egalitarian society."

My assignment was to introduce the women to "Feminist Analyses of the Woman Question" as these applied to the Asian/Pacific region. Before my section of the course, the group had shared their life stories and presented country reports documenting the position of women as encoded by custom and governmental policies. We had also gone on the first part of a series of "exposure tours," which brought into focus the jarring disjointedness and fragmentation that have become defining characteristics of urban life in developing societies.

These day trips within Manila and its vicinity included visits to an opulent mega-mall flaunting superfluous consumer items (an added attraction featured an exhibit on "the world's 'firsts,'" highlighted by a lecture from U.S. astronaut Eugene Ciernan, who taught his Filipino listeners that the history of U.S. space exploration is "your history"); a slum dweller women's association; San Agustin church, an imposing 16th-century cathedral; garment factories producing winter coats for export; a ballpoint pen factory shut down by striking women workers who had pitched makeshift shelters outside. The glaring disparities of class everywhere on display as we took in the sights were surely familiar scenes to these Asian/Pacific women. Something in the manner in which juxtaposed symbols of wealth and poverty converged as if solely for our perusal gave us pause, and, throughout, served as a backdrop against which to interrogate women's lives. By the time I began my session, the ice had been broken and the groundwork laid for exploring the terrain of feminist thinking.

Still, an appreciation of feminism requires, at the very least, the naming of women's oppression. Even though the UN-declared Decade for Women opened people's eyes to the subordination of women worldwide, "feminism" remains taboo for many in developing countries. Seeing consciousness-raising as my first task, I asked the group to bring up examples showing the ways in which women's experience differed from men's in the women's respective societies. The response was immediate and animated, and soon the discussion centered on traditional practices that threaten women's existence or constrain their behavior. The list was lengthy: dowry deaths, the taking of temple prostitutes, requiring proof of virginity on one's wedding night, female infanticide, taking multiple wives, women eating only after everyone else has been fed, submission to the husband's authority as "chief spirit of the household" (*Aing U Nut* in Burma), and so on and so forth. We also discovered in the process of assembling this cross-cultural inventory that "under the *saya*" (skirt), a taunt thrown at "henpecked" husbands, was a sexist phrase of common currency not only in the Philippines but also among Indians, Pakistanis, and Sri Lankans.

Prepared to meet some resistance, I was relieved not to encounter any. What I found most unusual was the enthusiasm, the vigorous flow of energy that generated this litany of misogynistic rituals and conventions. But even more intriguing was the relatively undisturbed state of mind maintained by the group as a whole. In my introductory women's studies courses in the United States, female students who first begin to glimpse the extent of women's oppression typically react with open rage. If not rage, one usually senses in the newly awakened a palpable tension, an impatience to extricate themselves from what all too suddenly has come to be a burdensome situation.

In contrast, here the response was calm, thoughtful, deliberate. Yasmin, a well-heeled Sri Lankan school principal, appropriately recognized her own victimization as being less pronounced than that of her subordinates: "What do I do with my maid? Should I raise her salary? Maybe I am oppressing teachers in my school, too." A few days after this discussion, Minah from Indonesia confided that she had written her parents telling them how women's consignment to the chores of cooking, washing, cleaning, and childcare constitutes oppression. Pratima, a Nepali lawyer, reported that she had done the same. Ma Paw from Myanmar, who regularly got phone calls from her boyfriend stationed on a traveling commercial vessel, joked that she was not going to get married anymore. If I must sum up the overall sentiment of the group, however, I would say that it was best captured by Barbara's solemn matter-of-factness as she spoke to me across the lunch table: "I've been married 24 years. Now I know that I'm oppressed, and that women in my country are oppressed. In our organization [in Zambia] we believe we must change ourselves first and then change others. So I must change my relationship with my husband. But what am I to do? How do I do this without divorcing?" Then she added, "Battering is something we all say we don't want. But how about housework?"

Individualism vs. Community

Without a doubt, the experiences and age range (21 to 46) of these women separate them from the average U.S. college student I teach in my women's studies classes. These factors alone can account for the difference in their responses. But another factor is the rootedness felt quite deeply by these Asian/Pacific women, their profound embeddedness in an intricate network comprised of family, clan, friends, workmates, acquaintances, and others in the community. Their identities, though inevitably influenced by the market (e.g., as workers and consumers), are not primarily defined by it. Subsequently, the discovery or "naming" of female oppression did not trigger the individualist impulse to escape that it often does among women in industrialized nations.

An example should serve to clarify my point. Bidya from Nepal, 25 and single, began to take a new look at arranged marriages as a result of our ongoing dialogue. Yet she continued to insist that, despite the freedom to choose allowed by her parents (she was, after all, a lawyer practicing in the city), she preferred not to take this route. "I don't have my parents' wisdom and judgment and wouldn't know on what basis to select," she explained. Afterward, she made quite clear her belief that families of origin are a solid anchor, implying that marriage is no more than a way of extending kinship connections. I did not get the impression that marriage might signal, as it could for some young people in the United States, a breaking away into adulthood and independence. "A husband is someone who is new to you, but you've known your family all your life," she declared, in a tone hinting that there was something strange in having to distinguish between an untested relationship and an established institution whose permanence ought to be taken for granted. As if foreseeing that her inexperience could lead to the wrong choice, she expressed anxiety over requesting her family's assistance should her marriage not work out: "I would really feel bad about that."

When I tell U.S. audiences about Bidya, what they almost invariably communicate back to me precisely proves my point. They consider her powerless—power being equated with the individual's ability to take action and choose freely, a market-impelled notion. For them, the possibility that arranged marriage may be beneficial to a kin system, the smooth functioning of which in turn ensures its members' survival and well-being, is an alien thought. (This is not to romanticize a custom that automatically cancels romance, or to propose cultural relativism.)

Given that individualism is a core Western value that neither class nor race appears amply capable of mitigating, it was hardly surprising that Ann, my U.S. student who enrolled in the course, found the dissonance in her new store of information unsettling. She told me how angry she was starting to feel about the distortion that U.S. policies, enacted through international monetary bodies, have foisted on the economies of developing countries. She was enraged to see with her own eyes the resulting havoc in people's lives. On the other hand, she also felt that her sympathy was somehow misplaced. In the face of her Asian/Pacific colleagues' seeming resignation to their fates, she "just could not imagine the lives of these women."

But, chances are, these women's lives were not as wretched as Ann imagined. They knew that although they were surely women, they were simultaneously many other things as well. Gender for them was not an autonomous category unaffected by other social relations, a point rather belabored in feminist writing in the United States and Britain. (Deconstructing the category "women," Denise Riley asks: "what does it mean to insist that 'women' are only sometimes 'women'?"[4])

Like Asian American feminists and other women of color in the United States and Britain, it did not seem to take much for these women to be conscious of their multiple, shifting, fluctuating identities, to use postmodernist jargon. For what else would have led to Yasmin's perceptive comments, her concern about her subordinates? By considering her maid and teaching staff instead of herself, she demonstrated an instinctive understanding of class as a shaping influence of no lesser consequence than gender. (This constituted a radical switch from the gist of her country report, in which she claimed gender parity for Sri Lankan women on the basis of laws granting them equal economic rights.) Moreover, being rooted in a community means feeling responsible, in your diverse roles and capacities, for those around you. Replying to her own question about what is to be done, Barbara later stated that altering her marriage to any significant degree was no longer possible, but she assured us all that she would definitely use her newfound knowledge about gender inequality to educate her children and the families and couples she counsels in her job.

Anti-Western Sentiments

Ironically, the powerlessness that U.S. audiences typically attribute to these women's equanimity, which supposedly derives from the absence of a viable alternative, is belied by what I saw as a keen awareness on my students' part of the existence of other worlds and other cultures. One can rarely say the same for many in the United States, who, presuming themselves to be situated in the hub of the universe, harbor little curiosity about anything outside. This is not to say that this group's ideas about other cultures were always accurate, but their interest was present and strong.

Let me explain what I mean. At breakfast one morning, Yasmin showed me an essay commending the protection afforded to women by Islamic religion. I assumed the author to be someone else, but on subsequent inquiry found out that she herself had written it "many years ago" as an address to teachers. The piece did not simply exhort women to be faithful to their domestic duties because doing so was valuable in itself, or because female piety would guarantee the stability of family life and, by extension, the society at large. Instead, it seized upon the social disruption plaguing the United States—worded in the well-worn conservative assertion that the untrammelled freedom of Western women has led to family breakdown which, in turn, is causing juvenile crime, drug addiction, wanton violence, and a pervasive moral collapse—and used that as a warning to keep Sri Lankan women in place.

At this point in the course I was convinced that Yasmin had taken hold of my feminist agenda and was mulling it over very carefully in her mind. So while there were two major points in her article, one anti-feminist and the other pro-Islam, it really was not feminism that she was against, nor was she necessarily urging conversion to Islam. Before long I began to realize that what Yasmin and others along with her had undertaken to staunchly defend was the matter of cultural pride, which, though now punctured by their cognizance of misogyny, remained over and above all a weapon to fight off a more feared specter—moral decadence and degeneration as they saw these manifested in the technologically advanced West.

This message was as explicit as it could be in the speech Yasmin wrote. Echoes of that sentiment resonated with others in the group, and, intoned again and again in various ways, this point of view simply could not be missed or misinterpreted. For example, I was shortly to learn from Gail (the other U.S. student) that she and Ann had received a tepid welcome from the start, in spite of the fact that everyone knew that the two of them had not received funding. As Gail was recounting events surrounding her arrival, I recalled a prior exchange during the country reports when her use of the terms "First World" and "Third World" immediately drew sharp criticism from a number of women who questioned the basis for the implied ranking. Moreover, the women's impression of the Philippines as not only heavily "Westernized" but worse, suffering from a "lack of their own culture" (observations that are hard to contest), operated to aggravate simmering antagonisms between those from the North and from the South. Giving voice to these conflicts, as the more outspoken women began to do, was, in my opinion, a perfectly healthy sign.

When Vibha of Pakistan announced, "We are proud of our own culture; we do not look up to America as our model," she unmistakably meant it for Filipino ears. I was glad to hear her say this, because I felt that it was important for my compatriots in the class to hear directly from other Asians how we, as Filipinos, are viewed. I felt that such comments would compel constant alertness to the often confounding ramifications in a neocolonial formation like the Philippines, where feminist issues intersect with questions of national sovereignty at every single juncture. Interestingly enough, no one impugned the vibrancy of feminism in the Philippines as a symptom of its acquiescence to Western values. Perhaps it was inevitable, after I encouraged this drift—by asking for examples of what someone had referred to as "Western behavior" in Filipinos—that Luzviminda, a Filipina organizer of domestic workers in Hong Kong, was described to her face as a "dominating" person who "talks too much," conduct in women that is purportedly antithetical to Asian values. It was mentioned privately to me afterwards that Luzviminda's keeping company with the two U.S. women was interpreted as a sign that she looked up to them and had taken them for role models, their closeness in age having been discounted altogether as another explanation. Also brought in for questioning was the advice that Señora Carmen, director and founder of the Institute, told us she had dispensed to a woman who was an object of repeated battering. "We'd never advise a wife to leave her husband," Vibha volunteered, risking accuracy or veracity to insinuate that this was somehow out of tune with Asian folkways. Ann was perceived as "acting just like her country" when one Saturday morning she got out of bed and, still groggy, grouchily asked the three women chatting in the room across the hall to quiet down or move so she could resume her sleep. And at a session one afternoon, Gail and Ann found themselves abandoned in their request for a schedule change, a turnabout from the previous night, when everyone had supported their proposal.

Is Sisterhood Global?

This development effectively laid to rest a prior worry of mine. All indications up until then had led me to believe that my efforts at consciousness-raising around inequalities of gender had produced the reductive notion that, since women share a common oppression, all women are sisters. The fact is, there was a push for just this stand among some Filipina facilitators—a predisposition bound up, I suspect, with the exhilaration infusing a women's movement in its initial stages. Extolling universal sisterhood on the grounds that all women, regardless of class, race, or other structuring relations, are potential victims of male violence, a Filipina feminist at one point spiritedly asserted that "a victory for women anywhere is a victory for us." I queried the statement by asking everyone to consider who the women are who are inclined to celebrate which women's victories. How many British (or U.S., French, etc.) women have celebrated as their own triumph the successes won by Philippine slum dweller women, assuming Western women even hear about such campaigns? Although I thought that the criticism I was making was clear, I failed to get my point across. To my chagrin, moreover, I noted that, in a collective project to create murals depicting the women's vision of a better society, practically all the drawings iterated the same essentializing motif of global sisterhood.

To place this assumption of sisterhood in perspective, I sought to draw out women's similarities and differences by situating us Asian/Pacific women squarely within the international economic order. I summed up our common experiences as elaborated in the country reports each participant had delivered early on: massive rural to urban migration, ever-increasing poverty and homelessness, militarization, cash-crop production and production of consumer goods for export, dominance of multinationals, external debt, structural adjustment dictated by international lending agencies such as the International Monetary Fund and World Bank. Within this framework, we discussed how large numbers of women migrate overseas as domestics or, in the absence of an opportunity to leave, stay home to do backbreaking labor or work in the informal sector; how women's "nimble fingers" and "docility" ("genetic" credentials authenticated by a garment factory president we interviewed, who also cited women's ability to sit patiently) qualify them for low-paid employment on the assembly line; how women succumb to being mail-order brides or to working in the "entertainment industry" when limited options for a living wage are available. In short, it became sufficiently manifest that there was no way we could speak of Asian/Pacific women without at the same time implicating unequal power relations between the North and the South.

Having explored the above issues, I expected the women to now apprehend commonalities and differences in another light. This they did, as the anti-Western posture described earlier attests. Not only had they withdrawn subscription to a universal sisterhood with "women everywhere," but they also pushed ahead of me. When they articulated "difference," the tone was not celebratory, and not a soul proclaimed the wonders of diversity.

Because our meetings averaged six-and-a-half hours every day, I was constantly in search of some activity or exercise to vary the pace of our sessions. I decided to start one morning with a narration of how some women in a poor neighborhood in Lima, Peru, organized around wife abuse. All the women had purchased whistles that they agreed to blow whenever a beating occurred, a strategy meant to embarrass or shame the perpetrator, and ultimately to bring him in line. I admired the Peruvian women's ingenuity and assumed that everyone hearing the account would, too. Reinforced by a Filipina friend who informed me that village women in a southern Philippine province had devised a scheme like it, substituting the clanging of pots and pans for whistles, I was positive that the story would go over well. I was wrong. Leilani from Papua New Guinea, strong and unafraid to speak, just about roared: "No! In my country that won't work! If women did that, the man would gather his relatives and they would all go and beat up the whistleblowers!" Taken aback, I asked why. With a little prodding from me, others eventually spoke up to reject the strategy, reasoning that it could only backfire. "Why, that is like broadcasting the woman's failings as a wife to the entire neighborhood!"

My mistake was to carelessly lump together in my mind, under the unspoken rubric "Third World," Peruvian women of one specific neighborhood with the group of "Asian/Pacific women" in my midst. By rejecting my proposal, Leilani and the rest forced my recognition of the group as separate and identifiable from one community of Peruvian women. In addition, their objection compelled me to reckon with the tremendous diversity within the group itself—disparities along the lines of race, nationality/ethnicity, class, caste, and religion, among other things, that had been concealed by the convenient geographic label "Asian/Pacific."

And what about within their own societies? It was evident that they were not oblivious to diversity there, either. For example, after having presented feminist theories offering explanations of women's subordination (liberal, radical, Marxist/feminist), I asked the group which paradigms would prove most applicable or relevant in their own countries. Rather than speaking for "women back home" as a unified entity, or on their own behalf as individuals (which no one did), many of the participants gauged the theories' worth in terms of the sector addressed, thus: for middle-class and rich women in the city, liberal feminism; for the poor in the city and agricultural areas, Marxist/feminism, and so on. This sensitivity to women's diversity was likewise confirmed in the course evaluation, when several class members noted their appreciation of the reminder I issued to constantly refer back to women's lives in their own societies; this they found to be a good means to help clarify the explanatory potential of these feminist theories, and also to test their own understanding. I should have also asked, along with the reminder, "which women?"

What was most instructive for me in this experience that might also be useful for Asian Americans? Above all, it was heartening to see that women could have their eyes wide open to the cleavages separating women and still remain committed to the search for a common ground for feminist solidarity. Here awareness of multiple standpoints did not appear to weaken presumptions of mutual agreement; in effect, solidarity (indeed, solidarity as "Third World" people demarcated by the metropolis/periphery divide) as both a guiding principle and a goal was assumed, differences notwithstanding. It must be remarked that the program itself was designed so that this aim remained in sight throughout. To illustrate, the final assignment in the last module required every participant to draw up a concrete plan of action, which each woman then shared with the rest, for the express purpose of exploring the possibility of collaborative ventures in the region. The participants, furthermore, had target populations with whom they were already involved—unemployed youth, illiterate women, domestic helpers, church organizations, to mention a few—and could envision the outcomes they were seeking.

The women's locatedness, a kind of surefootedness, if you will, secured them—plural, heterogeneous identities and all—to the unembellished realities of their "Third World" contexts. This is why the decision to dump hoary practices such as arranged marriage, however oppressive, can be neither reached nor carried out in any facile fashion. I think it is exactly their location in the "Third World" that makes people like this group of Asian/Pacific women painfully aware of social conditions, whatever their station in life might be. I wish to emphasize this factor—the beneficent burden of being unable to deny or ignore social reality—because I believe that it is only in contraposition to prevailing material, social, and political realities that social change can even begin to be imagined. By social change I include those everyday practices that affect women's lives and are at the same time indissociable from policies enacted on an international level.

Given that, neither essentialism nor difference feminism holds much utility for the struggles of Asian/Pacific women or, for that matter, for Asian American feminists. Both approaches are ahistorical. The latter, by focusing mainly on the cultural, has given up the goal of redistributive justice in favor of mere recognition.[5] Those of us on the margins cannot allow ourselves to be mesmerized by calls proclaiming the glories of difference when the material conditions shaping our lives are ignored or glossed over.

As the daily struggles of Asian/Pacific women testify, the basic contours of the world order have not undergone a transfiguration so profound during this so-called postmodern era that its systemic and hierarchical nature completely defies apprehension. My Asian/Pacific sisters consistently urged that relations of dominance and exploitation attendant on the world economic order be elucidated in order for emancipatory transformation to be at all conceivable. Unfortunately, the pragmatic skepticism of feminists who herald difference often plays right into the hands of international monetary agencies and transnational corporations who themselves in their daily operations cannot do without deploying a global, indeed totalizing, view of human affairs on a planetary scale.

Notes

1. Larrain, J. "Identity, the Other and Postmodernism." *Post-Ality: Marxism and Postmodernism.* Eds. M. Zavarsadeh, et al. Washington, DC: Maisonneuve Press, 1995. 271, 189.

2. hooks, bell. *Talking Back: Thinking Feminist, Thinking Black.* Boston: South End Press, 1989.

3. Ebert, T.L. *Ludic Feminism and After: Postmodernism, Desire, and Labor in Late Capitalism.* Ann Arbor, MI: University of Michigan Press, 1996; Soper, K. "Postmodernism and its Discontents." *Feminist Review* (1991): 39, 97-108; Segal, L. "Whose Left? Socialism, Feminism and the Future." *New Left Review* 185 (1991): 81-91.

4. Riley, D. *Am I That Name?* Minneapolis, MN: University of Minnesota Press, 1988.

5. Fraser, N. "From Redistribution to Recognition? Dilemmas of Justice in a 'Post-Socialist' Age." *New Left Review* (1995): 68-93.

IV. Awakening to Power

Leslie Mah, Selena Whang, and Margarita Alcantara
Photograph by Dominik Huber

Revolution's from the Heart

The Making of an Asian American Woman Activist, Yuri Kochiyama

By Diane C. Fujino

Yuri Kochiyama is one of the few Asian women activists with national stature. She has been the subject of hundreds of articles and interviews, most notably for her longtime involvement with radical international liberation movements and her alliance with Black liberation leader Malcolm X. Today, at 76 years of age, Yuri is an extremely popular speaker and continues her involvement in radical politics. She has inspired countless young Asian American women and others to enter activist politics.

I first met Yuri when I asked if I could interview her for my research on Asian American women's grassroots activism.[1] She graciously agreed, and I flew out to Harlem. I had planned to meet some comrades at her home and then go out to eat. But to my surprise, Yuri had already prepared a delicious meal for us. That night she placed keys to her home in my hands.

I found out later that what I considered extraordinary hospitality is standard practice for Yuri. During the height of the civil rights and anti-war movements of the 1960s and 1970s, activists both unknown and widely known, such as Malcolm X, Kwame Ture (a.k.a. Stokely Carmichael), and H. Rap Brown, would visit Yuri and her husband Bill (who passed away in 1993). One friend remembers, "People were everywhere, eating, talking, laughing, spilling out into the hallway [outside their apartment]. People were even in the bathroom. You couldn't close the front door because there were so many people inside."[2] Organizations such as the Black Panthers, Student Non-violent Coordinating Committee, Congress of Racial Equality (CORE), and

Revolutionary Action Movement met in the Kochiyamas' home.[3] Guests would stay for weeks or months at a time in the Kochiyamas' four-bedroom apartment, already filled with their family of eight. Their home was "grand central station" on weekends, and it continues to be to this day.

Political Awakenings

Born Mary Yuri Nakahara in 1921 in San Pedro, California, Yuri led a self-described "ordinary" childhood that ended in 1941.[4] On December 7, at 11 a.m., as bombs were dropping on Pearl Harbor, three FBI agents abducted Yuri's father, Seichi Nakahara, who had recently been discharged from the hospital. The family later discovered that he was in a federal penitentiary on Terminal Island because the U.S. government falsely suspected Japanese fishermen of spying for Japan.[5] During her father's imprisonment, his health deteriorated; when he was close to death, he was allowed to return home. The next day, January 21, 1942, he died, at age 60. Yuri recalls:

> As soon as the FBI heard the report of his death, we got a phone call from them and were told that anyone who came to the funeral service would be under surveillance. The Japanese people came in from Los Angeles, twenty miles away, despite a five-mile travel ban. And some of the fishing folks who were still left in Terminal Island and the farmers from the San Pedro hills came, too. Even our Caucasian neighbors attended. And sure enough, the FBI was right there in front of the funeral parlor.[6]

In 1942, the rest of the Nakahara family was sent to the Santa Anita "assembly center" and then to a concentration camp in Jerome, Arkansas. From camp, Yuri began writing hundreds of letters to nisei GIs and, along with other young nisei women, formed a USO for the nisei GIs who were discriminated against at the regular USO.[7]

It was at this USO that she met her future husband, Bill Kochiyama, a New Yorker in the racially segregated, all-nisei 442nd Regimental Combat Unit. After the war, they were married in New York and had six children: Billy, Audee, Aichi, Eddie, Jimmy, and Tommy.[8]

During the 1950s, Yuri's political consciousness continued to grow. The Kochiyamas' Friday and Saturday night open houses started out as social gatherings but turned into educational events. They invited people who were scheduled to speak at local universities, held cultural events, and also provided services to help people find jobs, housing, healthcare, and schools. It was during this time that Yuri visited and supported the Hiroshima Maidens, 25 female atomic-bomb survivors who came to the United States for plastic surgery. Yuri also briefly met Daisy Bates, the National Association for the Advancement of Colored People (NAACP) leader who had worked with the famous Little Rock 9 school desegregation case. "People were fighting for things that we had taken for granted," Yuri says. "I started to realize that I needed to fight for my civil rights, too."[9]

Becoming a Revolutionary Nationalist: Turning Action into Liberation

In 1963, three years after moving to Harlem, the Kochiyamas joined the Harlem Parents Committee to work on local community issues. Yuri, Bill, and their three oldest children attended the Harlem Freedom School to learn the basics of African American history. The Harlem Parents Committee and other organizations decided to close down every public school until the Board of Education reformed educational practices to better serve Black children. Yuri was up by five or six every morning to picket the schools. The committee also organized its children, including the Kochiyamas' two youngest, into a sit-down strike in the street to demand more traffic signs in the neighborhood. That summer, Yuri and her six children, ages four to sixteen, joined picket lines at the Downstate Medical Center in Brooklyn organized by CORE to demand construction jobs for Black and Puerto Rican workers. Yuri and her oldest son, Billy, were among more than 600 arrested during the demonstrations.[10]

Yuri met Malcolm X on October 16, 1963, when he went to the Brooklyn court where the 600 arrestees were being arraigned. Encouraged by a friend, Yuri hesitantly approached this famous figure, concerned that he would not want to speak to anyone who was not Black. She asked if she could shake his hand. He sternly asked why, and she replied, "To congratulate you for giving direction to your people." She then added that she did not agree with his strong stance against integration. Malcolm invited her to his office to discuss this.

Yuri began attending weekly sessions of the Organization of Afro-American Unity that Malcolm X had founded. After a couple of months, Malcolm X invited Yuri to attend the Malcolm X Liberation

School. Yuri attended each Saturday morning, learning about revolutionary nationalism, Black liberation, and liberation struggles in Africa from the head teacher, James Campbell, and other instructors. At a time when many were advocating civil rights and integration, Malcolm X and his supporters introduced Yuri to a radical liberation perspective. She says:

> [Malcolm X] opened my mind to see that the Black struggle...was about human rights, self-determination, sovereignty, and Black nationhood. And only through this path would Black people move toward real freedom.[11]

Yuri adds, "I came to see how correct Malcolm was—that integration would only hinder the struggle for freedom."

In 1964, the Hiroshima Nagasaki World Peace Mission visited Harlem. Three Japanese journalists who were *hibakusha* (atomic-bomb survivors) were eager to meet Malcolm X; Yuri arranged a meeting at her home. Malcolm X spoke of the connections between the struggles of the Japanese and Blacks in America: "You may have scars from the bombing. We were also bombed. The bomb they dropped on us was racism." He also spoke about his admiration for Mao Tse-tung for challenging government corruption, feudalism, and European encroachment into China. He warned about U.S. intrusion into Vietnam.

Malcolm X sent the Kochiyamas 11 postcards from his travels throughout the world, which Yuri keeps in a photo album with other memorabilia. Inspired by Malcolm X's example, Yuri became a Sunni Muslim for five years during the 1970s. She also became close to Malcolm's daughter, Attallah, who still refers to Yuri as "Auntie." Yuri was in the audience when Malcolm was assassinated on February 21, 1965, and it was she who ran up on stage afterwards and cradled his head.

After the assassination, activists met to plan how to sustain Malcolm X's ideas, to push for human rights rather than civil rights, and to appeal for social justice under international law to the United Nations rather than the United States. To pursue these goals, the Republic of New Afrika (RNA) was established in 1968.[12] Yuri agreed with RNA's aims and its articulation of the rights to Black nationhood and to defense of the nation through armed struggle, if necessary. In 1969, the RNA decided that non-Blacks who agreed with and abided by

RNA principles could become what they called "citizens of the republic," and they extended this invitation to Yuri.

By the late 1960s, Yuri's son Jimmy had renamed himself "Chikara"—a Japanese word meaning strength. Yuri's daughter Lorrie Aichi, who was already using her Japanese name, had been persistently prodding her mother to drop her "slave name." When she became a citizen of the RNA in 1969, Mary Kochiyama decided to begin using her Japanese name, Yuri.

Throughout the 1970s and beyond, Yuri has worked to free political prisoners targeted by the FBI's notorious Counter Intelligence Program (COINTELPRO), which continues under a different name to this day.[13] Many of Yuri's activist comrades were arrested on trumped-up charges and/or given unjustly long sentences as a result of COINTELPRO and other government campaigns. Throughout the 1970s, Yuri worked with the National Committee for the Defense of Political Prisoners. She visited prisoners, wrote to them, and attended their trials. She worked on numerous legal defense committees, including those of Assata Shakur, Sundiata Acoli, Mutulu Shakur, the New York Panther 21, Queens 17, Harlem 6, Rap Brown 4, RNA 11, and many Black Panther Party and Black Liberation Army cases. She has also worked to free Puerto Rican *independentistas*, Leonard Peltier of the American Indian Movement, anti-imperialist Marilyn Buck, and Yu Kikumura. No doubt these arrests resembled her own and her father's unjust imprisonment during World War II.

In 1977, Yuri was one of 30 activists who seized control of the Statue of Liberty to protest the imprisonment of Puerto Rican *independentistas.* In a nine-hour siege, activists closed down the Statue of Liberty and flew the Puerto Rican flag on the statue's forehead. Simultaneously, about 400 demonstrators gathered to support those inside the statue. In 1979, key Puerto Rican political prisoners were released with pardons granted by President Jimmy Carter.[14]

Yuri also worked with other revolutionary nationalist organizations, such as the Revolutionary Action Movement and the New Afrikan Peoples Organization. She supported others, including the African People's Party and the Black Panther Party. In addition, Yuri supported movements for American Indian sovereignty, the Palestine homeland, and many other anti-imperialist Third World liberation struggles.

In addition to her practice, Yuri attended revolutionary schools and political study groups, reading the works of Frantz Fanon, Patrice Lumumba, and Kwame Nkrumah, among others. Through her study and practice, Yuri has formulated strong political stances: she believes in revolutionary nationalism, that Blacks in the United States constitute a sovereign nation, that Puerto Ricans have a right to national sovereignty, and in the right to armed struggle.[15]

"We Are the Offspring of the Concentration Camps": The Asian American Movement[16]

Yuri was one of the earliest participants in the nationwide Asian American movement that started in the late 1960s, spurred by sentiment against the Vietnam War.[17] In 1968, Yuri was one of the few older niseis who responded to the call from Kazu Iijima, Minn Matsuda, and Mary Ikeda, three nisei women with histories of radical activism dating back to the 1930s, to start Asian Americans for Action, or Triple A, one of the first pan-Asian groups in New York. A primary concern of Triple A was opposing the Vietnam War, which they deemed imperialist and racist.

In 1979, Yuri began working with Concerned Japanese Americans (CJA), which organized to support Iranians in the United States during the hostage crisis in Iran. CJA believed the attacks against Iranians echoed earlier anti-Japanese agitation during World War II. CJA also advocated for redress for Japanese Americans to help offset the economic, cultural, and psychological damage of the internment. CJA holds annual Day of Remembrance events that commemorate the Japanese internment during World War II.

A decade after the demonstrations to gain jobs for Black and Puerto Rican construction workers, Yuri became involved in fighting for construction jobs for Chinese workers. Confucius Plaza was being built in New York City's Chinatown, yet contractors did not hire Asian construction workers. In addition, Yuri started working with students to establish or strengthen ethnic studies programs on college campuses in New York, and she supported the Vincent Chin, Chol Soo Lee, David Truong, and Detroit Philippine nurses' cases.

Today, Yuri is active in several organizations. She is a member of the New York Coalition to Free Mumia Abu-Jamal and the Asian Ad Hoc Committee for Mumia; in May 1996, Yuri marched with the

New York Coalition to deliver one million letters demanding a new trial for Abu-Jamal to Attorney General Janet Reno. Yuri supports the only Asian political prisoner in the United States, Yu Kikumura, a Japanese anti-imperialist given a 30-year sentence for the alleged possession of three explosive devices. She also helps support David Wong, a Chinese national convicted of killing an inmate, though evidence indicates he is innocent. She helps organize the annual Day of Remembrance events and works with the Malcolm X Commemoration Committee and the W.E.B. Du Bois Foundation. In addition, Yuri is a popular lecturer (often featured as a keynote speaker), and she travels the country on the college speaking circuit.

Yuri's Legacy for Asian American Women

How do we make sense of Yuri Kochiyama's years of dedicated and radical activism? How have gender and cultural prescriptions influenced her role as an activist? From a superficial reading, I would argue that society's construction of race and gender—and her internalization of this construction—has limited Yuri's role in the movement. For example, Yuri considers herself to be a worker, saying, "I'm just another activist and not a leader type.... I'm just one of thousands and thousands who participate in the movement." And indeed, she has not played the role of primary organizer, decisionmaker, strategist, or theoretician. But to stop here is to miss the essence of Yuri's leadership and political philosophy. While she acknowledges the need for dynamic, out-front leaders, and has worked with many of them, Yuri's philosophy echoes Philip Vera Cruz's: "Leadership...is only incidental to the movement. The movement should be the most important thing...It must be something that is continuous, with goals and ideas that the leadership can then build upon."[18]

I see Yuri's greatest strengths as her ability to build bridges between communities and movements, and her deep love for people, grounded in revolutionary politics. These two assets flow from her political philosophy. She believes polarization, or the creation of artificial divisions to separate people, substantially holds back the movement. Yuri is no stranger to political feuds and has had to develop political savvy to survive in social movements. Part of her practice involves a tendency to distance herself from conflict. Some would interpret this as a liberal tendency to refrain from condemning unprincipled tactics. But, Yuri stresses, "there has to be a certain amount of politics and truth to what you say, even if you lose some people. If you acquiesce and lower your standard, I just wouldn't be for that." At the same time, she says, "I didn't get involved [in conflicts]. . . . I saw how many groups judged each other by the organizations they were in, even though in organizations you get all kinds of people. I didn't want to become a part of it." Even in the midst of the 1970s, when Asian American leftists and other activists were trying to determine "the correct line" and at times viciously attacked others who differed from their position, few people attacked Yuri:

> I was lucky I was so much older; they didn't really attack me. Usually everyone was attacked by whoever they didn't agree with. A lot of people think, oh my God, Yuri just goes for any old thing. I think it's important to know about each group and where their differences are. But I think their [political] differences weren't as great; it became so personal.

Yuri recognized that the divisions among many activists in the 1970s were the result of their relative lack of political experience.[19] Given the small size of the progressive movement, Yuri believes the work of almost every activist and organization is important and needs to be encouraged. And her love for people has inspired hundreds, if not thousands, to participate in the movement.

As an activist, Yuri sustains a vision of both the larger political issue and the individuals involved. She does this in big ways, by delivering fiery, passionate, forceful, and radical speeches at colleges and community events nationwide; by using her artistic skills to liven up newsletters and picket signs; and by writing newsletter entries and innumerable leaflets.[20] She also does this in small ways, by talking to young people, remembering their names and asking about their activities; by constantly distributing flyers and petitions; and by connecting people. She is a master at building bridges. Many people say that Yuri has done more than any other person to bring together the Black and Asian movements.[21]

In all her work, Yuri does not lose track of the individual involved in the struggle. This is how she demonstrates a different concept of leadership, one usually devalued by Western frameworks. She nurtures activists to develop a multifaceted view of political leadership, to build bridges between different struggles, and to develop holistically as human beings. Yuri believes "a real revolutionary should have the highest principles and even standards of morality, not just in their politics but in how they live everyday, in the concern they have for people." As Glenn Omatsu notes, "There is a sophisticated view of political change embodied in Yuri's actions—sophisticated because she constantly carries out an all-sided approach to political work that combines bridge-building, leadership development, concrete acts of solidarity, training and nurturance, etc....And she does this in the context of her everyday life as a mother, a worker, and a comrade."[22]

In addition to polarization, Yuri believes the other major problem in society is racism. Her movement work clearly reflects this priority. But her emphasis on anti-racist work also limited her work in the women's movement. Acknowledging this to be one of her weaknesses, she says:

> The only women's organization I would have worked with if I had the time was the Third World Women's Alliance. I liked their line. It was so political, not anti-men, though it was against male chauvinism and against imperialism. So much of the White women's movement was about equal pay and upward mobility. They didn't really understand the damage of racism on the human psyche. Plus, I was too busy in Harlem, especially with support for prisoners and Black organizations, so I didn't join the two fine Asian women's groups: Organization of Asian Women and Asian Women United.

Neither does Yuri consider herself a feminist. Like many women of color then and today, Yuri equates feminism with an anti-male position.

> I'm not a feminist because I've always worked with men and women. I see feminism's main priority as fighting for women's rights. But I think we must fight for both women and men. I see my priority as human rights because it's for everyone, on both domestic and international issues.

Of course, many feminists consider the fight for women's rights to be intertwined with the struggle for universal human rights. While she refrains from directly confronting sexism in progressive movements, Yuri acknowledges that women's equality is an important struggle and that sexism affects her as an Asian American woman: "If I had lived in California, I probably couldn't do as much because the

Japanese community would put so much pressure and criticize me" for stepping outside her prescribed gender/cultural role. For Yuri, the struggle of Asian American women is linked with the struggle for international human rights; we must simultaneously oppose racism, sexism, capitalism, and imperialism.

Some may interpret Yuri's actions as those of a humble, nonconfrontational, other-focused, behind-the-scenes worker perpetuating the stereotypic passive role of the Asian American woman. But as a revolutionary nationalist, Yuri hardly fits this characterization. Whether or not she considers herself to be one, Yuri is a leader. She defies stereotypes, takes radical stances on controversial issues, inspires hundreds of young people to join the movement, and bridges various liberation struggles throughout the world. Herman Ferguson, one of today's foremost Black leaders, says:

> Yuri is a revolutionary soldier....A revolutionary soldier is committed to the destruction of the enemy in word and deed, is...someone you can trust fully,...who's not afraid of the enemy, who has cleansed herself of the negativity of humanity. I can count all the revolutionary soldiers I know on one hand and still maybe have a thumb left.[23]

Yuri Kochiyama, as a revolutionary soldier, stands out as a heroic figure in Asian American women's political heritage.

Notes

I would like to thank Sonia Shah and Lynn Lu for their helpful editorial advice and a collaborative working relationship. I am grateful to Yuri Kochiyama, Herman Ferguson, Matef Harmachis, Kazu Iijima, David Monkawa, Glenn Omatsu, and Emily Woo-Yamasaki for their editorial suggestions, keen political insights, and enthusiastic support.

1. Unless otherwise noted, information comes from interviews and interactions with Yuri Kochiyama, especially during the author's visit to Harlem, 8-11 December 1995; Yuri Kochiyama's visit to Santa Barbara, CA, 28 April-2 May 1996; and a telephone interview, 28 August 1996.

2. Ferguson, Herman. Personal interview. 19 June 1996.

3. Ibid.

4. For a fuller description of Yuri's early life, see *Fishmerchant's Daughter: Yuri Kochiyama, An Oral History*. Vol. 1. Video. Prod. Community Documentation Workshop, 1981.

5. The FBI, along with the Office of Naval Intelligence and Military Intelligence Division, had conducted surveillance of the Japanese American community since the early 1930s, a decade before the Pearl Harbor bombing. Numerous government investigations found no evidence of espionage, sabotage, or fifth-column activity by the Japanese in America. Yet, immediately following Japan's bombing of Pearl Harbor on 7 December 1941, the FBI abducted and incarcerated more than 2,000 Japanese Americans, mostly issei men who were fishermen, produce distributors, Shinto and Buddhist priests, farmers, influential businesspeople, and leaders of the Japanese American community. For more information, see Daniels, Roger. *Prisoners Without Trial: Japanese Americans in World War II*. New York: Hill and Wang, 1993; Kumamoto, Bob. "The Search for Spies: American Counterintelligence and the Japanese American Community, 1931-1942." *Amerasia Journal* 6 (1979): 45-75; and Weglyn, Michi. *Years of Infamy: The Untold Story of America's Concentration Camps*. New York: Morrow Quill, 1976.

6. *Fishmerchant's Daughter* 10.

7. "Nisei" refers to second-generation Japanese Americans, the children of immigrants.

8. Tragically, Yuri has lost two of her adult children; Billy died in 1975 and Aichi in 1989. Despite these heartbreaks, Yuri marches on, obtaining support and strength for her activism from her family. In particular, her late husband participated actively in the housework and childrearing, and graciously welcomed all who entered his home.

9. *Fishmerchant's Daughter* 28.

10. *Yuri Kochiyama: Passion for Justice*. Video. Dir. Rea Tajiri and Pat Saunders, 1993; Hohri, Sasha. "Because Movement Work is Contagious: Reflections of Yuri Kochiyama as told to Sasha Hohri." *Gidra* (1990): 6, 10; Kochiyama, Yuri. Personal interview. 8-11 December 1995.

11. Hohri 6.

12. Political literature and other papers and records from the Black Revolutionary Action Movement of the 1960s and 1970s. Indexed and microfilmed by Monroe Fordham Afro-American Historical Association of the Niagara Frontier, Buffalo, NY, 1979.

13. For more on how COINTELPRO programs killed, infiltrated, bombed, arrested, and otherwise neutralized radical activists and organizations, see Churchill, Ward, and Jim Vander Wall. *Agents of Repression: The FBI's Secret Wars Against the Black Panther Party and the American Indian Movement*. Boston: South End Press, 1990.

14. The political prisoners, Oscar Collazo, Griselio Torresola, Lolita Lebron, Rafael Cancel Miranda, Irving Flores, and Andres Figueroa Cordero,

were incarcerated for armed attacks against the president's home and the U.S. Congress in the 1950s to bring attention to U.S. colonization of Puerto Rico. Their goal was to denounce U.S. imperialism, not to kill politicians (their actions caused no deaths). Fernandez, Ronald. *Prisoners of Colonialism: The Struggle for Justice in Puerto Rico*. Monroe, ME: Common Courage Press, 1994; Tajiri and Saunders, op cit.; Kochiyama, Yuri. Public address on the Asian American Movement. University of California, Santa Barbara. 30 April 1996. Breasted, Mary. "30 in Puerto Rican Group Held in Liberty I. Protest." *New York Times* 26 October 1977.

15. According to Yuri, many people confuse narrow or cultural nationalism, which focuses on race and culture but lacks a class analysis, with revolutionary nationalism, what she also calls Pan-Africanism or revolutionary internationalism, which promotes self-determination based on an anti-capitalist, anti-imperialist economic system that is international and often socialist. Yuri believes Blacks constitute a nation within the United States whose land base is in five southern states. In contrast, some Pan-Africanists believe Africa is the land base for Blacks, and some leftists believe in integrating Blacks into a transformed, socialist United States. Yuri believes in armed struggle, when well-organized and appropriate, because history demonstrates its necessity to create genuine social change.

16. From a song by an Asian American movement group, A Grain of Sand, featuring Chris Iijima, Nobuko Miyamoto, and "Charlie" Chin.

17. Kochiyama, Yuri. Public address on the Asian American Movement. University of California, Santa Barbara. 30 April 1996; Wei, William. *The Asian American Movement*. Philadelphia: Temple University Press, 1993.

18. This is not to say that leadership and leaders are not important; clearly they are. But history has shown that it takes masses of people working collectively to create social change. Scharlin, Craig, and Lilia V. Villanueva. *Philip Vera Cruz: A Personal History of Filipino Immigrants and the Farmworkers Movement*. Los Angeles: UCLA Labor Center and Asian American Studies Center, 1992. 97. I am grateful to Glenn Omatsu for his political insights and help in interpreting Yuri's practice.

19. Omatsu, Glenn. Letter to author. 24 February 1997.

20. Yuri's family used to write a newsletter called *North Star* about movement activities, especially about political prisoners. With their own meager funds, they mailed the newsletter all over the country. Yuri continues to write an end-of-the-year newsletter to movement activists recounting the victories and defeats of the year and providing an update on the health of revolutionary activists.

21. Ferguson, Herman. Personal interview. 19 June 1996.

22. Omatsu, Glenn. Letter to author. 24 February 1997. Yuri often worked part-time as a waitress or a church secretary to supplement her family's sparse income. As a waitress, she worked in working-class restaurants where, in between serving dishes, she could talk to customers and distribute leaflets.

23. Ferguson, Herman. Personal interview. 19 June 1996.

Bringing Up Baby

Raising a "Third World" Daughter in the "First World"

By Shamita Das Dasgupta and Sayantani DasGupta

Shamita

For me, the mother of this mother-daughter writing team, attraction to this particular topic mounted as I watched my U.S.-born daughter grow into a "Third World"[1] activist. As a young and inexperienced Indian mother raising a child in the isolated and somewhat segregated world of a Midwestern town, my task had been complex, even disheartening at times.

As an immigrant to the United States from India in the late 1960s, I did not have the privilege of having my mother or any other female relative close by when my daughter was born. Thus, my early days of childrearing were fraught with self-doubt, advice from Dr. Spock, and a make-up-as-I-go quality. I knew that I wanted a politically aware, activist daughter, but did not have a clue about how to help her get there.

When I joined an undergraduate program in the Midwest as a psychology major, my daughter was three years old. I soon learned from my classes the many ways one can warp a child's mind and development. I became convinced I had already succeeded in doing so. I had surely thwarted my child's individuation by allowing her to sleep in our bed, by instructing her to share with others, by not providing her with a stable, stay-at-home mother. Every time my daughter got into trouble at school or with the neighborhood children, I was sure it was because of some maladjustment process that I had triggered. Later, when I expressed these feelings to my mother in India, she, in her characteristic disregard for psychology, quickly dismissed my fears: "Psychology, shmychology! You can't control everything in life or children. All of you overanalyze and hassle your children about everything. Being a sensible parent is all that one can do. Relax! No parent has ever been perfect up to now." Easier said than done. It took me many more years to realize that in much of Western psychology, the context of an Asian Indian is wholly missing, let alone that of an Asian Indian immigrant.

During the early days of my training in feminism, a white American friend in my consciousness-raising group asked me whether, given a choice, I would have opted to have a child. The assumption, of course, was that I had little choice in the matter. Despite women's socialization by patriarchal mores and the presumed absence of free will in the indoctrinated, I could never deny my need to be a mother. For me, the problem was not motherhood, but finding help and advice about how to be a good mother. Feminism and the mainstream women's movement gave me no such direction, but added to my confusion by casting aspersions on my feminist convictions. This need to rear future generations has stayed with me over the years, as I have grown to mentor a new generation of young women, students, and activists.

When I joined the university and began moving in feminist circles, my community predicted dire consequences for my husband and daughter. My friends told me that I was sure to neglect my family's well-being because of my involvements. Nothing good could come out of feminism since it went against family solidarity and attachments. Many of my husband's male acquaintances told him that they pitied him, that they would never allow their wives to be "corrupted" by me. Even my women friends made snide comments about my motives, insinuating that there must be marital discord between my husband and myself. Others told me that my aggressiveness and politics were sure to break my family apart.

Recently, a young activist friend of mine came to me in tears. For some time, she had been trying to move out of her parents' apartment to secure literal and figurative personal space. Even though she had been trying to discuss this move with her parents for a considerable period, they had avoided speaking about it openly. When finally confronted with the inevitable, her parents were horrified and took her move as a rejection of their family. Although her new apartment was close to her parents, her mother swore never to step inside it. To their friends and neighbors, the uncles and aunties of the community, the truth was never revealed. Everyone in her family kept up the pretense that the move had never taken place. It seemed too shameful to admit that a "good" Indian girl could want to live alone.

When five of my friends and I founded Manavi, a battered women's organization for South Asian women, and began addressing the issue of domestic violence, we were quickly dubbed homewreckers and dismissed as fanatic feminists (read: Westernized). Our discussions about incidents of domestic violence within the community usually met with disbelief and skepticism. Even the most sensible members of our community told us that leaving a marriage, regardless of its abusiveness, could never be an option for women from our culture. This attitude of the community is imposed on battered women who end their marital relationships. Most women who decide to leave their abusive husbands anticipate relentless condemnation from the community and terminate their relationship with the latter as well.

Because I and my daughter started writing together on feminist issues, our picture appeared on the cover of the national women's magazine, *Ms.* Although our community friends maintained a stony silence, one of my husband's colleagues sympathetically warned him about the danger of such explicit declarations of our politics. Since no one in our community takes kindly to a nontraditional woman, the colleague explained, my feminist daughter was really hurting her chances of marriage. Besides, who would want to establish a marital alliance with someone whose mother was a feminist?

Sayantani

What's the big deal?, I keep asking myself. What's the big deal about my mother and me? I'm not sure I realized exactly how we started getting attention as a "feminist mother/daughter team." For us, we've always been a team. From my days in elementary school, I remember going straight from the school to my mother's college campus. When most kids were playing with other children, I was spending my time playing with my mother's graduate-student colleagues. I was almost constantly with her. On our car rides back and forth from grocery stores, schools, universities, we discussed courses she was taking, books I was reading, our personal thoughts. As I grew older, we started collaborating on writing and other projects. We became collaborators and friends, as well as mother and daughter.

As a medical student, I can't envision spending the same kind of quality time with my future children as my mother did with me. All the way from her bachelor's degree through her Ph.D, and then throughout her career, my mother kept me beside her. We read together, played together…she even watched *Sesame Street* with me every single day. I think it was the sheer amount of time we spent together that taught me my politics. I never remember her formally teaching me to be an activist, yet she encouraged me to read and discuss with her everything I could get my hands on. She took me along on the journey of her feminist consciousness. I remember attending progressive rallies and listening in on most of her consciousness-raising meetings; when she formed the South Asian women's group, Manavi,[2] I was right there with her. Yet as I envision the long years of residency and medical practice ahead of me, I don't know how I will teach my children the same lessons my mother taught me. I'm not just scared of raising non-activist children, I'm petrified I will screw mine up! Will my children blame me for not being like their grandmother?

I'm not sure the Great White Foremothers of feminism would call most of the women in my family feminists. Then again, I'm not sure I like the label, either. The narrow definition leaves no room for diversity. But I learned about women's strength from my elderly white-sari-clad grandmothers as well as my activist mother; I had the privilege of meeting their friends, octogenarian grannies who turned out to be nationalist freedom-fighters, double Ph.Ds, or black-belts in judo. A tradition of women's strength leapt out at me from the pages of myth, from stories of the courageous Rani of Jhansi to the tradition of the Durga Puja festival for Bengal's favorite, the warrior goddess.

As a little girl, I remember taking Indian singing and dance classes, attending pujas, and participating in all variety of talent shows, musical dance-dramas, and traditional poetry readings. While I, like most Indian American little girls of my generation, was spending my time swathed in saris and decorated with paper flowers, our Indian American brothers had more freedom in dress, movement, and activity. It was a dual life of being American during the school week and then magically transforming ourselves into perfect little Indian girls during the weekend. I've spent most of my adult life trying to overcome this image of good Indian girlhood.

"You're becoming more and more American every day," my mother would tell me, particularly when she was afraid I was paying too little attention to academics, or too much attention to boys. It was a tricky tension she was referring to, I realize now. While she and I were a constant pair at most mainstream feminist events, we were also Indian women in the U.S. Midwest. My childhood consisted of being ultra-aware of my brownness, my strangeness, my difference. Even at mainstream feminist events, we were two of the few non-white faces. While she had to defend Indian culture to her progressive friends, who were convinced that Indian culture was comprised of nothing but sati, daughter disfavor, and other oppressions, my mother was faced with challenges from within our Indian community about her views. She was balancing my upbringing between two worlds, each with problematic politics.

"It would be much easier if you were a lesbian," friends have joked with me when we have attempted to come up with a list of eligible Indian men for me. The thought being, of course, that there are manifold more interesting South Asian women of my political persuasion than South Asian men. And even though I've used this joking comment frequently in my writing, I know it's not true. As a South Asian woman who dates men, sexuality is a difficult enough arena to negotiate. Yet the uniform silence our community maintains about lesbianism and bisexuality is a veritable minefield. My friend Sarita, 32, who has always been fairly close to her Indian immigrant parents and came out to them a few years ago, still has to field arranged marriage offers from them. "I tell them about my girlfriend," she complains, "and they seem to understand. Then in the next breath, they suggest I meet some nice young man. They seem to think being a lesbian is a phase." This parental reaction is a reflection of larger community attitudes: what doesn't fit their image, they ignore, perhaps thinking that if they ignore it long enough, it will go away.

The Indian American community convinces us that our natal culture consists of nothing but singing, dancing, and happy faces. And yet every time I go to India, I realize how anachronistic the monolithic Indian culture we learn in the United States is. My Indian cousins, who dated and behaved like most U.S. teens, used to appear utterly American, while I, who had been brought up in the Indian American community, fit a more traditional picture of Indianness.

There was also more space for me among my Indian relatives than the Indian American community. In fact, while most of the Indian community chided my parents for sending me away from home for college (subtly suggesting that the money would be better spent on my wedding), my grandmother continued to urge me to begin an ambitious career. She seemed to think I had a higher destiny than traditional womanhood, that I could be granted the space of the *virangana* (warrior woman).

Our latest feminist gathering was a mother-daughter event at which we were invited to speak. It had been a long time since either of us attended a primarily mainstream U.S. feminist event, but this one, a speaking engagement for an anthology of feminist mother-daughter oral histories, struck home. But while everyone else was expounding on how moving, revealing, and inspirational it was to be interviewed, neither my mother nor I could figure out what to say. What's the big deal? I kept thinking, we've talked about all of this before. Then someone asked us to relate how the mother-daughter interview process affected our relationship as feminists. We couldn't avoid the question.

"It hasn't," my mother says, smiling at me, "I have been discussing feminism, activism, and politics with my daughter for years. I've been teaching her and learning from her for as long as she's been in my life."

"It's nothing new," I add, "this is what we do together. This is our life!"

Mothers-Daughters, Professionally Speaking

In this chapter, we try to articulate our experiences of becoming activist adults in the United States. Being mother and daughter, we are able to view the topic from two differing vantage points: becoming and being brought up as feminist activists. Our own experiences of being a mother and daughter are separated by time and space, as well as circumstances and conditions, since one of us grew up in post-independence India and the other in the post-1970 United States. Our chosen areas of work are also different, with one concentrating on violence against women and the other on healthcare systems. Yet we feel that there are systematic and complementary meanings to be found in our experiences.

How do we, South Asian diasporic mothers, raise activist children, especially daughters, away from our native cultures and our own histories? How do we, as diasporic daughters, accept the teachings of our South Asian mothers, whose lessons often feel culturally inappropriate? Who guides us as we become immigrants and South Asian American activists? Where do we find time-tested templates or our own role models?

Research on relationships between mothers and daughters is scant even in the Western world, let alone in the Third World. In fact, the mother-daughter dyad suffers from deep scholarly neglect, perhaps stemming from the oversight all women have historically experienced in society. When mothers have come into focus, it has been to make them responsible for what has gone wrong with their children. In the recently published anthology of mother-daughter oral histories, *The Conversation Begins*, Barbara Seaman expresses the result of this ubiquitous mother-blame: "For many women—and I am among them—the way you spell mother is G-U-I-L-T. I once began writing a book called "The American Mother: Whatever You do, It's Wrong." I never finished it. I was too 'guilty.'"[3]

Feminism Does Motherhood

Psychodynamic inquiries have focused on the importance of the mother-daughter dyad in women's emotional well-being.[4] This research suggests that mutuality in mother-daughter relationships is involved in women's social adjustment and the evolution of their self-esteem.[5] Feminists, on the contrary, have examined the same relationship in terms of the development of female autonomy. From the latter explorations two basic arguments have emerged: (a) that mothers stunt their daughter's individuation process; and (b) that being a mother is an obstacle to adult women's independence.

Academic and popular writers advancing the first argument have discussed how mothers have historically instilled guilt in their daughters and consequently have obstructed their metamorphosis into autonomous women.[6] According to these scholars, daughters seem to find their mothers restricting and silencing, rather than empowering compatriots.

Conversely, Western feminists have also openly discussed the constraints of motherhood and its inhibitory influences on women's individual development.[7] Perhaps reacting to the conflation of womanliness with motherhood, these feminists have been most eager to disentangle the two. In favor of encouraging the independent feminine self, at times this effort has led to the denunciation of motherhood itself. Unfortunately, such condemnations have only helped to alienate the majority of women for whom motherhood is still desirable. Even among the praetorian feminists, the issue of motherhood evokes more ambivalence than any other topic. Motherhood, a reality for most of the women on this planet, can hardly be dismissed summarily. Yet the controversy surrounding it is palpable in many feminist analyses.[8] The majority of these investigations have centered on the appropriateness of motherhood in a feminist's life rather than examining the various factors involved in this critical relationship or the vital part it plays in feminist struggles.

After years of neglecting motherhood, we have only recently seen a change of heart among Western feminists. Articles and books about mother/daughter feminist pairs are becoming *de rigeur*.[9] The common perception appears to be that these mothers, products of the 1960s feminist movement, are the first set of women to raise feminist daughters, negotiate relationships with them, and then attempt to "launch" them into the world while retaining strong friendships with them.[10] This perspective may not only be historically egocentric, but culturally narcissistic as well.

Although information about historic mother-daughter relationships in the West is scarce, we manage to catch a glimpse of these through letters and travelogues left behind by some women.[11] No such evidence seems to exist for South Asian women. Yet South Asian women have had a long history not only of activism,[12] but of close-knit female communities. As is wont in segregated societies, South Asian women have depended on each other on a day-to-day basis in the *andar mahal* or *zenana* (women's quarters)[13] and other women's congregations.[14] They have educated, affirmed, and taken care of each other through various *vrata*, or folk rituals.[15] Yet we know little about the relationships women have had with their mothers or daughters. Part of the reason for this silence may be the fact that South Asian women spent very little time in their natal homes due to the traditions of early marriage and patrilocal residency. However, given the numerous high-achieving and activist women in South Asia, such as

Pandita Ramabai, Rokeya Sakhawat Hossain, Indira Gandhi, Pritilata Waddedar, Sirimavo Bandaranayake, and Khaleda Zia, it is not easy to understand this total blackout of mother-daughter relationships.

Women, by Men

Motherhood, as defined by patriarchy, has historically been problematic for women. In the West, motherhood implies a lack of mobility, an unbreakable chain to home and hearth, and powerless self-sacrifice. In South Asia, motherhood brings with it more complexity. On the one hand, the birth of daughters traditionally brings social shame to women, whereas the birth of sons fortifies their power.[16] This initial reaction at birth translates into widespread daughter disfavor and son privilege in society. On the other hand, motherhood is highly venerated as a powerful role. The association of mortal mothers with the great goddesses in India provides some measure of cultural strength, however hidden or theoretical. It is with this heritage that Asian Indian immigrants arrive at U.S. shores. However, this is not the only factor that influences the relationship between mothers and daughters within our immigrant community in the United States.

Although immigrants from India entered the United States first in the early 1800s, the major influx occurred after the passage of the 1965 Immigration and Naturalization Act. The modified immigration policies that facilitated the passage of Indians to the United States also artificially created an upper-middle-class, Western-educated, technologically oriented homogeneous community within the first decade. That this group would quickly find financial and occupational success in this country is thus of little wonder.[17] In fact, the phenomenal economic achievements of Asian Indian immigrants procured for them the label of "model minority." The tag was created in the 1970s by the media, which presumed that Asian Indians were free from all social ills such as racism, drug addiction, intergenerational discord, social maladjustment, violence, and unemployment or underemployment. Such assumptions resulted not only in exempting Asian Indians from most governmental assistance, but in creating rifts with other minority groups. In addition, Asian Indian immigrants themselves internalized this myth and became preoccupied with living up to it.

With the acceptance of this immaculate image of themselves, Asian Indians have created a public face that is unblemished by conflicts, dissension, and diversity. This deliberate creation of an uncontentious Indian monolith is typical throughout North America. A speaker at the Federation of Indo-Canadian Associations once said, "The strength of Indians and other South Asians in Canada depends on their ability to project themselves as a united force." He further added, "the whole issue of South Asian unity has to be redefined by South Asian Canadians in the 1990s [to] sell that reality and image to other Canadians."[18] In the process of creating and maintaining this ideal image, Asian Indians have constructed certain icons that are symbolic of the community's cohesion and integrity. Foremost among these is the image of our community's women as loyal, passive, chaste, modest, and obedient. To the immigrant Indian bourgeoisie seeking to establish culturally "familiar essentials" around them, "[T]he woman becomes a metaphor for the purity, the chastity, and the sanctity of the Ancient Spirit that is India."[19] Thus, the validity of our community's image rests on the submissiveness of its women.[20] Lata Mani articulates this issue succinctly: "the burden of negotiating the new world is borne disproportionately by women, whose behavior and desires, real and imagined, become the litmus test for the South Asian community's anxieties or sense of well-being."[21]

In the immigrant community, direct and implicit censure confine both generations of Asian Indian women within boundaries that limit their activities.[22] Mothers are assigned the task of socializing their daughters within prescribed roles, and a daughter is taught to be "a good Indian girl...who does not date, is shy and delicate, and marries an Indian man of her parents' choosing."[23] A letter written to the editor of *India Abroad* by a U.S.-raised young woman speaks of this socialization eloquently: "As Indians, we are taught to respect our elders, to remain silent unless spoken to, and especially to be obedient."[24] These strict rules are enforced in the name of preserving the natal culture, the perpetuation of which has become a priority for the community.

The issue of preserving the "Indian culture" has taken on great importance as the children of immigrants have started to come of age in the United States. Asian Indians recognized early on that they are at risk of losing their native culture to ferocious assimilationist pressures in the environment as well as at the hands of their own U.S.-raised children. However well-adapted they may be economically, over the years Asian Indian immigrants have resisted total acculturation and opted to maintain a distinct cultural self. In addition, they believe that the future of their beloved culture depends upon the loyalty of the community's women, especially daughters, who will be socializing agents of the next generation.

Relegating women to the role of keepers of culture, hearth, and home is not a new phenomenon in South Asian traditions. However, to simplify the passage of values, Asian Indian immigrants have fabricated a mythical culture that denies all variability. To be considered an authentic Indian in the Indian community, an individual has to unquestioningly accept an upper-class, heterosexist, Hindu-centric, hierarchical, and sanitized version of "Indian culture." For example, in almost all the regiono-linguistic conferences that take place each year in the United States, such as the Bengali, Tamil, Assam, Havik, Punjabi, and Telegu conferences, activities are limited primarily to Sanskritized versions of visual and performing arts. *India Abroad* described the 1996 Bengali conference as "a strictly cultural event." "Religion and politics were left out of the platform....[W]e waxed philosophical, sang, and made merry," stated one of its organizers.[25] Even when a few seminars are included in these conferences, they are sidelined and stripped of all controversies. Furthermore, in most seminars, issues pertaining to race, class, and sexuality are not discussed, while there is an overall absence of working-class people and their concerns. This reconstructed culture relies heavily on a blatantly androcentric model of gender relationships that is promoted in the community as "true traditions" of India.[26] A letter to the editor of *India Abroad* summarized this communal attitude:

> I wonder what will make a woman happy in the developed world. In India women are happy just being women. It appears that in the U.S. women don't want to be women, but to be equal to men. But they simply can't be because God never wanted that. It is frightening to visualize the direction toward which the feminist activists are leading unsuspecting women, by destroying the element of love between the sexes.[27]

To be fair, this reformulated Indian culture is not just for the expediency of the immigrants. It is also a reaction to the dominant U. S. culture that seems to view diversity as deficiency, a view that is paralleled by the recent rise of the highly militant Hindu fundamentalist movement in India. In both the Indian and U.S. forms of this fictional

Indian culture, women have been rendered the emblems of purity and authenticity. Consequently, women in general, and the second generation in particular, feel obligated to play the passive, unprotesting, ritual-bound, gender-typed role of a "good Indian woman." Transgressors of these strictures are labeled "Westernized" and are often psychologically, and sometimes literally, banished from the community. "In the U.S., the worst fear of Indian parents by far is their children are becoming 'American.'"[28] Thus, to counteract the host culture's influences and inculcate the children in "authentic" traditions, classes in music, dance, Indian languages, and religion are proliferating all over the United States.[29]

In this mission to sustain the "Indian culture," both young men and women are targeted, but it is second-generation women who bear the brunt.[30] Any questioning of "traditions" are considered cultural betrayals and dealt with harshly. "Many Indian women," writes a reader of an ethnic newspaper, "fully realize the tolls of challenging age-old traditions. They could be ostracized from families."[31] This penalization is not confined to individual levels only, but extends to institutional spheres. A prime example of this was the 1995 India Day parade in New York City, where the organizers, the Federation of Indian Associations in America (FIA), barred groups focusing on battered women, gay and lesbian rights, communal relations, workers' rights, and anti-racism activities from participating. Each of these groups represents a segment of the population that belies the trouble-free image that the Asian Indian immigrant community has been trying to maintain.

Women on Women

As women of the community, mothers and daughters play a vital role in the preservation of this re-created Indian culture. Besides being bearers of culture, mothers are positioned as monitors of their daughters' conduct, and their punishment for disregarding the community's dictates is to be identified as "bad mothers." Daughters, on the other hand, are even more restricted within the community's prescriptions, and their transgressions are deemed gross betrayals of the culture. Thus, both generations of women who question "traditions" or express autonomy, diversity, and independence in their behavior are treated as destroyers of the community.

Rejecting the constraints of the Asian Indian immigrant community is not always possible. It is this community that provides us with shelter from mainstream racism and the day-to-day difficulties of negotiating multiple cultural identities. Nonetheless, unquestioning compliance of community rules that strengthen the upper-class patriarchal hierarchy is not possible. As mothers we have to resist the inclination to take the path of least resistance, not only in our own lives, but in the upbringing of our daughters.

Internal cultural critique does not, however, imply cultural betrayal, as the leaders of our immigrant communities would have us believe. Neither feminism nor activism are alien to our culture—they are nested within our heritage.[33] We can draw strength from the tradition of the *virangana,* or "warrior woman," which visualizes women as inherently powerful.[34] In addition, the *virangana* is not marginalized in our natal societies. Rather, she is revered as a savior whom parents urge their daughters to emulate. Claiming this legacy for ourselves and our daughters would only help to empower us. Furthermore, we cannot erase our history of resistance and social change work from the version of "culture" we present to our children. Our "culture" does not only consist of songs and dances, literature and art, but includes activism and the pursuit of social justice.

A Mother-Daughter Dialogue

Since the Asian Indian immigrant community rejects feminism as a Western phenomenon, many young activists tend to believe that progressive activism and their heritage are incompatible.[35] Thus, young women of Indian descent are often forced to make a choice between their politics and their communities. Those who choose the latter are restricted by the monolithic picture of "good" Indian womanhood that their communities have constructed, their questions silenced by the fear of cultural excommunication. On the other hand, the women who choose the former are not only isolated from their communities, but they often reject their heritage themselves as inherently "backward." By adopting a Western model of feminism, they also run the risk of developing an individualistic feminist politics.

As Third World feminist mothers, we have a responsibility to extend our daughters' social consciousness from the individual to the collective, from the local to the global. In the 1960s, U.S. feminism ran on a platform of "being what you want to be." Despite its superficial inclusion of other agendas, this idea of individual progress has persisted into the feminism of the 1990s. In an interview with *The New York Times*, Katie Roiphe, the author of *The Morning After*, stated, "I thought feminism was a train that you took to end up somewhere better."[36] It is this type of individualistic, looking-out-for-number-one feminism that is particularly dangerous for women from marginalized communities. Indeed, the mainstream feminist movement has a history of exclusion on the bases of class, sexuality, race, and other identities. In the 1990s, U.S. mainstream feminism is trying to overcome this history of oppression by including "other" women—in numbers only. Indeed, it continues to be insensitive to other ideas, agendas, or methodologies.[37] For Third World feminists, our strength arises from our history of collective rather than individualistic action. This does not imply that we should ignore our new environment. Indeed, in the United States we may learn from other minority groups including African American, Latino/a American, and Native American communities, as well as other Asian communities.

As Third World feminist daughters, it is critical to question from within the community and to root our politics in the rich history of feminist activism in South Asia and the rest of the Third World. A global vision of feminism can only develop if we can extract the empowering parts of our heritage for ourselves and our children. By informing our analyses and work with understandings of race, class, sexuality, and nationality, we broaden our feminist thinking. This process can only take us toward an intergenerational sisterhood, a complex and multidimensional understanding of the forces of oppression at work around us.

Feminist development is a constant process, an interaction rather than merely individual growth. It is dissension, collaboration, and communication with the women around us, our mothers, our sisters, our daughters. It is a pattern of learning where there are no teachers, only participants with different viewpoints. It is a process that grows and continues with the realities of our lives.

Notes

1. We use the term "Third World" in all its subversive power that stems from a history of oppression and resistance. We define the "Third World" activist as a person who recognizes the roles that sexism, classism, racism, im-

perialism, heterosexism, and nationalism have played in the power differential between the two-thirds and Euro-American worlds and who brings this understanding to his/her social-change agenda.

2. Manavi is the pioneering organization that focuses on violence against South Asian women residing in the United States. It was established in early 1985 in New Jersey.

3. Baker, Christina L., and Christina B. Kline. "Barbara Seaman: A Mother's Story." *The Conversation Begins: Mothers and Daughters Talk About Living Feminism.* New York, NY: Bantam Books, 1996.

4. Chodorow, Nancy. *Feminism and Psychoanalytic Theory.* New Haven, CT: Yale University Press, 1989; and Jordan, June. "The Meaning of Mutuality." *Women's Growth in Connection.* Eds. Jordan, J., A. G. Kaplan, J. B. Miller, I. P. Stiver, and J. L. Surrey. New York: Guilford, 1991. 81-96.

5. Sholomskas, Diane, and Rosalind Axelrod. "The influence of mother-daughter relationships on women's sense of self and current role choices." *Psychology of Women Quarterly* 10 (1986): 171-82; and Goldberg, Joan E. "Mutuality in mother-daughter relationships." *Families in Society* 75 (1994): 236-42.

6. Friday, Nancy. *My Mother, My Self: The Daughters Search for Identity.* New York: Delacorte Press, 1977; Flax, Jane. "The conflict between nurturance and autonomy in mother-daughter relationships and within feminism." *Feminist Studies* 4.2 (1978): 171-189; Rich, Adrienne. *Of Woman Born: Motherhood as Experience and Institution.* New York: Norton, 1976.

7. Rich, op cit., and Firestone, Shulamith. *The Dialectic of Sex: The Case for Feminist Revolution.* New York: William Morrow and Company, Inc., 1970.

8. Hochschild, Arlie R., and Anne Machung. *The Second Shift.* New York: Avon Books, 1990.

9. Webb, Marilyn. "Our Daughters, Our Selves: How Feminists Can Raise Feminists." *Ms.* 3.3 (1992): 30-35; Debold, Elizabeth, Marie Wilson, and Idelisse Malave. *Mother-Daughter Revolution: From Betrayal to Power.* Reading, MA: Addison-Wesley, 1993; Glickman, Rose L., *Daughters of Feminists.* New York, NY: St. Martin's Press, 1993; Rosenzweig, Linda W. *The Anchor of My Life: Middle-Class American Mothers and Daughters, 1880-1920.* New York: New York University Press, 1993; Baker, Christina L., and Christina B. Kline. *The Conversation Begins: Mothers and Daughters Talk About Living Feminism.* New York: Bantam Books, 1996; and "Mothers and Daughters: Honest Talk about Feminism and Real Life. *Ms.* May/June 1996: 45-63.

10. Webb 30-35.

11. Payne, Karen, ed. *Between Ourselves: Letters Between Mothers and Daughters, 1750-1982.* Boston: Houghton Mifflin, 1983.

12. Only 190 years of this history have been recorded, by Kumar, Radha. *The History of Doing: An Illustrated Account of Movements for Women's Rights and Feminism in India, 1800-1990.* New York: Verso, 1993.

13. Chughtai, Ismat. "The Quilt." *The Quilt & Other Stories.* Trans. Tahira Naqvi and Syeda S. Hameed. New Delhi, India: Kali For Women, 1990; and Minault, Gail. "Other Voices, Other Rooms: The View from the Zenana." *Women As Subjects: South Asian Histories.* Ed. Nita Kumar. Calcutta, India: Stree.

14. Oldenburg, Veena T. "Lifestyle as Resistance: The Case of the Courtesans of Lucknow, India." *Feminist Studies* 16.2 (1990): 259-287.

15. Dasgupta, Shamita D. "Nijaswasthan: Bangali nareer brata," (Personal space: Folk rituals of Bengali women). *Sixteenth North American Bengali Conference Magazine.* Ed. Chandralekha Sadhu. Houston, TX: Tagore Society of Houston, 1996. 158-160.

16. Cranney, Brenda. "Son Preference in India." *Diva,* 1.2 (October-December 1988): 35-46; Bumiller, Elisabeth. *May You Be the Mother of a Hundred Sons: A Journey Among the Women of India.* New York: Random House, 1990; and Warrier, Sujata. "Patriarchy and Daughter Disfavor in West Bengal." Diss. Syracuse University. Syracuse, NY, 1993.

17. Jensen, Joan M. *Passage from India: Asian Indian Immigrants in North America.* New Haven, CT: Yale University Press, 1988; Helweg, Arthur W., and Uma M. Helweg. *An Immigrant Success Story: East Indians in America.* Philadelphia: University of Pennsylvania Press, 1990; Agarwal, Priya. *Passage from India: Post 1965 Indian Immigrants and Their Children: Conflicts, Concerns, & Solutions.* Palos Verdes, CA: Yuvati Publications, 1991.

18. Jain, Ajit. "Finding a South Asian Identity." *India Abroad* 48 (28 August 1992).

19. Bhattacharjee, Anannya. "The Habit of Ex-Nomination: Nation, Women, and the Indian Immigrant Bourgeoisie." *Public Culture* 5 (1992): 19-44.

20. Dasgupta, Shamita D., and Sayantani DasGupta. "Public Face, Private Space: Asian Indian Women and Sexuality." *"Bad Girls"/"Good Girls": Women, Sex, & Power in the Nineties.* Ed. Nan B. Maglin and Donna Perry. New Brunswick, NJ: Rutgers University Press, 1996. 226-243.

21. Mani, Lata. "Gender, Class, and Cultural Conflict: Indu Krishnans Knowing Her Place." *SAMAR* 1 (Winter 1992): 11-14.

22. Dasgupta, Shamita D. "The Gift of Utter Daring: Cultural Continuity in Asian Indian Communities." *Women in Asian Indian Communities.* Ed. Sucheta Mazumdar and Jyotsna Vaid. Forthcoming.

23. Agarwal, Priya, op. cit.

24. Nigam, Lori. "What Do Women Want to Be? Facing Two Fronts." *India Abroad* 4 (22 January 1993).

25. Easwaran, Ashok. "Bengali Conference: Bengalis Weigh Cultural and Women's Issues." *India Abroad* 42 (19 July 1996).

26. DasGupta, Sayantani, and Shamita Das Dasgupta. "Women in Exile: Gender Relations in the Asian Indian Community in the U.S." *Contours of the Heart: South Asians Map North America.* Ed. Sunaina Maira and Rajini Srikanth. New York: Asian American Writers Workshop, 1996.

27. Nirvitananda, Balaram. "What Do Women Want to Be? Too Much Feminism." *India Abroad* 4 (22 January, 1993).

28. Chandran, Jayanti. "Growing up in America." *India Tribune* 20 (May 1995): 23.

29. Anand, Tania. "Instant Initiation." *India Today.* North American special ed. (July 1993): 40e; Tilak, Visi R. "Route to Roots." *India Today.* North American special ed. (31 December 1994): 64c, 64e, 64g; and Jha, Alok K. "Not for God's Sake Alone." *India Today.* North American special ed. (10 April 1995): 64b-64c.

30. Agarwal, Priya, op cit.; and Mani, Lata, op cit.

31. Nigam 4.

32. Names of individuals have been changed to protect their privacy.

33. DasGupta, Sayantani, and Shamita D. Dasgupta. "Journeys: Reclaiming South Asian Feminism." *Our Feet Walk the Sky: Women of South Asian Diaspora.* Ed. Women of South Asian Descent Collective. San Francisco: Aunt Lute Press, 1993; Dasgupta and DasGupta, "Public Face, Private Space" 226-243; and DasGupta and Dasgupta, "Women in Exile."

34. Both Hinduism and Islam believe in active and aggressive feminine forces. In Hinduism, Prakriti and Shakti are representatives of feminine power with the former being the source of all cosmic dynamism and the latter symbolizing autonomous sexuality. For further explanations, see Mernissi, Fatima. *Beyond the Veil: Male-Female Dynamics in Modern Muslim Society.* Cambridge, MA: Schenkman, 1975; Mookerjee, Ajit. *Kali: The Feminine Force.* New York: Destiny Books, 1988; and Wadley, Susan. "Women in Hinduism." *Women in Indian Society: A Reader.* Ed. Rehana Ghadially. Newbury Park, CA: Sage Publications, Inc., 1988.

35. Puar, Jasbir K. "Writing My Way 'Home.'" *Socialist Review* 24.4 (1994): 75-108; and Dasgupta and DasGupta, "Public Face, Private Space" 226-243.

36. Noble, Barbara P. "One Daughter's Rebellion or Her Mother's Imprint?" *The New York Times.* Late New York ed. (10 November 1993): C1, C12.

37. Lorde, Audre. "An Open Letter to Mary Daly. *This Bridge Called My Back: Writings by Radical Women of Color*. Ed. Cherríe Moraga and Gloria Anzaldúa. New York: Kitchen Table—Women of Color Press, 1981; Davis, Angela Y. *Women, Race & Class*. New York: Vintage Books, 1983; hooks, bell. *Feminist Theory: From Margin to Center*. Boston: South End Press, 1984; and DasGupta, Sayantani. "Reinventing the Feminist Wheel." *Z Magazine* (September 1994): 12-14.

Searching for the Ox

The Spiritual Journey of an Asian American Feminist Activist

By Cheng Imm Tan

I spent my first 20 years on the island of Penang, off the northwest coast of Malaysia. With its green, forested hills and white, sandy beaches shaded by tall casurina and coconut palm trees, Penang has been called the "Pearl of the Orient." Besides being a well-known tourist spot, Penang is also known locally for its delicious food and its spiritual heritage.

In 1968, when flood waters wreaked havoc in many parts of Malaysia, Penang was spared. Many Penangnites, including my mother, believed that this was due to the religiousness of the Penang people, who had been consistently faithful and had prayed fervently to avoid the disaster.

Like the rest of Malaysia, Penang is multiracial, composed predominantly of Malays, Chinese, and Indians. It is also a place where several of the world's religious traditions—Buddhism, Hinduism, Christianity, and Islam, as well as local belief in spirits and ghosts—coexist side by side. Early Hindu and Buddhist influence first came to Malaysia by way of Indian traders who, as far back as 1700 years ago, crossed the Bay of Bengal to engage in trade. These Indian traders brought Hindu and Buddhist influences, deepening and enriching the Malay culture. Chinese immigrants who came to work in the tin mines also exerted a Buddist influence. The British, who colonized Malaysia from 1786 until 1957, brought Christianity.

My family were practicing Buddhists. When I was a young girl, I did not really know what this meant, except that we practiced ancestral worship (i.e., offering food and praying to departed ancestors during their death anniversaries or on special occasions, such as Chinese New Year and weddings), prayed to an array of Taoist and Buddhist deities, and celebrated many religious festivals. Chinese Buddhism is syncretic, containing many elements of Confucianism as well as Taoism. Religion was not just a Sunday phenomenon. It was very much a part of the culture and part of the life of the community.

Despite, or perhaps because of, growing up in an environment steeped in religious symbols, rituals, and meaning, I had many spiritual questions as a child. Where does life begin? What was I, and what were other human beings before we were born? Was there a time when we did not exist, and will there be a time when we will cease to exist? Is the world we live in really what we think it is? Perhaps we are merely a figment of someone's imagination, or perhaps we are but a micro-universe within a much larger and complex one that we know nothing about—like a colony of ants inside an old tree trunk, unaware that there is more to the world outside. These were the questions that I used to ask myself when I was five years old.

My mother had little interest in such metaphysical questions. She was more interested in teaching me about ethics and how to achieve a better, happier, and more successful life. So instead of answering my questions, she taught me not to steal, tell lies, engage in immoral deeds, or cause harm to others. If I stole, she said, after I died, I would have my hands cut off, and if I lied, I would have my tongue cut off. If I looked at pornography, I would have my eyes poked out. If I borrowed something from someone and did not give it back, I would have to pay the person back in my next life. If I disobeyed my parents and was unfilial to them, my own children will be unfilial to me. If I caused someone harm or suffering, I would reap the consequences of my actions later on in my life or suffer at the hands of the people I wronged in my next life. If I was too attatched to food, I would be reborn as a hungry ghost. On the other hand, if I was good, if I practiced kindness, compassion, and generosity, I would be amply rewarded in my next life. I would be reborn into a rich and happy family, and be respected and treated well by everyone. I would know no suffering, and my former enemies would serve me. If I were really, really, really good, kind, generous, and compassionate, I might be reborn in the heavenly realm where all one's desires are fulfilled instantly. The suffering or happiness that one experienced in this life, my mother taught me, were the consequences of past actions.

This was the law of karma, a fundamental tenet of Buddhism as taught by my mother; every action had a reaction, and none of us could ever totally escape the consequences of our actions—but we could ameliorate them with acts of kindness and prayer to the pantheon of gods and goddesses who govern different aspects of earthly life. For example, one could call on Kuan Yin, the Bodhisattva who is the embodiment of compassion, the goddess of mercy, if one had difficulties. Kuan Yin, the "hearer of cries" would come to the aid of anyone who invoked her name. Traditionally, she was also appealed to for help with conceiving children, and was the goddess who looked after the welfare of sailors and fishermen at sea. Then there was Tua Pek Kong, the god of prosperity, the patron god of all capitalists, who could help make businesses succeed, and Kong Chu Kong, the god of education, who could help students do well in exams. There was also Omitabha, the future Buddha, to whom one could appeal in times of trouble, danger, or fear. All one had to do was to call on him by repeating "Namo Omithohud" several times.

My mother was a pious woman who burnt incense sticks, chanted, and prayed to the gods twice a day for the well-being of her family, once in the morning and again in the evening before she went to bed. She went to different temples whenever she felt a need to ask for special favors, or on special festival days and birthdays of the gods.

Kuan Yin, the goddess of compassion, was my family's patron goddess. Because I was a sickly child, I was given to her as a godchild, so that she would bestow her blessings and protection on me. As a godchild of Kuan Yin, I was directed to abstain from eating beef as an act of compassion. Cows had toiled so hard for humankind in the fields that it would be cruel to eat them. We believed that after a person dies, his/her soul would travel. If I ate beef, my soul would not be able to travel across water after my death, impeding my progress in the "other" worlds. To a child for whom death seemed very distant, this threat was not much of a deterrent, but there was not much beef around anyway. Our household almost never bought beef because several people in my family and extended family with whom we lived were also Kuan Yin's godchildren, including my mother herself. Eating beef was not much of a temptation, except when my father would bring a few pieces of curried beef home. My mother would admonish him for being cruel as he sucked down the juicy pieces of meat while we watched with wide, round eyes.

Around us, there were also Christian churches and Hindu temples. To ensure maximum protection from evil, bad karma, and to obtain adequate guidance and blessings, my family also worshipped at churches and Hindu temples that were particularly known for their effectiveness in helping people in need. We also participated in Christian and Hindu festivals dedicated to particular saints or gods.

We did not go to mosques or take part in Islamic religious life, because only Muslims were allowed to. If we had been allowed to, we probably would have done so. However, we were exposed to Muslim prayers that were broadcasted publicly, and we participated in the Muslim New Year by visiting our Muslim friends.

To live a happy, successful life, not only gods but spirits too had to be appeased. We believed that the spirits of ancestors who had passed away were still very present in the lives of the living family. Proper homage, prayer, and offerings to deceased ancestors would bring blessings. On the other hand, failure to attend properly to deceased ancestors could incur their wrath, resulting in illness among family members, or misfortune. It was also the common local belief that spirits inhabit nearby trees and rocks. Paying respect to these spirits was also necessary if one desired a peaceful and happy coexistence. I grew up with a host of stories about ghosts and spirits.

As a fourth-generation Chinese in Malaysia, I had many ancestors who had gone before me. Stories of these ancestors and other spirits appearing to some family member or other used to scare me so much, I would not go anywhere alone when I was young. To show respect to, to appease, and to gain blessings from these ancestors, offerings of food, drink, prayers, and paper money were made to the ancestors on the anniversary of their death, on festival days, or on important family occasions. On festival days, such as Chinese New Year, we would also offer food to the other spirits that inhabited the trees or rocks near our home.

This was the backdrop against which my theology and spirituality were shaped. Because of my exposure to and participation in different religious traditions, I grew up with a healthy respect for many religious traditions, as well as for the supernatural. There was much more to life than what we could perceive through our five senses.

There was space for the intercession of the transcendent. Life and death were part of a continuum. All of life, visible and invisible, was intricately interconnected.

When I was seven years old, I was sent to Catholic school. Because Malaysia was a British colony, going to missionary schools was the upwardly mobile thing to do. The Convent of the Holy Infant Jesus was just a short five-minute walk from our house. My mother and her sisters had also gone to school there. Across the street from the Convent was St. Xavier's Institution, the Catholic boys' school that my father, uncles, and brothers had attended. In spite of my family's openness to different religious practices, my mother did not want her children to convert to another religion, particularly to Catholicism, which was opposed to ancestral worship—the foundation of Confucianism, and the basic fabric of Chinese family structure. I vaguely remember my mother's reminder not to get too involved with Catholicism when I started first grade, but soon I got deeply involved.

Unlike my first- and second-grade teachers, who were very strict, my third-grade teacher, Sister Sabine, was my role model—I worshipped her and wanted to be just like her. She had a gentle voice and rewarded us with pretty, colorful Christmas cards if we did well on a quiz or test. Sister Sabine was very religious. Every day, after morning assembly and prayers, before classes began, after recess, and before school let out, Sister Sabine would pray with us and teach us to sing hymns. I loved the hymns and can still remember many of them. She taught us about God and creation. She told us about the Garden of Eden, about Paradise, about Adam and Eve and how wonderful things were in the Garden—and then she told us how Eve, because she was female and weak, succumbed to the Devil's temptation to disobey God's command not to eat the apple from the tree in the Garden of Eden. Not only did Eve eat the apple, but she got Adam in trouble as well by giving him the apple and persuading him to eat it. Alas, because of Eve, humankind was forever cast out of the Garden of Eden. Then, Sister Sabine told us that because we were female, we had to be extremely careful because, like Eve, we were the gateway to the Devil and were particularly weak and susceptible to the Devil's temptation. We were admonished to repent, to be self-effacing and vigilant at all times.

But all was not lost, she told us. Because God loved humankind so much, "He" would not let us be cast out of Eden for ever. In fact, God, in his infinite love, had taken human form as Jesus Christ to save us from the Devil and this imperfect world of acrimony and suffering, and return us to Eden. However, God was killed by sinners and would come again at the end of the world to judge us. Those who were good would go to heaven and live with God, and those who were bad would burn in hell forever. The end, according to Sister Sabine, was imminent.

I was enthralled by this story. At last, someone had given me some answers to the questions I had been asking about life's origin. What I could not find answers for, I was told simply to believe and have faith in. Faith was the supreme test of one's complete dedication to God.

I thought that Catholicism was superior to the mundane Buddhism that my mother practiced and the seemingly tit-for-tat law of karma that she taught me. I was particularly touched by the notion of an all-loving and forgiving God who, despite my "badness" and "sinful" condition as a female, gave his life for me and still loved me. At age nine, I resolved to give up all worldly desires and attachments and to dedicate myself to the love and service of this one true God. I tried my very best to imitate Jesus Christ and to be a saint. This meant honing the skills of complete self-denial, service, sacrifice, and endurance of suffering for the love of God.

As the years passed, I lost some of my resolve to be a saint. I certainly did not live up to the rigors and demands of sainthood, despite constant practice in the arts of self-denial, service, sacrifice, and endurance. However, the way I saw myself as a woman was deeply influenced by Sister Sabine's teachings—until I discovered feminist theology in graduate school.

In 1978, I came to the United States to go to college. It was the first time I had left my country. There were all kinds of new experiences that I did not know how to make sense of or name at the time. It was also the first time that I encountered the academic study of religions.

For the first time, I was not expected to simply believe or rely on faith, but I could openly ask all the questions that I had always wanted to ask. How can an all-loving, all-knowing, all-powerful God allow bad things to happen to innocent, good people? Why did God put the tree of knowledge in the Garden of Eden, knowing that Eve would be tempted by the Devil to eat its fruit? I was able to analyze and explore various religious traditions and philosophies. I no longer had to simply rely on faith alone for answers.

I also began to study Buddhism. I had had very little understanding of Buddhist philosophy. In college, I became acquainted with the Buddhist analysis of suffering, of impermanence, of interdependence, of liberation and the means of liberation. The study of Buddhism gave me a new appreciation for it, and I was able to go back and reclaim my own Buddhist roots. I began to identify myself as a Buddhist Christian.

In graduate school, I became politicized. The study of feminist theology exposed the underpinnings of sexism. I realized how the image of God as male, male-dominated religious language, the exclusion of women in the religious hierarchy, and explicit statements of female inferiority or subordination were used to maintain and justify the discrimination and mistreatment of women. The dualism and hierarchical mentality within much of Christian theology pit good against evil, soul against body, spirit against matter, flesh against nature, transcendent against profane, and men against women. This was a model whereby reality was divided into two distinct, clear-cut, and separate levels, the superior and the inferior, the good and the bad, and the two did not mix in any way—one always had to dominate and overcome the other. It was a perfect model and justification for the domination of women and the environment/earth since both the earth and women were identified as negative.

I began to understand how my oppression as a woman was directly linked to church doctrine and theology. As a female living in a sexist society, I had been taught in numerous ways that I was inferior. As a result, for years, I distrusted my own thinking. I followed instead of led, I had no sense of myself and felt inferior, inadequate, bad, and sinful. My inferiority was justified by my femaleness, which was identified with flesh, the profane, and the sinful. After all, it was my femaleness, like the femaleness of Eve, that made me inherently weak and inadequate and susceptible to the temptations of the Devil. I felt completely betrayed. I had given my loyalty to the one True God, only to discover that the image, language, symbolism, and religious hierarchy of this one True God was the very mechanism that justified, maintained, and sustained the oppression of women and the environment. Eventually, I stopped identifying myself as a Christian. I was furious. It was as if the very ground I walked on had been yanked from under my feet and I was simply floating in a vacuum with no center, nothing to hold on to.

Understanding sexism also opened the door to understanding other oppressions as well—racism, class exploitation, adultism, homophobia, imperialism, etc. As an immigrant Asian woman, I had been aware only of racism against Blacks, which I had read about and seen on television when I was in Malaysia. At least in Malaysia, I knew what ethnic conflicts existed. I knew what to look out for, what to do, what to avoid, how to be. As an immigrant Asian woman to the United States, there were no roadmaps, no guides to help me navigate my way through the particular U.S. brand of racism. In many ways, it was a new game with new rules, and I did not know how to play. As a result, for the first few years, I did not know how to conceptualize and make sense of my discordant experiences. I was constantly overlooked, ignored, tokenized, made invisible, pressured to blend in and bleach out or assimilate, labeled as a foreigner/outsider, and sometimes I was mocked and threatened with violence—yet I did not identify this as racism.

As an Asian woman, I often did not seem to exist. When I spoke up in a discussion, my words often fell into a vacuum. No one would follow up on what I said. Yet a white person would make a similar point, and everyone else would respond. Often when I was with other white people, they would be greeted, and I would be ignored. I would be asked to be part of a group or sit on a Board because I am Asian, but nothing in the way the group or Board did business changed to reflect my reality and participation. When discussions on racism were held, people referred only to racism against Blacks. No one said the issues I brought up were unimportant, but no one would respond, and there was simply no follow-up discussion or corrective action.

For immigrant Asians in particular, because racism against Asians has not been acknowledged publicly, there is no framework, no context, no language in which to place our experiences. We know that something is wrong, but we can't name it. We begin to think we are crazy, blame ourselves, internalize the message that we must really be at fault and that we are less smart, less good, less capable, less knowledgeable, less everything.

In 1982, I met Katie Cannon, a Black woman ethicist who was teaching at Harvard Divinity School at the time. Katie helped me name what was happening to me as racism. All of a sudden, all the pieces of the puzzle began to fall into place.

I began to understand that racism was more than simple prejudice and hatred on the individual and interpersonal level. I began to comprehend the structural and institutional nature of societal and systemic oppression. Understanding structural oppression was useful in counteracting the internalized oppression of self-blame and self-hatred that keeps victims of oppression suppressed.

In order to "fit in," I have learned to talk, dress, and act in a way that is acceptable. I've learned to say "thank you" when someone pays me a compliment instead of denying it (which my culture teaches me to do, to inculcate humility). I've learned to dress acceptably, which means I have to calculate when an ethnic attire would be deemed appropriate. I've learned to lower the pitch of my voice, to not giggle and smile as much so as to be taken seriously. I have learned that if I want to be heard, I often have to loudly repeat myself many times. When I succeed in getting myself heard, I am often criticized for being "pushy" because I no longer fit the stereotype of a nice, quiet, Chinese woman who does not make waves.

By the early 1980s, I was no longer satisfied with the academic study of religion and spirituality and the limitations within the walls of Harvard University. In those early days, I became involved in a fledgling coalition called Women of Color Unified, a group that was trying to articulate a vision of unity and empowerment among women of color. It was a group that was started by a handful of local women activists who organized a Women of Color Conference. It was a valiant effort, but this group eventually fell apart because no one had yet figured out how to effectively address the internalized sexism and racism that made it difficult for us to build real understanding, closeness, and true appreciation of our differences. What held us together for a while was the experience of racism. But organizing around our pain could not last, and we had not yet learned how to organize around our strengths.

Perhaps my most significant involvement was with Renewal House, a battered woman's shelter in Boston. I joined Renewal House as a student intern in 1982 because I was impressed with the founder,

Rev. Elizabeth Ellis Hagler, a Unitarian Universalist minister, and wanted to work with her. However, once I started working at Renewal House and listened to the women tell their stories, I understood even more how sexism could kill and how internalized sexism often made it so hard for women to be emotionally, physically, and economically independent. I understood how difficult it was for women to retain a sense of who they were, confident in their self-worth and capacity to live a good life without a man.

As a woman who had struggled with the forces of sexism in my own life, it was clear to me that violence against women was a key tool for maintaining control over women and keeping women subservient and oppressed. It was also apparent that violence against women existed on a continuum of discrimination, emotional and psychological abuse, harassment, rape, and battering. Although not all women have endured physical abuse, all women have endured emotional and psychological abuse. All women have been overlooked, ignored, put down, or discriminated against at some point in their lives. Almost all women have endured some kind of sexual harassment and live in fear of battering or rape. The imposition of fear in women's lives is a key ingredient of keeping women "in their place."

The idea that no woman is safe until all women are was consistent with my Buddhist theological framework that all life is interdependent and interconnected, and I became completely committed to the work of stopping violence against women and achieving women's empowerment.

During the early days of my domestic violence work, I was still struggling with my spirituality. I had stopped identifying myself as a Christian. I liked philosophical Buddhism but had not developed a personal practice in Buddhism. At one point, Krister Standahl, a professor at the Harvard Divinity School at that time, commented that feminism seemed to be my religion. But feminism in and of itself was not enough for me. It fed my intellect but left my soul empty. It never was and never pretended to be a path for inner knowledge, inner transformation or for the cultivation of wisdom and compassion. It did not set out to teach its adherents the meaning of life and death or the art of loving fully and living a life in tune with reality. It was merely a useful framework for understanding gender oppression and envisioning women's liberation.

Moreover, feminism itself was mostly a white construct that had to be translated for cultural, racial, and class relevancy. Western feminism's focus on personal choice and personal freedom is very individualistic. As an Asian woman from a culture that stresses relationships—of the individual to the family, the family to society, the personal to the communal—Western feminists' focus on personal choice and personal freedom missed the bigger picture. It is the art of balancing the personal and the communal that makes Asian communities work.

During those transition years of the early 1980s, Rev. Hagler introduced me to Unitarian Universalism (UU). I liked the inclusiveness of UUism, its respect for the dignity of all life, its understanding of the interdependent web of all life, and its ability to respect and learn from the truths in diverse religious traditions—but I was not ready to become a Unitarian Universalist yet.

During these same desert-like years, both my parents passed away in Malaysia within a year of each other. In 1985, I returned to Asia for a year to work on women's issues. I connected with many women's groups in Asia, participated in the World Conference on Women in Nairobi, and came back to the United States to write my dissertation on international sexism, classism, and racism as expressed in the global sexual and economic exploitation of Asian women. It became clear that the oppression of women worldwide was connected. It was the disconnection and the separation that enabled the oppression to go on.

It has been very important to me to have an international perspective on women's liberation. It is only when we understand the connections and uncover how women around the world have been used and pitted against each other that we can begin to stand in solidarity and stand up for each other.

As an Asian woman, culture and history also inform my activism and my spirituality. I am connected to and affected by the history and experiences of my ancestors and my people. It has been a history affected by oppression, war, colonialism, and modern-day economic and cultural imperialism. The hopes, aspirations, struggles, and fears of my people, passed down from generation to generation, still live within my veins and haunt my subconscious dreams. Therefore, while I may have a strong sense of connection to the larger human family as a whole, I have chosen to base my activism and ministry within the Asian, refugee, and immigrant communities.

As an Asian, I've been socialized to strive for "perfection" or incur scorn, criticism, or humiliation. I've been trained to push myself hard and often. As a woman, I've been socialized to be "seen and not heard." Within this context, spirituality is not only about bringing compassion to the world but to myself as well, since I too am intrinsically part of the world. It is also about reclaiming love for myself, my roots, and my culture as well as my complete goodness, connectedness, and power as an Asian woman.

In 1986, I decided to take up the practice of Buddhism seriously and began to incorporate meditation into my life. For the first time in years, I began to feel spiritually centered again. To be spiritually centered for me means to be aware of the whole of life, of one's place in relationship to all life, of the meaning and goal of one's life, and of the reality of the interdependence of all existence. It means the cultivation of a path of inner knowledge, of inner transformation, of wisdom and compassion. I started to cultivate the practice of mindfulness. The cultivation of mindfulness is the cultivation of self-awareness, of letting go of preconceptions, constructs, and expectations, of simply being, of compassion, of interconnectedness and insight into the nature of self, phenomenon, and reality.

As I grounded myself in my spiritual practice, a sense of the preciousness of all life and the deep interconnectedness of all life began to emerge. A calling to ministry began to articulate itself. I came to see my involvement with battered women beyond the context of women's liberation. I began to see my work within the context of ministry, that is, within the context of human liberation—not only liberation from oppression, but a reclaiming of our full humanness and interconnectedness, of our capacity to value all of life and be in right relationship with one another and the sacred.

Perhaps for some people, the cultivation of the spiritual life is not that important. For me, it is the very ground on which I stand and operate. It is the well from which I draw my inspiration to live well and love fully. It is the center from which my life and actions are shaped and which informs my political activism.

In 1986, I was invited to a Unitarian Universalist Conference that was seeking to establish a new category of ministry called "community ministry." It was a radical group of UUs who were committed to some of the same issues that I was concerned with—women's issues, community issues, urban issues, justice issues, poor people's issues—issues outside the walls of the parish. I can still remember the passion and commitment of this group of UUs to a "larger" sense of ministry. We shared a common vision of a call "to respond to a world shaken by the massiveness of human suffering, to bear witness to that suffering, and to participate in its transformation and to affirm the inherent glory of life" (as the Society for the Larger Ministry Proclamation stated). I decided to join this group and became one of the first to be recognized as the new breed of UU community ministers. In 1992, I was ordained as a UU minister.

While metaphysical questions are sometimes interesting to ponder, what has become more important to me is how I live my life in relationship to all life. Today, my spiritual life is enriched by the teachings of many religions, including Christianity. Religious truths, I have learned, transcend institutions, structures, teachings, symbols, images, and language.

The divisions of gender, color, ethnicity—the differences that have been used to divide and pit human beings against one another—are fundamentally superficial differences. As human beings, we are more alike in our essential nature than we are different. One of the most inspiring passages that informs my spirituality and activism is from Santideva's *Guide to a Bodhisattva Way of Life*: "We are all alike in wanting happiness and not wanting pain. What is so special about me that I should strive for my happiness alone?" As human beings, we are essentially the same in our hummanness and are part of a complex web of life.

We exist in a relationship with all life, with every expression of the universe. If this is true, how can I turn away if a part of the universe is being abused? If a member of my human family is hurt? Is being oppressed?

Unfortunately, we live in a world that has lost the sense of the sacred and the holy, the sense of our wholeness and interconnectedness. We live in a culture that loves to divide and separate. As a result we live in a world where the use and abuse of large numbers of people and of the environment is pervasive, as though our well-being were not connected. We live in a world that is full of pain, violence, competition, alienation, exploitation, and fear. How does one live in a world where there is so much suffering? The U.S. popular culture is one that abhors facing pain and suffering. The consumer society encourages people to forget their pain through all kinds of distractions that can harden us or help to numb out the pain through consumption of sports, entertainment, alcohol, drugs, food, and other products.

Those of us who are not numbed are sometimes immobilized by fear and despair at the state of the world we live in. Others are spurred into action out of anger and hatred for the "enemy" or the "oppressor."

But how to clearly see and act effectively against injustice, inequality, and oppression is not an easy task. I am more than aware that all kinds of atrocities and violence have been carried out in the name of goodness and love, and in the name of God.

How do activists who care deeply about the elimination of injustice and oppression avoid getting caught in our own egos, our own agendas, our own delusions, or in recreating yet another set of oppressive structures? And what are the best strategies to use? Does one fight violence with violence, for example? Where are the guides, the wisdom, and the "how to's" with which to wisely address and dismantle injustice and oppression?

I am humbled by these questions. Good and bad are not always so clear-cut and so easy to differentiate. Sometimes, good is called bad, and bad often comes packaged in the guise of good. Sometimes it takes real wisdom and courage to tell them apart.

There is no question in my mind that oppressive systems, structures, and institutions need to be changed, but how does one relate to those who are the agents of oppression? Do we draw a sharp line between "us" and "them"? Do we try to annihilate, overpower and destroy "them," or do we try to transform "them" with love and compassion?

We live in a society that loves to hate and to oversimplify; that loves to say, "here is the problem and this is who is to blame." However, the line between victim and oppressor is often not clear-cut. All of us have been victimized, and all of us have acted as agents of oppression or colluded with the oppression of others knowingly or unknowingly. We are all victims and agents of oppression at some point in our lives.

We live in a society that loves to put things and people in separate boxes, as though life were disconnected and separated. However, from a spiritual standpoint, the lines are much more blurred. If, as human beings, we are essentially the same in our humanness, sharing the common capacity for great generosity and compassion as well as the capacity to ignore our connectedness to each other, the seemingly clear lines between victim and oppressor, friend and enemy, may not be as sharp as we think.

The Dalai Lama, Thich Nhat Hanh, and Aung San Suu Kyi of Burma are some inspiring models of justice-oriented, spiritual activists. Theirs is a model of activism with compassion, with open-heartedness rather than hate, constriction, and separation. In the face of great aggression, they have consistently advocated policies of nonviolence and speak of their "oppressors" with compassion. Aung San Suu Kyi says that there is no "enemy," only people who are in pain, confusion, and suffering. The Dalai Lama speaks of the Chinese government that refuses to acknowledge him in the same way, with compassion. At the same time, these spiritual leaders are very clear about speaking out and interrupting injustice and oppression while remaining mindful of human connections.

Anyone who has ever felt wronged or victimized knows how difficult it is to deal with anger and sometimes hatred towards the perceived perpetrator. Anger has sometimes been a helpful fuel to energize and give determination and confidence to our activism. But from a spiritual perspective, an activism that continues to be fueled by anger and hatred, which lashes out with the intention of revenge, in the long run cannot be effective. When activism is fueled by anger and hatred, we end up objectifying the "enemy" just as we have been objectified.

What about the enemy within? The fears, the despair, the confusion, the doubts, the self-criticism, the internalized oppression that prevents us from being as effective as we could be? If we meet these internal "enemies" with anger, resistance, aversion, and rejection, they often grow stronger or are replaced with a legion of other inner "demons."

Meeting these "internal enemies" is the spiritual work of self-love and acceptance. For me, this means opening my heart to those parts of myself that I do not like, to the parts of myself that I reject or judge harshly, and embracing them with the same spirit of acceptance, gentleness, and love that I try to hold the world in. This is the spiritual work to embrace all of myself with a loving heart.

Only in this place of unconditional acceptance is there transformation. Our preciousness as human beings can never be destroyed. It is only hidden behind ignorance, defenses, fears, distance, and separation.

Some people think that spirituality is not justice-oriented, that spirituality is otherworldly and has nothing to do with the affairs of the world. To me, spirituality has to be incorporated into every aspect of our lives. Spirituality calls us to care deeply and to be involved, to realize our interconnectedness, to let our hearts "break" open by daring to see clearly the pain around us and to act against injustice, inequality, and oppression with compassion and wisdom.

Spirituality may seem complicated. In essence it is about uncovering and reclaiming our connection to ourselves and to all of life. Spirituality is about rootedness and connectedness to all life. It is the center that embraces all of life, visible and invisible. It is the holy and the sacred. Spirituality is a path of living in right relationship to all of life, including ourselves. It is about loving fully, freely, and deeply.

> Put away all hindrances, let your mind full of love pervade one quarter of the world, and so too the second quarter, and so the third and so the fourth. And thus the whole wide world, above, below, around and everywhere, altogether continue to pervade with love-filled thought, abounding, sublime beyond measure, free from hatred and ill-will.
>
> —adapted from the *Digha Nikaya*,
> translated by Maurice Walshe[1]

Notes

1. Kornfield, Jack, ed. *Teachings of the Buddha*. Boston and London: Shambala, 1993. 9.

Yellowdykecore: Queer, Punk 'n' Asian

A Roundtable Discussion

With Margarita Alcantara, Leslie Mah, and Selena Whang
Moderated by Selena Whang

Punk Rock

SELENA: Do you want to talk about how you got involved in the punk movement and what attracted you initially about it, even if it was many years ago?

MARGARITA: Well, with me, it was because I was growing up in Pittsburgh, where they didn't have many minorities in the first place and all the minorities that were there were trying to be white, so I was trying to find out how I fit in and everything; and then, I guess because I felt so different I kind of flaunted it, in a way. But at the same time, it also kept me safe in a way to flaunt it, so the music I started to listen to was because of girlfriends who felt the same way. Then, once I graduated from college pretty much, I just let myself go.

SELENA (to Leslie): Okay, and how about you?

LESLIE: Man, I got into punk rock probably like 15 years ago now. And I was really into heavy metal and just being really rebellious because I was brought up to be really nice and good and quiet and polite and sweet and just that whole stereotype of the Asian girl and the little Catholic girl. And usually what happens is that pre-puberty hits and you go nuts, and then I discovered punk rock, and it was more obnoxious than heavy metal, and I just got really into it. And I really started to like the music and the variety of the ska[1] and also that women were in the bands. I grew up in a town that was probably 98 percent white, and so I was always made aware that I had this unique situation. And I think I really relate to what Margarita said about already feeling like a freak. And also, I knew I was not like other people because I wasn't white. And the other Asian people around were adopted Korean babies, and that was about it! I didn't fit into that category, either. When I was about that age [puberty] too, there was all this pressure to date boys, and I tried that a little bit. But with punk rock it was more about androgyny, and you didn't have to fulfill this feminine image. And that really attracted me to punk. And if I dyed my hair blue and shaved the side of my head, then, you know, boys wouldn't pay any attention to me in that kind of sexual way, and I wouldn't have to worry about dating boys or having to play that heterosexual game. So, in a way, it was sort of a cover-up for being queer, too.

Because I knew I was a freak, but I didn't really have to come out and say, "Well, it's just because I'm a dyke." It was like, "Oh, well, I'm a punk. And I just look weird." And people are going to see that before they're going to maybe examine me further and realize that I'm queer. And just flaunting it and just getting shit anyway, and it's like, "Well, of course I'm getting shit because of the way that I'm dressed or my haircut or something."

SELENA: You said you got pressure to date boys? Your [Chinese American] father raised you?

LESLIE: Yeah, my father raised me. I mean it wasn't from my family at all. But it's just like society in general. You go to junior high school and everybody's on this rampage of going steady.

SELENA: With my family, my parents were such strict Korean parents that they wouldn't let me date, because they didn't date that young in their generation. So they didn't want me to go out with guys!

LESLIE: Yeah, my father, definitely, was not into it. But, I mean, like I said, I was raised by my father, but in a very Americana culture.

SELENA: He had married your [white] mother, right?

LESLIE: Yeah.

SELENA: So he probably wasn't as strict as my parents were.... I got into punk rock when I was a teenager too, and I think that was one way I could somehow reconcile wanting to hang out with both guys and girls, not having to date, because I really couldn't in a way. I mean, I could have snuck out of the house, I snuck out to go to clubs and stuff, too, but somehow I could kind of do what my parents wanted me to do, but I could also do what I wanted to do. I had it justified in some weird way. I remember I would go out and I would get all these boys' phone numbers and stuff. (Leslie laughs.)

But I didn't do anything sexual with any of them when we went out. I would just call them up and talk to them about punk rock. And growing up in Los Angeles, everyone lived all over in the suburbs, and so I'd be calling all over L.A. And that was exciting for me too, because I grew up in South Pasadena, a small suburb.

MARGARITA: Yeah, it would have been nice to be with more people who were into punk. Because with me, it was just me and two or three of my girlfriends, and so we just were like hanging out together all the time. We'd get into the music and we'd go to concerts together and stuff, but I just really wished that at that time there were more people that I could have been with and everything. And because it was so sheltered over there, I did date a lot of guys, but I always knew there was something else there, but I never really identified what that was. I had always known that I was queer, I guess, but I didn't know what the label was supposed to be. I thought about it a lot but I didn't see it so I didn't delve into it as much, until I realized what it was and then I explored it.

LESLIE: It was okay to play androgynous and asexual in the early years for me. And then I got my first girlfriend and she was also a punk, and it was kind of strange because everyone knew that we were a couple, but people didn't talk about it. And we weren't really out. So it was definitely weird, being called a dyke then was a real put-down. It was really harsh.

MARGARITA: Really?

LESLIE: Yeah. And we had a band called ASF. And we were pretty much some of the only girls that were in a band in Colorado at the time. A lot of the boys were pretty intimidated by us just because we wanted to be more in the scene than just the drunk little punkettes. (Margarita laughs.)

But it was a really isolating feeling too, at the same time, because I always identified more as a punk than a lesbian or anything like that. I really felt we were the only ones.

MARGARITA: What was really funny was that when I was growing up, I always wanted to go to California. I'd see those John Hughes movies and stuff and would be like, "God, they're so accepting over there, of people who are so different!" (Selena laughs.)

Because I was also dealing with my ethnic makeup or whatever you call it, so it didn't really seem like I was hooking up with people who are of mixed ethnic backgrounds and stuff. Because I'm Filipino, Spanish, and Irish. Everyone was really, really Filipino or really Asian or really white. There was no middle ground. In California, it seemed like there were a lot of different people of different mixes who are supportive of each other being different, whether that be punk or whatever they were into. And I just thought that was really cool.

SELENA: I remember going to a show in the late 1970s. I kind of got into punk in '79. I saw this Chinese guy with blue hair all teased out. That was the fashion, to have longish hair all teased up. And I thought, "Oh, wow, there's another Asian!" And I remember there were these two other young Asian girls, I think they were twins or sisters or something, that would hang out. Yeah, but there were just very few Asians that early on.

LESLIE: Yeah, there were none in Colorado. And so it was hard for me to even identify myself. Because there was nobody else for me to look at. There'd be all my friends, who were white, pretty much.

SELENA: Punk is such a white scene.

MARGARITA: It is very white. It's very white-boy.

LESLIE: The first time that I saw other Asian punks was in California, when I hitchhiked out there when I was 19. That was really cool. And then I also realized that I could do things like get my hair to dreadlock and stuff, because I saw Japanese kids with dreadlocks. (Margarita laughs)

Race

SELENA: Maybe we should move into talking about race? I think it's interesting that we're all coming from different racial mixtures and backgrounds. Leslie, your mother is white...

LESLIE: She's Irish and German.

SELENA: And your father's Chinese. Which is not the more standard Eurasian mix in this country. (Usually the Asian parent is the mother, the white parent the father.) With you, Margarita, being from the Philippines—I've heard it's such a mixed country to begin with, and then there's all these levels of mixtures.

MARGARITA: From what I understand, the colonizers and also the traders were Indian, Malaysian, Chinese, Japanese, Spanish. And I guess there might be some others in there somewhere, but those were the main ones. It was really confusing for me to get my identity.

I guess I'll always still be kind of focusing, finding out exactly what it is...maybe one day I'll just be like, "Fuck it, I don't care anymore!" But it was really confusing me to find my identity racially because there were all these different things, and when I was growing up I got that "chink" stuff.

SELENA: In this country?

MARGARITA: Yeah, in Pittsburgh. And so I just figured I was Chinese. But then when I asked my mom, she said, "Well, no, you're Filipino." And then I found out that my mom is mixed and that my dad also has some Chinese as well, that brought more to the picture.

LESLIE: I mean right now I just feel myself being really sensitive racially and just always being aware and like what you said, maybe someday I'll wake up, it won't matter anymore because for so long I tried not to deal with it. But when my band [Tribe 8] plays shows and we're out on the road and we play to a crowd that's almost all white, I find it really disturbing.

MARGARITA: Really?

LESLIE: Yeah, I find it really disturbing. And in the Midwest, well, that's why they call them minorities, you know! There's just not many nonwhite people. But, yeah, I find it kind of annoying because [when I'm performing], I'm not fucking here to entertain all straight people or like all these boys or all these white people! Although I try to judge people on an individual basis, but when you're looking out on a group of people and it's all...

SELENA: Why is it that every time it gets repeated the same way like that?

LESLIE: That kind of goes back to the kind of music I'm playing, which has its roots in a lot of white culture. Even though the actual roots of rock music are in black culture.

SELENA: Yeah, but the black origins of rock music have been really repressed successfully in terms of people's awareness.

LESLIE: I'm not sure how to identify myself because a lot of people don't see how I feel in a lot of other ways too. And so, do I call myself a woman of color? I'm fair-skinned, you know? But, I'm also, well, don't call me white!

SELENA: Right, well, I think woman of color, that phrase, it's not so much a physical melanin thing, I think it's more psychological. Like Cherríe Moraga...

MARGARITA: Who is she?

SELENA: She wrote *Giving Up The Ghost*, she's a well-known lesbian writer and playwright, and she's half Chicana and half white, and she looks white. A lot of people who are half Latino and half white tend to look really white, but she strongly identifies as a woman of color.

LESLIE: Yeah.

SELENA: And I think it's cool because it's almost like that identity comes not so much from her pigment but from her commitment to community and what she writes about. She's really writing about her identity and the Chicano/Latino gay and lesbian community.

MARGARITA: I know with my 'zine *[Bamboo Girl]* and what I write about, when people ask me what it is, what kind of stuff I write about, I hate that question! I just pretty much say, it's by, but not exclusive to, women of color! But that's just a total blanket statement. Because I don't really know what to call it! I guess I will just say I'm a woman of color to make things simpler. That's still an issue for me about developing what exactly I am to myself and my own identity, because I don't think I have much color physically, but I'm not treated as a white person. So, I look at myself as, I guess, a woman of color.

SELENA: Do you feel also that culturally and psychologically people don't have a place for you, like in the Asian community or the white community?

LESLIE: Yeah. I feel really frustrated with it. It's frustrating because I think generally in society it's like you're white unless otherwise. You're straight unless otherwise. I feel that when people see me, they see a straight, white girl. And that's really hard for me.

SELENA: With tattoos! (Laughs) Do people see you also as a generic ethnic person…

LESLIE: I feel sort of ethnically ambiguous. I could be Latina, I could be part Native American, I could just be some dark-skinned European or something.

MARGARITA: So you get frustrated with that?

LESLIE: I do. I get frustrated. And I get frustrated culturally because there are times when Chinese people see my last name and start to speak to me in Chinese, and I'm just standing there, like, "Can't you tell that I'm just a dumb white girl?" And it is infuriating. The first time I went to Chinatown in San Francisco by myself, I was so overwhelmed, and I was like, "Oh my God, all these Chinese people. And maybe I'm related to some of them. And this is my culture, this is my heritage." And I got all teary-eyed and sad and everything. I had to sit down, and this old Chinese guy came up to me, and he's like, "Hey, what are you doing? Hey, do you want to come party with me?" And I just really got annoyed! (Laughs.) It burst my bubble, and I went home. (Margarita laughs.)

LESLIE: So, it's hard, and that's something that I've talked about with other Chinese women, mostly dykes. There's such a big difference between just being biologically Chinese and being culturally Chinese—knowing the language and being more accepted into the community. And it's hard because the dyke community is kind of based on white, middle-class feminism. Something that I feel that I'm unable to relate to. And the queer community is based on white-boy angst or something! And just trying to feel who I am...

MARGARITA: Do you feel like you're trying to find a niche with you being ethnically who you are and being a girl and this punk scene which is so typically white-boy straight?

LESLIE: I don't really feel I'm looking for a niche in the punk scene anymore. I feel I've paid my dues, and if anybody has any judgments about what I'm doing, or who I am, or am I selling out, or am I this, or am I that—well, fuck them. I did my prerequisite hairdos and tattoos and have been playing in bands, being on tour, you know. If people can't accept me at this point, then I really just don't give a fuck. And I'm not really looking to be accepted. In fact, when I started to feel that the punk dyke thing was being accepted, it started to make me sick.

SELENA: What do you mean, accepted by whom?

LESLIE: Like I'm not the only [punk dyke] anymore in the middle of nowhere. There's like a small community.

SELENA: Which your band kind of started, I think, with help from other bands.

LESLIE: Yeah, [Tribe 8] gave it sort of a focal point or something.

SELENA: Yeah. I always thought it was really important for people of mixed race to get together. I've probably told both of you guys this individually, but for the record, when I went to this Asian Lesbian/Bisexual Conference at U.C. Santa Cruz in 1989, they had different panels and workshops. There was a workshop for women of mixed race, and it was only for mixed race so I couldn't go, but I heard it was such a powerful workshop and that people were just crying the whole time!

And it wasn't just Eurasians, there were people mixed with everything. There were so many different combinations of Asians and whatever else. But another thing that happened at the conference was the whole issue of what "Asian" meant. Because the South Asian women in the conference were really pissed off because they felt they weren't being heard. And I've heard certain complaints from Pacific Islanders. They feel that "Asian" is just like…

LESLIE: Eastern Asia.

SELENA: Yeah, Japan and China, basically.

LESLIE: Fair-skinned.

SELENA: Yeah, northeast Asia really. There are these people on one of my queer Asian e-mail lists, and they're trying to figure out—they want to have a queer Asian conference—but they don't know what to call it. Because they want the South Asians to come, and these people who are South Asian are saying, "Well, we're not going to come, unless it's just South Asian. Because when it's just Asian, we're going to be subsumed again." It's just interesting about identity and what terms you use. And on whose terms you base it.

LESLIE: I think it's really good to come up with some sort of definition like, "This is what it is to be a lesbian, this is what it is to be Chinese," so you can go find other people with those characteristics, and you can start this community, and you can be strong. You know who you are, you have the definition. But then several years down the line a lot of people will say, "Fuck these definitions, they're so rigid, I'm not going to label myself a lesbian because of the fucking definitions." People see you just this one way. So, defining who you are is a really powerful thing, but then, eventually you have to smash all those definitions, continue to rebuild it, and start all over again.

SELENA: Yeah.

LESLIE: Being mixed is really hard, the identity, well, where does that lie? And how important is that? For some reason it's so important to me. And, it's always going on in my head. At least every day.

SELENA: Has this been recently, or all your life?

LESLIE: Not all my life. In the past several years. A lot of it started when I began to meet other Eurasian people, and especially queers. But even if they were just Eurasian punks or Eurasian dykes or just musicians or something. It's incredible to meet somebody like that. It used to be, when I was 15, meeting another punk rocker…

SELENA: Right, right!

LESLIE: "Oh, this psychic connection!" And then it was like meeting another dyke, "Oh, my god, we're sisters." And now it's like, oh, meeting another Eurasian person, "Oh, we're like psychically connected, we're sisters, it's really special!"

SELENA: I feel that way when I meet someone Korean. Definitely, there's a connection. Do you feel that way with Filipinos?

MARGARITA: With Filipinos, only because traditionally I know where they're coming from. And so yeah, but in the entire picture, not really. Because I feel different from them…

SELENA: I mean Fil-Ams.[2]

MARGARITA: Fil-Ams? I still feel quite different from Fil-Ams because a lot of the Fil-Ams, the boys are really into the homey look and into a black boy kind of thing, and everyone is so heterosexual. Everything is beauty-queen oriented. With the girls, they're always dressing in the hopes of competing in some kind of beauty pageant kind of thing. And I don't identify with that at all. And with the Filipinos, they have this coming-out party when you're 16 or 18, I forgot which one, and I just refused to have one of those. I'm just like, "Well, Ma, I just want to have a party with my friends, and that's it." So I don't identify with Fil-Ams really. It's nice to talk with them so I can exchange ideas and stuff, but that's pretty much it for me because I have not really met a lot who are into punk in general.

SELENA: Yeah, in a way, racially, I've been more attuned. I was into punk rock and stuff, but I felt my identity was influenced more racially than by [typical] sexual orientation. Especially because I was bisexual for so long. Even though for a lot of that time I identified as queer too, queer and bisexual.

But race was always more important to me. So when I did meet someone Korean I would feel more of a connection no matter who they were. But I find that as I've gotten more into being queer, being lesbian, it's almost like they have to be Korean and queer for me to feel connected to them!

MARGARITA: Even more specific.

SELENA: Yeah, we get more specific with whom we identify with.

MARGARITA: I know with me, I seem to have more of a connection with Filipinos if they're queer. I used to hope that I would meet someone who was Filipino and punk and all that other stuff. And that would have been really cool. And now I have friends who are like that, but there's not really anything more than friendship going on. I seem to have more of a connection with people who are queer.

SELENA: Oh, really? Well, what about Kilawin?[3]

MARGARITA: I still feel like a mutant among Kilawin because I'm the only punk chick. And at first it took them a long time to get used to me, because they thought I was a little bit overpowering, because I pretty much say what's on my mind. I don't hold back when I swear. With Kilawin they're all very prim, they censor everything.

But it's cool now because we've come to a point where we all look at each other in a cool way. And they'll look at me the way I am. They're not judgmental and stuff. If they were, I think I'd have a problem.

SELENA: Right, you wouldn't be involved. Even in terms of my race consciousness, I wanted to go back to when I was bisexual, it was in a way more important to me what race that person was that I was going out with, [rather] than their gender.[4] I found that of all the different groups of people—white women, women of color, and white men and men of color—personally, it was hardest for me to access men of color in terms of dating, because of the kinds of scenes I was involved in. So I didn't even realize I was doing this but I kind of focused on them [men of color] for a while! (Everyone laughs.)

Because I'm just really curious about people, and I wanted to know what they're about psychologically and what are their issues and stuff. What are straight Asian men's issues? And I guess I have a problem when I hear a lot of white lesbians saying, "Oh, yeah, I want to know about race," but they never take time to really know about men of color issues, or to read stuff about men of color, which is really integral to knowing about race. Not just knowing what Barbara Smith wrote or what the "dyke of color du jour" wrote.

MARGARITA: Yeah, I think it's important to know not only what your issues are but what other people's issues are, if they're different than yours. Because then it helps you to understand exactly what their struggles are so that you can say, "Well, I understand what your struggle is, but this is mine." And to be able to discuss it and get somewhere with it. If you can kind of understand where the other person's coming from but also be very adamant about your position, I think that's when you can actually get somewhere.

SELENA: I sense that in the lesbian community, race is dealt with more as an afterthought than as really structurally integral to identity. I feel like we keep getting subsumed under the white lesbian's needs or her values somehow. Because when you're talking about race, you're talking about a whole community of people in this country.

LESLIE: I think dykes of color are definitely a bit on the outside of their communities in general; I mean that's where her family is and that's where her culture is, that's where so much of her identity is. And just to take her and say, "Oh, well, she's a dyke." And then she's a "woman of color." It's just fucked up. "We want her to add spice to our little [dyke] community."

SELENA: Yeah. "We want to hear *her* point of view."[5] (Everyone laughs.)

LESLIE: Yeah! And it continues to put the Amerikan[6] white culture as the standard to which everybody else is being compared to. And I just find that, and this has happened in the punk community as well as the queer community, "Oh, we're color-blind. It doesn't matter what color you are." And you hear white people saying that, and what that actually means is, oh, everybody's white!

Lesbian Community

SELENA: I'm not really that interested in being surrounded by a white, dyke community. I feel that I can be here, and I can be with the white dykes, and I can be with my friends of color, straight or gay. But I also feel that through e-mail and my academic work I'm developing a community of queer people of color and queer Asians that's not a physical community in a city.

LESLIE: The miracles of modern technology.

SELENA: Yeah, and working on books like this anthology. And it's great, like I'm on these queer Asian lists, and I realize, well, I can go to all these different cities and I know people in them now.

MARGARITA: That's cool.

LESLIE: That is really cool. I'm jealous of people nowadays because, well, when I was a girl in the punk scene, you didn't have Riot Grrrl, and we didn't have queercore, and we didn't have e-mail. And I always felt so isolated, and now people have access. If they have the resources, there's a lot out there. So hopefully people won't have to be so isolated anymore.

I don't know, I just find that in my life, I do have a certain amount of affirmative action that I practice with the people that I put time and energy into having around me. And it's been really important for me to include people who aren't white. It can be a challenge to try and do that. But I do consciously do that. I had a white girlfriend, lover, some of my best friends are white, whatever. But she was pals with a lot of straight white boys. And you know, a lot of times with your lover, it's like "Oh, I don't like to hang out with your friends."

And I felt, am I being really fucked up? Am I closing off people that might be my friends otherwise? But it's just—no—I have a limited amount of time. I grew up with all the straight white guys. And it was really hard for me to convey that to her. In some way, it seemed it was fucked-up in one perspective, but just for me, this is just my personal life, and I feel I'd rather put time and energy into dykes, women of color. I feel like it's this conscious thing.

MARGARITA: It reminds me of what Lynn [Breedlove] said when I was interviewing you guys [Tribe 8]. Straight people might ask, "Why do you have to be so obvious, why do you have to so in-your-face about being a dyke?" And Lynn said, "Well, it's not in your face, it's always in our face, that there's all these people having the straight lifestyle and are holding hands, kissing in the theater, that kind of thing—and it's natural for me, why does it have to be that I'm being in your face about it?" I can see where she's coming from because I have some straight white girlfriends who I get along with very well, but I sometimes feel I'm trying to reach out to them but I don't know if they're reaching out to me as much as they could.

SELENA: Like you've got to bridge the gap.

MARGARITA: They might not really have to as much. I'm so familiar with the straight lifestyle but they're not with the queer lifestyle. Does that make any sense?

SELENA: Yeah. Do you want to say anything about the lesbian community in New York?

MARGARITA: I just feel that the lesbians in New York—it's more like a white lesbian thing. I'd like to see more lesbians of color that are around, that are more supportive of each other. Especially with Asians, because the Asian women seem to be more factioned off from each other than they really should be. There should be more of a network, it should be more supportive. We're technically minorities, and we should be supporting each other since no one else really will.

SELENA: And I would like to see more Northeast Asians and Southeast Asians and South Asians, really reifying their differences, recognizing that we do have different cultures…not conflating them all as Asian. And really making everyone understand each other's culture as queers.

Let's talk about sex now…(Everyone laughs.)

Sex and Gender Performance

SELENA: I don't know, we could talk about anything. We could start with top and bottom stuff. Because I was talking about this in my "Public Sex" class, and I was saying how, for me, being Asian, it's really political to me. Let's say if I was to do a public sex act, (laughs) with a white woman or something, let's say an S/M scene or an erotic dance or something. I would feel weird being the bottom. It's weird how race connects with desire.

MARGARITA: Oh, yeah, it does.

SELENA: It was funny because I have a friend who is a gay Filipino guy, and he was saying that they were in this float, in the parade this past year, the New York Pride March, and he's in APAL, which is this AIDS activism group, and they were doing displays of public sex on the float. And it was him and this Latino guy, and they were trying to decide who should be on the top or bottom! Like what would be politically correct to the audience? Because they were both gay men of color.

LESLIE: Well, we [Tribe 8] just made this video to this song called "Femme Bitch Top." And it was just by these two girls, it wasn't professional at all, but it was a really fun thing that we tried to get all our friends to participate in.

SELENA: In San Francisco?

LESLIE: In San Francisco. And we tried to get varieties of different kinds of people. Unfortunately, some people were sick and couldn't show up. It just sort of ended up that almost all the women of color were being portrayed as the bottoms. And it was just like, "Oh, can we do this? People already have an issue." It was S/M, some people might consider it a big deal and some people would be like, "It's nothing, you know, just depending on what they're into." It was really frustrating. To try to take the footage and make it seem like, "Okay, we don't want to portray all the women of color as slaves!" (Everyone laughs.)

LESLIE: But it's like, well, what can you do? I mean, well, there are black women who enjoy that role.

SELENA: Yeah, obviously. I mean, play is about being flexible and versatile. On some level.

LESLIE: Yeah, an image of something that's an S/M activity can be interpreted completely different than how it feels to the participants, and that's something that just applies to any S/M image. People don't really understand that unless they've tried it.

SELENA: Yeah, right! Well, it's just because we live in such a sexually repressed culture. So, what are you going to do about the video?

LESLIE Well, there were some scenes that we ended up not using.

MARGARITA: Because of the way they're portrayed?

LESLIE: Yeah, it might look bad. There's this one scene of Lynn Payne, the bass player, crawling on her hands and knees, and everyone is flicking their ashes on her. But then everyone who was doing it was fair-skinned, and it was like, "Oh, we shouldn't use this."

SELENA: Were there any scenes with you topping people?

LESLIE: Yeah.

SELENA: So, that's something.

LESLIE: So, we're not going to use the black-girl-as-ashtray scene! (Everyone laughs.)

LESLIE: On the one hand it's like, okay, who is your audience? How sophisticated are they going to be? And basically I don't really give a fuck. Because this is my culture, this is from my heart, and if you have a political problem with it, I can argue it. But then if you really want to have something really out there, people just interpret you through their own fucking filter, and almost all the time, it's like straight white male reviewers talking about, "Oh, well this dyke band is so holier than thou and so fucking fascist." And I'm like, "You're calling this multicultural group of dykes fascist, straight white boy?" You know?

I'm just going to disregard you then, okay? But it happens a lot. And people just not even getting simple things, like this is a different culture than yours, so, when they say, "Oh, they're just like men trying to get women to take their shirts off." And you completely overlook the whole political implications of what we're saying and that we have our shirts off and we're girls. It's just like you can't even explain that to people, so it's like, do you want these people to see this image of women of color being bottoms? And then what are they going to be thinking? Already there's this whole movement—backlash—of white men just saying that affirmative action is unfair to them.

Okay, first and foremost, we're just artists, we're just having fun. And that's important. But after a while you just have to take all this responsibility for the images that you're putting out there. And already you're misunderstood. So, it's like, well, just fuck with it, but then, I don't want to offend other women of color.

SELENA: Yeah. Especially those who aren't into S/M or young women of color who are like, "What the fuck is that?"

(To Margarita) How do you feel about the top/bottom stuff? Do you think race plays a role, are you even into those categories?

MARGARITA: I can only relate from my experiences about the top/bottom stuff. I don't like being put into one or the other. I like playing around with both.

SELENA: She switches.

MARGARITA: (Laughs) I like being flexible. Sometimes it's just more of a fun thing, when I'm with my partner and stuff, I want to arouse that person as much as possible, if sometimes it arouses them that I might be the top then I'll just do that and I'll just take over. But then sometimes I kind of like being the bottom. So it just really depends.

In terms of racially, I can probably say that I'm only thinking of experiences with people who are Asian who are darker-skinned than me. That it might be kind of like a turn-on for that person in that I'm so light-skinned, there is that correlation of the white-skinned Filipino mestiza who's with a darker skin.

LESLIE: Something that drives me crazy is that in all Asian pornography that I see, the women are always portrayed as the masochists, being the bottoms, being really young and helpless, like the schoolgirl. And sometimes for me, it's a real turn-on, because it's that twisted thing of something that you're always fighting against.

Whatever's taboo to me is a turn-on. Sometimes it gets really complicated. But I have yet to see Asian men being portrayed in Asian pornography as being bottoms and being submissive (except gay porn) and sometimes I wonder if that's because they're trying to assert their masculinity and their power through this pornography in general.

They're being victimized, and therefore they're going to overcompensate by always portraying themselves as being, "Well, at least we can handle our girls." And also like [to white men], "We know you really want our women, these exotic chickie-babes, and they're at our feet." But then there's that image of the really mysterious Oriental-dominatrix type, too.

SELENA: But she's only a dominatrix in a certain way. She always has long nails, long hair, in a vinyl bodysuit and a skinny sort of body. She wouldn't be a butch dominatrix.

LESLIE: But the image of butch Asian women is so incongruous with all the stereotypes. I think it's really rad.

SELENA: When Jenny Shimizu first started appearing in the Calvin Klein ads, a lot of white women would say to me, "Oh, she's not butch." Because they were reading her race first. They didn't think she'd be butch, they really thought that, and I'm like, "Yes, she's butch." And they're like, "No, she's androgynous." And if she was white or black or whatever, they would assume she was butch.

LESLIE: Yeah, I mean, I think race is definitely genderized where Asians are seen as being feminine and Africans are seen as being masculine. White people are neutral.

SELENA: Well, they're "normal." But, I wonder, where do the Asian American fagdykes like me fit in, who act fruity in a gay male kind of way, but definitely have a dick in bed?

Can you imagine if all the dykes of color just started going out with each other? Like the white dykes would freak out! It's the same thing, like if all the people of color got together in this country and talked to each other more than they talked to the white powers that be...

MARGARITA: Or talked about each other.

SELENA: Yeah, in a constructive way. Then I think that would make the white status quo very, very nervous. Because my first female lover was black, and so I just think that happened for a reason. Besides attraction.

MARGARITA: That's very interesting considering you were going out with white guys . . .

SELENA: I had slept with one or two effeminate, hippie white guys, then I slept with her. Like she was my second lover. I think in some way, I do feel more comfortable with women of color. Like there's a certain ease I feel.

MARGARITA: Yeah, I know I feel more at ease with women of color. And especially with women who might be also ethnically Asian-mixed. Just because they might come from a similar background is a little comforting to me. So it doesn't feel like I have this massive pressure of having to get to know them totally from scratch. You have things you can talk about.

Notes

1. A very multiracial genre of music that is a fusion of punk and reggae, popular in England during the late 1970s and early 1980s.

2. Filipino-Americans as opposed to Filipinos from the Philippines.

3. Kilawin Kolektibo is a New York City-based Filipina lesbian collective.

4. In retrospect, I'd have to say my sexual orientation was more "affirmative action" or "people of color" than bisexual!

5. A common phrase in white lesbian circles.

6. Amerikan is spelled this way to distinguish it as the United States, versus the other "Americas."

About the Contributors

DELIA D. AGUILAR is an associate professor of Ethnic Studies and Women's Studies at Bowling Green State University in Ohio.

KARIN AGUILAR-SAN JUAN teaches Asian American Studies and Sociology in southern California. She is the editor of *The State of Asian America: Activism and Resistance in the 1990s* (South End Press, 1994). Delia Aguilar is her mom.

MARGARITA ALCANTARA is the editor of the 'zine *Bamboo Girl.*

ANANNYA BHATTACHARJEE is currently working with Workers' Awaaz in New York City. She is a co-founder and member of the editorial collective of *SAMAR* magazine. She is the former Executive Director of the Committee Against Anti-Asian Violence and former Program Coordinator and founding member of Sakhi for South Asian Women.

KSHITEEJA BHIDE is a psychotherapist in Connecticut. She has worked extensively with women and provides consultation and counseling for corporations and their employees with special linguistic and/or cultural requirements. She is the current president/coordinator of SNEHA. She is also one of the founders of Women's Entrepreneurial Trust, an organization based in Pune, India, which is dedicated to the education and empowerment of women toward economic and social self-sufficiency.

GRACE CHANG is the author of the forthcoming book *Gatekeeping and Housekeeping: The Politics of Regulating Women's Migration*. She is co-editor of *Mothering: Ideology, Experience, and Agency*. Her essays on undocumented women's labor migration have appeared in *Radical America* and *Socialist Review*. She is completing her Ph.D. in Ethnic Studies at Berkeley.

PAMELA CHIANG works at the Asian Pacific Environmental Network and has organized garment workers.

MILYOUNG CHO is working for the National Asian Pacific American Women's Forum. She has worked with the Committee Against Anti-Asian Violence in New York and recently finished school in traditional Chinese medicine.

SAYANTANI DASGUPTA is an MD/MPH student at Johns Hopkins University and a freelance writer. Her essays have appeared in publications such as *A. Magazine*, *Ms.*, *India Currents*, *Z Magazine*, *Contemporary Pediatrics,* and *Journal of the Annals of Behavioral Science in Medical Education* and anthologies such as *So…What Are You Doing After College?*, *Our Feet Walk the Sky*, and *Contours of the Heart: South Asians Map America.* She and her mother, Shamita, have co-authored a book entitled *The Demon Slayers and Other Stories: Bengali Folk Tales* (Interlink, 1995).

SHAMITA DAS DASGUPTA is one of the founders of Manavi, the pioneering organization for battered South Asian women based in New Jersey. She is the editor of an anthology on South Asian women forthcoming from Rutgers University Press. She is an assistant professor of Psychology at Rutgers University.

DIANE C. FUJINO is an assistant professor of Asian American Studies at the University of California, Santa Barbara. She teaches courses on Asian feminism and Asian American social movements, and does research on Asian women's political activism. She is a socialist feminist and a founding member of Asian Sisters for Ideas in Action Now!, a radical political organization in Santa Barbara.

ELAINE KIM is a professor of Asian American Studies and Chair of Ethnic Studies at the University of California at Berkeley. She co-edited *Dangerous Women: Gender and Korean Nationalism* (Routledge, 1997), *Making More Waves: New Writing by Asian American Women* (Beacon, 1997), and *East to America: Korean American Life Stories* (The New Press, 1996).

YURI KOCHIYAMA is a longtime human rights activist. She lives in New York City.

MIRIAM CHING LOUIE works with the Women of Color Resource Center and has worked with Asian Immigrant Women Advocates. She helped organize roundtables on migrant and women workers' centers and on organizing among ethnic and racial minority women at the 1995 United Nations Fourth World Conference on Women NGO Forum in China.

LYNN LU is an editor/publisher in the South End Press collective.

MEIZHU LUI worked in a hospital kitchen for 20 years, and became the president of her union local. She is a community organizer around healthcare issues and is starting a project for immigrants access to health care.

LESLIE MAH is the lead guitarist of Tribe 8.

SIA NOWROJEE is a consultant in sexual and reproductive health, specializing in the impact of gender on women's health. She has worked with a range of organizations in the United States, East Africa, and South Asia. She is a fifth-generation Kenyan of Indian origin who recently became a U.S. citizen. She is a board member of the National Asian Women's Health Organization.

JULIANA PEGUES is a writer and activist living in Minneapolis. Her current political commitments include ongoing work with the Garment Workers Justice Campaign and work with the Women's Prison Book Project.

BANDANA PURKAYASTHA, a core member of SNEHA, is an educator and community activist. She combines organizing experience in India with activism in the United States. Her current research focuses on gender, transnational influences, places, and discursive politics.

SHYAMALA RAMAN is a founder/member of SNEHA. She is an associate professor of Economics and International Studies and Director of International Studies at Saint Joseph College in West Harford, Connecticut. Her interests include interdisciplinary curriculum design, feminist economics, theories of the firm, methodologies of economics, technological empowerment for women, and transformative pedagogies.

PURVI SHAH lives and works in New York City. She is active with Sakhi for South Asian Women and serves as a literacy tutor for Sakhi's ESL classes.

SEEMA SHAH is a student at Oberlin College in Ohio.

SONIA SHAH is an editor/publisher at South End Press and a freelance writer. Her essays on feminism and Asian American issues have appeared in *Ms., Sojourner, Z Magazine, The Indian American, Nuclear Times, In These Times,* and *Gay Community News*, and have been widely anthologized in books including *Listen Up! Voices from the Next Feminist Generation; The State of Asian America: Activism and Resistance in the 1990s; A Patchwork Shawl: Chronicles of South Asian Women in America; Frontline Feminism, 1975-1995; Women Transforming Politics; Reconstructing Gender: A Multicultural Anthology; Experiencing Race, Class and Gender in the United States;* and *Nationalism and Ethnic Conflict.* She is the editor of *Between Fear and Hope: A Decade of Peace Activism* and was formerly managing editor of *Nuclear Times* magazine. She has co-founded two South Asian women's groups in the eastern United States. She is not related to Purvi Shah; Seema is her sister.

JAEL SILLIMAN is an assistant professor of Women's Studies at the University of Iowa. She is currently board chair of the National Asian Women's Health Organization and board member of the Pro-Choice Resource Center, the International Projects Assistance Services, and a steering committee member of the Committee on Women, Population, and Environment. She has been an activist for women's rights in the United States and abroad and has worked particularly on population, environment, and development issues.

JULIE SZE is an organizer with the New York City Environmental Justice Alliance, a coalition of individuals and community-based organizations working for environmental, economic, and social justice in communities of color throughout New York City. She is a PhD student in American Studies at New York University studying constructions of race, nature, and environmental justice.

CHENG IMM TAN is a Senior Associate Minister at the Unitarian Universalist Urban Ministry, and organizer and co-founder of the Asian Women's Task Force Against Domestic Violence in Boston.

SELENA WHANG is a Ph.D. candidate in Performance Studies at the Tisch School of the Arts, New York University. She teaches at New York University and Parsons School of Design. She has toured widely with her lecture and film/video clip show "Queer Colored Girls: The End of Innocence and the Beginning of Violence and Desire" at film festivals and universities. She has published in the journals and 'zines *College Literature, Documents, Bamboo Girl, Outpunk, Girl Germs, Riot Grrrl NYC,* and in the anthology *Bi Any Other Name* (1991, Alyson Publications). She is also featured on the CD compilations *Music in Multicultural America* (1997, Schirmer Books), *There's a Dyke in the Pit* (1992, Outpunk and Harp Records), *It's all True* (1994, Big Cat Records), and the *Lucy Stoners* (1993, Harp Records), as well as the soundtrack to the film *Frenzy* (1993, Jill Reiter).

HELEN ZIA, the daughter of Chinese immigrants, is a writer and journalist; her writings appear in many books, magazines, and other publications. A contributing editor to *Ms.*, where she was formerly executive editor, she recently wrote about the Hong Kong handover's impact on women. She is also a featured columnist for the webzine www. ChannelA.com. A longtime activist for social change, she serves on the boards of and volunteers with numerous organizations, including the Asian Women's Shelter of San Francisco and the Asian Pacific American Women's Leadership Institute in Denver. She resides in the San Francisco Bay area and is at work on a book about the political and cultural impact of Asian Americans, to be published by Farrar, Straus and Giroux in 1999.

INDEX

About South End Press

South End Press is a nonprofit, collectively run book publisher with over 200 titles in print. Since our founding in 1977, we have tried to meet the needs of readers who are exploring, or are already committed to, the politics of radical social change. Our goal is to publish books that encourage critical thinking and constructive action on the key political, cultural, social, economic, and ecological issues shaping life in the United States and in the world. In this way, we hope to give expression to a wide diversity of democratic social movements and to provide an alternative to the products of corporate publishing.

Through the Institute for Social and Cultural Change, South End Press works with other political media projects—*Z Magazine*; Speak-out, a speakers' bureau; Alternative Radio; and the Publishers Support Project—to expand access to information and critical analysis. If you would like a free catalog of South End Press books, please write to us at: South End Press, 7 Brookline St., #1, Cambridge, MA 02139. Visit our website at http://www.lbbs.org.

Related Titles

The State of Asian America
Activism and Resistance in the 1990s
Edited by Karin Aguilar-San Juan
$22.00 paper; $40.00 cloth

Beyond Identity Politics
Emerging Social Justice Movements in Communities of Color
Edited by John Anner
$14.00 paper; $40.00 cloth

When ordering, please include $3.50 for postage and handling for the first book and 50 cents for each additional book. To order by credit card, call 1-800-533-8478.